First published in Great Britain in 2012 by
St Andrews Film Studies
99 North Street, St Andrews, KY16 9AD
Scotland, United Kingdom
Publisher: Dina Iordanova

Secure on-line ordering:
www.stafs.org

British Library Cataloguing-in-Publication Data
A catalogue record for this book is available from the British Library.

ISBN 978-0-9563730-7-6 (paperback)

University of
St Andrews

The book is published with the assistance of the Centre
for Film Studies at the University of St Andrews and The
Leverhulme Trust.

St Andrews Film Studies promotes greater
understanding of, and access to, international cinema
and film culture worldwide.

The University of St Andrews is a charity registered in
Scotland, No. SC013532

Front cover design: Duncan Stewart.

Cover and pre-press: University of St Andrews Print & Design.

Printed in Great Britain by Lightning Source.

Contents

Acknowledgements

I would like to thank Dina Iordanova for inviting me to participate in the Dynamics of World Cinema project, which gave rise to this book, amongst several other publications. The project has been funded by The Leverhulme Trust; it was through their generous funding that I was able to spend time with colleagues at the Centre for Film Studies at St Andrews in 2009 and cement what has been a productive collaboration.

Stuart Cunningham

I would like to thank all of the contributing authors for making this book what it is. I would also like to thank The Leverhulme Trust, for sponsoring this volume, which we are publishing as part of the Dynamics of World Cinema project (2008-2011); Alex Marlow-Mann, for book production and editorial assistance; Steve Blackey, for copyediting; Mike Arrowsmith, for advice on IT issues; Duncan Stewart, for designing the cover; Margaret Smith for typesetting the book; and my son, George, for introducing me to many aspects of cinema's on-line presence. Acknowledgement is also due to the Research Associates on the Dynamics of World Cinema project: Dr Ragan Rhyne, Dr Ruby Cheung, Dr Alex Fischer and Mr Thomas Gerstenmeyer. Thanks also to colleagues who hosted talks at the University of Manchester, Hong Kong Baptist University, Cines del Sur film festival in Granada (Spain), The Image Conference in San Sebastian (Spain) and the inaugural Busan Cinema Forum (South Korea), as well as to my colleagues from the Board of Trustees of the Centre for the Moving Image, the parent company of the Edinburgh International Film Festival. Recognition is also due to the senior management at the University of St Andrews, who helped me to accommodate work on this project in parallel with my responsibilities as Provost.

Dina Iordanova

Contributors

Stuart Cunningham is Distinguished Professor of Media and Communications at Queensland University of Technology and Director of the Australian Research Council Centre of Excellence for Creative Industries and Innovation. He has written extensively on film and television history, culture and policy, including *Featuring Australia: The Cinema of Charles Chauvel*, *Framing Culture: Criticism and Policy in Australia*, *Contemporary Australian Television* (with Toby Miller), *Australian Television and International Mediascapes* (with Elizabeth Jacka), *The Media and Communications in Australia* (with Graeme Turner) and *In the Vernacular: A Generation of Australian Culture and Controversy*. Among many appointments, he has served as Commissioner of the Australian Film Commission and foundation Chair of QPIX, Queensland's screen resource centre.

Marijke de Valck is Assistant Professor in the Department of Media Studies at the University of Amsterdam. She specialises in research on film festivals and has published widely on the topic. Her articles have appeared in *Cinema Journal*, the *International Journal of Cultural Studies* and *Film International*, as well as in the *Film Festival Yearbook* series. She is the author of *Film Festivals: From European Geopolitics to Global Cinéphilia* (2007). Together with Skadi Loist, Marijke founded and manages the Film Festival Research Network (www.filmfestivalresearch. org).

Alex Fischer is The Leverhulme Trust Research Associate at the Centre for Film Studies of the University of St Andrews where he works as part of the Dynamics of World Cinema team. His forthcoming monograph examines basic film festival operation through an open system paradigm. Alex's film festival-related work experience includes: the University of St Andrews 60 Hour Film Blitz (as CEO), the Brisbane International Film Festival (as Programme Manager, 2009), the Q150 Travelling Film Festival (as Project Coordinator, 2009) and the Gold Coast Film Fantastic (as Festival Director, 2008)

Michael Franklin is a Research Associate at the Institute for Capitalising on Creativity at the University of St Andrews and Film Investor for Creative Scotland. Michael holds degrees from the Universities of St Andrews and Edinburgh and from Cass Business School. As a Research Assistant at Cass, Michael worked on film marketing and is now continuing this work as part of his PhD research. His work focuses on managing uncertainty using digital technologies, including their application to feature film marketing and distribution campaigns. Within the film industry he has worked as a consultant for Northern Alliance advising the UK Film Council, Arts Council England, Film London, EM Media and NESTA.

Michael Gubbins is a film and entertainment industries analyst and writer, and a frequent speaker and chair at leading international industry events. He is the former editor of *Screen International* and Director of Content at Music Week. He has authored reports on the current state of cinema for Cine Regio and works with Power to the Pixel.

Dina Iordanova is Professor of Film Studies at the University of St Andrews in Scotland and Provost of its St Leonard's College. She was principal investigator on the Leverhulme Trust-sponsored project Dynamics of World Cinema, which produced the research for this volume. She has written extensively on transnational cinema, film festivals and the global creative industries, including *The Film Festival Circuit* (2009), *Cinema at the Periphery* (2010), *Film Festivals and Imagined Communities* (2010), *Film Festivals and East Asia* (2011) and *Film Festivals and Activism* (2012). She is Fellow of the Institute of Directors and of the Royal Society of the Arts and serves on the Board of the Edinburgh International Film Festival.

Mark David Ryan is a Research Fellow and Lecturer in Film and Television in the Creative Industries Faculty at Queensland University of Technology. He is an expert on Australian genre cinema and is currently working on research projects exploring transmedia screen production. He has written extensively on popular genre cinema, industry dynamics, creative industries and cultural policy. His research has been published in the *New Review of Film & Television Studies*, *Media International Australia: Incorporating Culture and Policy*, *Continuum: Journal of Media & Cultural Studies* and *Studies in Australasian Cinema,* among others.

Jon Silver is Senior Lecturer in Film and Television in the Creative Industries Faculty at Queensland University of Technology. His research focuses on strategic issues facing the movie business. A key focus is on the impacts of new technology on distribution and exhibition. Relevant publications include: 'Digital Dawn: A Revolution in Movie Distribution?', 'Rates of Change: On-line Distribution as Disruptive Technology in the Film Industry', 'Chindia: Innovation in On-line Film Distribution', 'Are Movie Theaters Doomed? Do Exhibitors See the Big Picture as Theaters Lose Their Competitive Advantage?' and 'Hollywood Dominance: Will It Continue?'. He has worked in film production, distribution and exhibition.

Ben Slater's writings on film have been published in numerous books, magazines, catalogues and websites including *Cahiers du Cinéma*, *Screen International*, *Vertigo*, *Indiewire* and *Criticine*. He is author of *Kinda Hot: The Making of Saint Jack in Singapore* and was script editor and consultant on the feature films *Helen* (2008, UK) and *HERE* (2009, Singapore). He is based in Singapore and currently works as a lecturer at the School of Art, Design and Media at Nanyang Technological University. His infrequently updated blog about 'outsider' films set in Singapore is at www.sporeana.blogspot.com.

Glossary and Abbreviations

3D	Three-dimensions
ADSL	Asymetric digital subscriber line
DCI	Digital Cinema Initiative
DIY	Do-it-yourself
DRM	Digital rights management: technologies used by content providers and copyright holders to limit the use of digital content and services
DTH	Direct-to-home
DTO	Direct transfer object
DVD	Digital Versatile Disk
FAQ	Frequently asked questions
FTTH	Fibre to the home
FVC	Film Value Chain
iOS	Mobile operating system (originally iPhone operating system)
IPTV	Internet protocol television
ISP	Internet service provider
P2P	Peer-to-peer
PPV	Pay-per-view
VOD	Video-on-demand

DIGITAL DISRUPTION

Digital Disruption: Technological Innovation and Global Film Circulation

Dina Iordanova

'The Internet is changing the way in which people experience watching movies.' Geoffrey Gilmore, Chief Creative Officer, Tribeca Enterprises, 2011

This book is concerned with the novel ways in which people can experience a cinema conditioned by digital innovation and the wider possibilities for the global circulation of film. Traditional distribution – where studios control box office revenues by releasing films for coordinated showing in a system of theatres and then direct them through an inflexible succession of hierarchically ordered windows of exhibition and formats – is radically undermined by new technologies. Chances are that film distribution as we have come to know it will soon represent a fraction of the multiple ways in which film can travel around the globe. The result will be a new film circulation environment: a more intricate phenomenon that includes a plethora of circuits and, possibly, revenue streams. Along with it come conditions conducive to the free flow of previously rarely seen cinematic material which, due to the vitality of growing alternative channels of dissemination, can now be seen and appreciated by anyone with a data connection.

Cinema is in the process of moving on-line. In this book, we are exploring various manifestations and aspects of this process which, even if still in their early period, may well accelerate and overrun previously known patterns of film circulation.

In this introductory chapter I summarise some of the main arguments advanced in the volume. My focus is on the profound nature of digital disruption and the increased chances that it brings for the transborder flows of niche and peripheral content. I also explore the gradual changes affecting dissemination intermediaries and the arrival of new business and circulation models that lead to a rethinking of issues of intellectual property, trigger mutations in the film festival landscape and give rise to a new type of cosmopolitan cinéphilia.

Disruption All the Way

In 2011, *The Wall Street Journal* listed the DVD, games and video rental industry among the top ten dying industries, along with newspaper publishing and record stores (Izzo 2011). Around the same time, *Fortune* magazine chronicled the swiftness of disruption in a variety of business areas, such as mail, book and record sales, as well as film distribution (Cendrowski 2011). In all of the instances discussed by *Fortune*, the disruption had been preceded by a period of relative quiet in which intense technological bubbling below the surface was followed by a blitz of radical disruption, to a disastrous effect for those who were not able to ride the wave of technology.

The same pattern is repeated across a number of industries. The demise of traditional mail delivery services – the triumph of e-mail over snail mail – is one of the earliest examples of such disruption; it evolved over the course of less than a decade. Then there is the downfall of traditional booksellers, with the corresponding ascent of Amazon and on-line booksellers. In 2011, the sales of electronic books, which had only been in existence for about five years, surpassed the sales of paper books for a first time. Kindle sales now account for more sales than all hard copy books on Amazon, and Borders filed for bankruptcy in February 2011. Traditional music sellers crumbled soon after the debut of iTunes in 2003; retailers such as Tower Records and HMV shriveled and folded in response to the devastating effects of the new on-line distribution model, while sales of songs on iTunes grew more than a million percent over the same period (Cendrowski 2011). Another example lies in the sphere of traditional video rental services: in about a decade Blockbuster withered from a 4000-store strong operation to bankruptcy (in September 2010), whereas Netflix, founded in 1997, reached market capitalisation of U.S.$2.2 billion and grew sales by 43,000%. Since it began streaming content directly to a variety of devices in 2010, Netflix has reached 24 million subscribers in the U.S. alone, up from about 15 million just a year earlier (Hastings 2011).

Writing in this volume, Michael Franklin confirms these trends by outlining digital disruption as the clash between exponential rates of technological change on the one hand, and incremental rates of change in society, economics, politics and law on the other.

Will film be next in line for a radical shake up? In their investigation of On-line distribution, Stuart Cunningham and Jon Silver reiterate that we are dealing with a phenomenon that is still marginal and quite far from being dominant. Could it be, however, that we will soon see rapid and radical developments similar to those that swept across other industries and left them radically changed? The degree of technological innovation is similar across the board, and so is the pattern of a lengthy period of bubbling under the surface, accumulating energy for a hot spring-like eruption.

Ever since the bankruptcy of U.S. video-chain Blockbuster in 2010, the answer to this question has been becoming more and more obvious. People see new films in new ways. It is commonly acknowledged that technologically-driven change takes place in all areas and is radical in nature.

The processes, as they affect film, may still appear peripheral, yet technological innovation creates enormous potential. YouTube only began in November 2005, but by 2010 had already become an indispensable site, ranked third in the world, as shown in Appendix 3 and Marijke De Valck's essay in this volume. Speaking at the Edinburgh International Film Festival in June 2011, the founder of the Internet Movie Database (IMDb) Col Needham suggested that rights holders in film should look at what is happening with music and take a lesson in the application of technology, because it is only a matter of bandwidth before it becomes possible to legitimately pay for and download a full-length TV episode, and eventually a feature film in mere seconds (Needham 2011).

Could it be that the time for the anticipated dramatic change in film has come? Could it be that things have bubbled up for long enough and that film is the next one in line for the surge in radically disruptive new ways of circulating content that we have been witnessing elsewhere?

Disintermediation

A process whereby direct access to content makes the intermediary in a supply chain obsolete – disintermediation – is perhaps the main trend that characterises the digital disruption that Franklin, Cunningham and Silver, and Alex Fischer discuss in this volume. In this instance the intermediary is the traditional film distributor.

The disintermediation trend leads to the gradual narrowing of clearly distinguishable consecutive windows: content is often released across platforms simultaneously (Macnab 2010). Previously, theatrical distribution enjoyed a secure run of at least several months in its 'window' to enable the maximisation of revenues before other exclusive deals, such as pay-per-view (PPV), could kick in; only later could the so-called 'auxiliary' distribution modes such as DVD/video releases enter the play, before the circle was completed by the broadcasting of the content on terrestrial television networks, sometimes up to 24 months after a film's original theatrical release. Today, a number of films are being simultaneously released across platforms; such situations are still more common for indie films, but this new distribution paradigm could soon enter the mainstream as well. Even where they are preserved, traditional windows get narrower and narrower, with the greatest pressure now being felt in the changing relationship between the theatrical and premium video-on-demand (VOD) windows, which are often closely positioned next to each other. Global cinema operators could soon be facing a showdown with Hollywood studios over plans to show films on demand less than two months after they have been released in the cinema (Davoudi 2011).

Traditional distribution channels, where the producers of a film enter a contract with distributors for certain territories, are being undermined, particularly in independent and low-budget filmmaking; the cycle of film circulation is frequently limited to the interaction between the content owner and the exhibitor. Peer-to-peer (P2P) technologies enable content owners to deal directly with individual customers or groups; most of this interaction takes place over the Internet, and its costs are significantly lower. This results in a diminished role for intermediaries; it creates a situation where distributors see themselves cut off from previously lucrative opportunities and resist the change. In turn, digital businesses that are poised to bracket out intermediaries, content providers and cable operators, are set to profit. Many of the new digital providers (such as TiVo, Netflix or DirecTV) are rushing to enter agreements with rights owners on the one hand (for films and prime television content from the likes of Comcast, HBO, Universal, Relativity Media or the independents), and to secure new exhibition platforms on the other (such as Apple's streaming of film content directly to its iPad and iPhone devices, or Sony's streaming to PlayStation platforms). The overall decline in DVD sales is compensated for by an increased interest in VOD. As shown here by Cunningham and Silver, on-line distribution is typically engaged in by innovative small to medium scale enterprises, although it is also being utilised by larger corporations that are not the Hollywood majors.

The processes of disintermediation are most clearly felt at the periphery for now. Situations that involve indie, documentary, foreign and other niche films actively embrace the new digital and on-line tools available. This helps them to avoid any studio and distributor dependency, to finance production and distribution via crowdsourcing sites such as Kickstarter, or to sell content and DVDs directly from websites (Boudway 2011).[1]

Internet distribution guru Peter Broderick, who specialises in helping independent filmmakers get direct access to audiences, talks of a 'New World Distribution' based on principles of greater control via global direct sales; of customised strategies, reduced costs and separate revenue streams, as well as direct access to core audiences and true fans. To Broderick, distribution is 'a hierarchical realm where filmmakers must petition the powers that be to grant them distribution' (Broderick 2008). Independents who manage to secure exposure for their work without giving total control of the marketing of their films to distributors prove most successful. His chart juxtaposes 'Old World' and 'New World' distribution and reveals the main areas of disintermediation: (see Table 1, page 6)

Even as disintermediation leads to improved exposure for independent content, 'Old World' distributors are struggling to preserve the traditional windows of distribution established by the powerful Hollywood model. These windows – sequentially-positioned phases granted to secure the uniqueness of a certain form of exploitation of content for a given period of time – are shrinking across the board in a radical and deep rearrangement that dramatically affects the mediators. In a recent move, for example, a number of Hollywood studios agreed to reduce the theatrical-only window to just two months before releasing new films on 'premium video-on-demand basis' (Garrahan 2011). New pressures originating from the growth of VOD are likely to lead to a further narrowing, or even the closure of distribution windows, with traditional distributors no longer controlling the order of the platforms onto which a film will be released, nor the timing or the sequence of such a release. In a range of releases that were seen more as experiments than as standard practice at the time – from the pioneering quasi-simultaneous theatre/cable/DVD release of Stephen Soderbergh's *Bubble* (U.S., 2005) to the cross-platform première of Franny Armstrong's *Age of Stupid* (UK,

2009) – content owners have opted to release films simultaneously over a variety of platforms, consciously ignoring the prescribed hierarchical order of windows as understood by traditional distribution.

Table 1: Peter Broderick's Comparison of Changing Distribution Patterns

Old World Distribution	New World Distribution
Distributor in control	Filmmaker in control
Overall deal	Hybrid approach
Fixed release plans	Flexible release strategies
Mass audience	Core and crossover audiences
Rising costs	Lower costs
Viewers reached through distributor	Direct access to viewers
Third party sales	Direct and third party sales
Territory by territory distribution	Global distribution
Cross-collateralised revenues	Separate revenue streams
Anonymous consumers	True fans

Source: Peter Broderick (2008) 'Welcome to the New World of Distribution'. On-line. Available HTTP: http://www.peterbroderick.com/writing/writing/welcometothenewworld.html (20 June 2011).

To a large extent, the closure of exhibition windows is dictated by the need to counteract the speed at which pirated material can now travel over the Internet; but it is not just that. The disintermediation processes reflect activist work towards reinstating various other channels of exhibition that were previously pushed aside. And consequently the concept of 'distribution' gradually dissolves, whilst a new concept – one of film circulation – becomes ever more viable.

How does what I have previously termed 'peripheral cinema' (Iordanova 2010a) benefit from such circulation opportunities? First, smaller players now come to be on a par with the bigger players; the latter may still exert a degree of control over the international theatrical distribution, but they no longer possess an efficient means of barring alternative content from seeking exposure on the Internet. Various inventive on-line channels for the distribution of independent and international cinema are mushrooming and niche products – such as independently produced features or international documentaries – come within easy reach. In an unprecedented move to reach out to wider audiences, more and more filmmakers bypass the gatekeepers and jump on the bandwagon; for the first time in history they have at their disposal the means to access previously distant audiences who may not be particularly large, but are sufficient to provide the modest revenue needed to keep going.

Transborder Flows

Stuart Cunningham and John Sinclair's volume *Floating Lives* (2001) was one of the first studies to trace circulation channels catering to the increasingly active diasporic audiences around the world. It recognised that while film production centres may be based in one country, audiences could be located in another, and that the consumption of what is created 'here' would quite likely be taking place elsewhere. The study also recognised that diasporic consumers were compartmentalised and scattered across different locations around the globe; they could only be thought of as a compact audience if they were connected through a medium that could reach out simultaneously to all far-flung communities.

In a world where substantial populations live in a diasporic condition or in a migratory mode, more and more audiences are turning to the Internet for cultural consumption that transcends borders. An increasing variety of studio-produced films have become available on the Internet for streaming or downloading, but content is not limited to mainstream choices. A huge and diverse range of alternative international offerings is now equally accessible as well. Niche content that was traditionally left out from the mainstream channels of distribution now finds its way to audiences through the global exposure granted by on-line circulation. In the new configuration, the flood of product erases national borders, becoming a tide that, as Henry Jenkins observes, is driven along both by commercial strategies and by grassroots tactics; it is 'apt to be multidirectional, creating temporary portals or "contact zones" between geographically dispersed cultures' (Jenkins 2006: 154).

Indeed, long before many of the Japanese manga animations appeared on DVD in Western stores, one could view all episodes of popular manga and anime series via YouTube, Veoh, Tudou and other similar sites. Such sites soon came to be seen as treasure troves of content announcing the existence of an untapped universe of alternative cinematic content. They carried musical video clips and trailers not only of Western films, but also of internationally-made blockbusters – like the hugely popular hybrid rap numbers from *Singh is Kinng* (Anees Bazmee, India, 2008), featuring Snoop Dogg and Akshai Kumar – which, with hundreds of thousands of views, tremendously assisted their popularity. More and more rare films were made available in their entirety on YouTube, cut into ten-minute-long segments, while file sharing via BitTorrent enabled the formation of lively communities that converge around the partaking of rare material in a variety of languages.

In this new context of transborder circulation, a much larger number of products are available from film content sites that operate entirely on-line. Technological innovation makes it easy to access niche material that was never likely to be stored in the limited physical space of the neighbourhood video stores, or even specialist ones. In addition, such niche material is now available to a much wider client base than could be reached previously. As Michael Gubbins notes in this volume, the ability to aggregate audiences beyond national borders may improve the economics of specialised film. New audiences, many based internationally and in peripheral locations, now receive the same exposure to content as those based in Western urban hubs. Both Gubbins and Franklin talk here of the innovative model of the Brazilian operation Moviemobz/RAIN.

Previously, scattered diasporic audiences were only partially reached (if at all) in the context of an export-import business model that, in order to effectively link production and distribution, had to rely on dedicated outlets that targeted specific, singular user groups for particular cultural imports. The last decade of the twentieth century and the early years of the twenty-first have been marked by the emergence and growth of innovative networks that use new technologies to enable concurrent outreach to previously discrete diasporic groups. The area of transnational television underwent rapid growth, too, and brought the transnational linking of production and consumption into reality. Soon, the proliferating local and global satellite channels became major players in the transborder circulation of television and cinematic content aimed at global diasporas.

Initially, the amplification of such outreach was driven by Hollywood's interest in conquering new audiences and was marked by the emergence and transnational growth of TV channels that relied on extensive libraries: Turner Classic Movies (TCM), or the Metro Goldwyn Mayer (MGM) channel or those showcasing their own content made for TV, such as HBO.[2]

The TV channels that rely on Hollywood film content, however, soon became only a fraction of the similar and rapidly proliferating enterprises that showcase cinema transnationally. A growing number of television channels specialise in screening film content that is otherwise unavailable theatrically because it is of marginal interest, whether it be an independent arthouse film or of interest to specific ethnic or other groups of audiences that are best reached via dedicated (often subscription) channels. For example, Hong Kong-based Celestial Pictures, which has the rights to a significant part of the Shaw Brothers library, runs three TV channels: Celestial Classic Movies (showcasing older films), Celestial Movies (showing new acquisitions from around the region) and Wah TV, which specifically programmes for youth audiences (Shackleton 2010). Another model has been developed by the World Movies Channel, which originated in Australia and is carried by cable providers in a number of countries: it showcases indie and international feature films that have been acquired for TV distribution from various film festivals around the world.

In the new environment, where film is expected to fit and be seen on 'any size of screen', the lines between feature films and made-for-TV films are becoming increasingly blurred, as both ultimately receive their widest circulation through transnational television.

In a trend that can be traced as far back as Krsyzstof Kieslowski's Polish-German TV-work *Dekalog* (*The Decalogue*, 1989), which spun off films like *Krótki film o zabijaniu* (*A Short Film about Killing*, Poland, 1988) and *Krótki film o milosci* (*A Short Film about Love*, Poland, 1988) and Lars von Trier's 1990s series *Riget* (*The Kingdom*, Denmark/ France/Germany/Sweden, 1994), fewer and fewer films in circulation are necessarily conceived or created for exhibition on the big screen. French distributor Vincent Maraval of Wild Bunch even claims that French cinema is essentially produced for television (in Tartaglione, 2010). The fact that some of the most popular Nordic films today – such as the Swedish *Wallander* (Henning Mankell, Sweden, 2005-2009) or Danish *Forbydelsen* (*The Killing*, various directors, Denmark/Sweden/Norway, 2007) – find international circulation chiefly through television, does not prevent them from being recognised as key contributions to the region's cinematic revival. Simultaneously, a number of films originally made for the big screen get their widest exhibition when they are broadcast and circulated transnationally through the medium of television.

Transnational television channels catering to diasporic audiences – Indian, Nigerian, Chinese to name but three – have undergone a global expansion. Divya McMillin indicates that global television networks featuring Indian cinema – such as the India-based Zee TV or private networks such as B4U, Sahara, Sony and Sun TV, and the variety of their subsidiaries – reach out to an international audience based in 120 countries (McMillin 2010: 118). Of these, Zee TV, which is available in the United States, United Kingdom, Ireland, Malaysia, Singapore and Israel, boasts 532,000 subscriber households in North and Latin America, 174,000 in Europe, 73,000 in Africa, and two million in the Asia Pacific region (McMillin 2010: 125). Thus, through the emergence of this specific business model of transnational television, Indian cinema retains a global reach, even in countries that lack compact populations from the subcontinent. Several other similar companies cater to further diasporic audiences, using a similar business model.

The massive output of Nigerian cinema seems to reach destinations in the West mainly through dedicated cable channels of transnational television. Nigerian films run 24/7 on channels such as Nollywood or Nigeria Movie, and rely on transnational television distribution as much as on other forms of circulation, such as the sale of DVD copies. More recently, many of these outlets have started moving on-line and are in the process of embracing Internet television.

The effects of easier transnational flows that have been enabled by the advent of sites such as YouTube are multifarious and profound. The first book to address these issues, Jean Burgess and Joshua Green's *YouTube: Online Video and Participatory Culture* (2009), focused predominantly on YouTube's role in enhancing and diversifying participatory culture, in facilitating the 'rise of the rest', and in reaching out to geographically dispersed audiences; the study asserted YouTube's function to secure better visibility for independents and smaller players, and improve access for players from remotely-based, minority or diasporic groups.

Building on the ease of transborder flows, some of the most innovative approaches were brought about by transnational individuals, who seem to be acutely aware of the buoyancy of global audiences.

Indian-American businessman Gaurav Dhillon, the founder of Jaman, started building his streaming business by asking 'Why couldn't a really good film made in Europe be enjoyed by somebody in India?'

(Dhillon 2010). Jaman evolved out of Dhillon's realisation that the Internet presented the best way to bridge the gap between audiences in the West and elsewhere. Even though it needs to comply with zoning restrictions imposed by rights holders and does not have license to stream all of its films to all territories, Jaman still reaches out to a wide transnational community of users. It invests in the cultivation of an international user community of film buffs who are interested in non-mainstream cinema. As discussed here in a dedicated case study by Cunningham, Silver and Mark David Ryan, Jaman does not even try to woo Hollywood's big players to license content, but opts to target niche audiences with a variety of international films, Sundance-films and other indies, or Bollywood classics. 'Less than one percent of the films produced on planet earth get distribution in the United States,' they say in their promotional materials. It is the alluring market opportunity of the untapped 99 percent of cinema – the periphery – which Jaman's team is committed to pursuing.[3] Like a 'Sundance on the Web', Jaman allows the user to watch a film, review it, recommend it and see what are the favourites with other members of its on-line community (Dhillon and Galaria 2007).

Another of these new global digital art cinema entrepreneurs is MUBI's founder, Efe Cakarel, who originates from Turkey. In an interview, he describes how he came up with the idea of the service at precisely the moment he realised that content which would be at his fingertips in North America was out of reach in Asia – MUBI's whole development has been driven by this realisation.

The activities of these new businesses have led to a situation where more and more previously unseen international films are becoming available for on-line viewing, rental or purchase, often through content providers based either in a diaspora or in their respective countries. Most previously-rare Polish or Hungarian cinema, for example, is now available from various distributors on-line, and it is now possible to order rare documentaries from Malaysia (at Red Films) or titles from Ghana (at All African Movies). More importantly, these films have become available to viewers based in locations that were previously beyond the reach of such niche material, by virtue of their geographical remoteness.

There has been a significant growth in websites based in Asia that feature diverse transborder content. The major on-line players in China, for example, are invariably owned by videogame companies or search engines and benefit from cross-border investments from the likes of Hulu or from venture capital firms; the latter include Ku6, LeTV, Qiyi (owned by Baidu), Tudou, Voole and Youku (Shackleton 2011b). Many have entered revenue-sharing deals with the likes of Sony or Warner Bros, and in many instances a significant proportion of the content comes directly from the U.S. studios, while the rest is sourced from Asian producers. Although the majority of, for example, Youku's content comes from Asia, Disney sought to strike a deal with the site, since such a partnership helps the North American associate to bypass China's restrictions on foreign content in cinemas. The revenue for these Chinese on-line sites in 2010 was estimated at U.S.$687 million (Shackleton 2011a).

It is particularly important to stress, though, that such transborder collaborations do not come about merely to create channels for the penetration of Western-made entertainment. In fact, they have greatly facilitated the increased reverse flow of Asian goods into Western markets, and are assisted by three groups of players identified early on by Jenkins (2006): national or regional media producers, multinational conglomerates, as well as niche distributors. And while it may appear that adaptable mainstream players use advanced marketing savvy to enter transborder on-line alliances, the main beneficiaries are the peripheral players who, while still small, now receive a much-widened transnational access and exposure.

New Business Models and Intellectual Property

The theory and practice of intellectual property rights in relation to all cultural businesses is another area experiencing drastic change. Whilst previously the signing away of rights was an inevitable part of the deal of getting into distribution, nowadays copyright holders are more and more likely to opt to retain rights to the content they create; solely acknowledging their moral right to authorship no longer seems to suffice. Content creators are growing increasingly conscious of the commercial realities of ownership and look to increase the technological savvy that allows them to engage in gainful exploitation of their product. More and more commercially successful artists opt to keep the copyright to their works and engage in dissemination strategies over which they have direct control. The old model that required the signing away of copyright was imposed under the reasoning that special expertise was needed for the reproduction and distribution of the work of art in order to make it widely available. Digital developments now make it quite easy for the content creator to handle both production and dissemination and thus eliminate the middleman: disintermediation.

Where once writers were routinely signing away to publishers the exploitation rights for all formats, the trend in recent years has been dominated by movement in the opposite direction: authors retain rights, control publication and sell content out of their own outlets. What was started experimentally by Stephen King's self-publishing undertakings during the late 1990s and early 2000s (often dubbed 'the publishing industry's worst nightmare') was adopted by a number of other high profile authors and has led to such enterprises as the recently-inaugurated Harry Potter site (Pottermore) owned by J.K. Rowling, who, to the dismay of publishers, had retained all rights to the electronic exploitation of her material and is now expected to capitalise massively on it. In the fine arts, popular artist Jack Vettriano opted to retain the rights to his best-selling work and sell it alongside the work of other chosen artists through his own outlet, Heartbreak Publishing. In music, Radiohead became the leaders in copyright retention with their self-released *In Rainbows* album (2007); and more recently, Kaiser Chiefs launched *The Future Is Medieval* (2011), an album that was distributed exclusively peer-to-peer (P2P) through on-line word of mouth. These initiatives have deployed innovative approaches to user input and payment methods, such as an honesty box or fixed price using PayPal, and include the option for purchasers themselves to turn into distributors.

Filmmakers are similarly embracing the idea of retaining copyright. For the time being such an approach to intellectual property is mainly practiced in the sphere of indie filmmaking (Dargis 2010). Still, in an environment where more and more high profile film actors – Will Smith in Hollywood and Aamir Khan in Bollywood, for example – establish and run their own production and distribution companies, it won't be long before we see challenges to the way intellectual property is tackled in mainstream cinema as well.

The evolving conceptualisation of piracy ought to be considered hand-in-hand with these developments. 'The sense that the Internet is a Wild West to be tamed,' notes Michael Gubbins in his contribution to this volume, 'has been typified by the fight to impose the same intellectual property rules that have prevailed in the physical business and in the view that piracy is the fundamental barrier preventing recovery'. He concludes that insistence on the traditional ideas of content ownership and exploitation rights is an idea that 'will be severely tested in both the courts and by consumer behavior'.

Traditionally, large Hollywood studios and the MPAA (Motion Picture Association of America) have fought the line of intellectual property infringement by engaging in extensive global monitoring and by commissioning consultancy reports aimed at estimating the alleged losses incurred as a result of piracy. Such monitoring of illegal activity has traditionally been limited to Hollywood content; there is no readily available data on the extent of piracy in relation to other content owners. Indian distributors have alleged that rampant piracy affects Bollywood imports to North America, yet they have no access to the elaborate research or to the protection mechanisms from which Hollywood benefits.

An increasing number of authors exploring the global dynamics of cultural industries are writing about the lack of understanding of piracy and the untenable, exaggerated and inflexible model still used by the larger players in the West. Henry Jenkins (2006), for example, has observed that a much wider range of content is being pirated and that it is not only American studios, but also a number of other international players who could raise concerns over the piracy practices related to their own products. Scholars who have explored the circulation of films in non-Western contexts, such as Ziauddin Sardar in Indonesia (2005 [2000]) or Brian Larkin in Nigeria (2008), have highlighted specific considerations, insisting on a more flexible interpretation of what constitutes 'piracy', and subjecting to critical scrutiny the inflexible economic practices that facilitate it. Ravi Sundaram has spoken of a 'cluster of legality and non-legality' as being typical for Indian technoculture; he speaks of a 'pirate modernity', which is not a manifestation of counter-cultural anti-corporate trends, but much more 'a simple survival strategy' (2005 [2001]: 45).

More recently, Chris Anderson (2009) has shown that the alleged growth in digital 'piracy' is to be attributed to the rapidly diminishing costs and ease of distributing content via digital reproduction; in a context where film travels mainly through P2P networks, he is right to point out that the traditional views on piracy no longer apply. Anderson advises that piracy be estimated not so much in terms of loss but more in terms of lesser gain (2009: 71) and recommends strategies to accept as legitimate much of what is now seen as pirated material, thus making it available for free as part of innovative business models.

There have been calls to better understand the reasons behind piracy by seeing it from point of view of the cultures in which it thrives. Dropping the artificially maintained high pricing of film content would easily bring 'piracy' in places like China or India to an end; one cannot possibly insist on maintaining a certain level of pricing in a context where the cost of reproduction keeps falling drastically and content becomes more easily accessible all the time. The need to fight piracy by readjusting the inflexible stance that large studio players have taken on the matter is addressed in various essays in this volume. In discussing critic Alexis Tioseco's film viewing in Manila, for example, Ben Slater indicates that, in a non-Western context, piracy is regarded simply as a phenomenon of the local economy. In an interview for our case study on Jaman, CEO Gaurav Dhillon indicates that research has revealed that in Jaman's case if film content could be offered across countries at affordable local prices 'there may be greater incentive for consumers to purchase titles legitimately, rather than downloading them illegally via BitTorrent sites' (Dhillon 2010). Such possible adjustments would also involve overcoming the territorial and zoning restrictions, which still apply and limit the reach of dissemination, as the case study reveals.[4]

There have been radical and rapid developments in other areas, where knotty issues related to intellectual property, levels of payment and piracy have been addressed by activists inspired by uncompromising radical thinkers such as Lawrence Lessig (2005, 2009) and by the open-source movement behind the Creative Commons license. Again, the music industry leads the way here by taking decisive action, with varying degrees of success, to shut down illegal download sites (Napster, The Pirate Bay) while offering alternatives in easily accessible and affordable services (such as iTunes or Pandora); even if the newly modified versions have to comply with geoblocking technological restrictions. Indie filmmakers such as Spanner Films are looking at similar models; a range of independent filmmakers are engaged with ideas and projects are that are 'in effect creating a virtual infrastructure' (Dargis 2010) and advancing approaches that utilise the new channels for the dissemination of alternative content. There is no confrontation with Hollywood and its take on piracy in these activist models; the studios are squarely bracketed out of the emerging circulation infrastructure.

Parallel developments in film are somewhat delayed; advanced P2P technologies such as BitTorrent are still regarded as mainly backing illegal downloads; their innovative potential is still to be recognised.[5] The success stories in film are still few and far between: in this volume Michael Gubbins discusses Jamie King's VODO service, launched in 2009 and billed as 'free-to-share films available through BitTorrent', which has seized on the potential of P2P network file-sharing to distribute content for free while soliciting donations, hoping that even a small percentage of payments could make a significant difference if they originate from a large enough audience.[6]

Most of these new approaches, which still appear to be in the DIY domain, rest on the premise that new technology significantly lowers costs and can inexpensively secure the widest possible access to content in a context where rights are being retained by the filmmakers. New business thinking, inspired by radical innovative approaches, such as the 'Blue Ocean Strategy' (Chan Kim and Mauborgne 2005), and enhanced by an improving grasp of the 'freemium' models discussed by Chris Anderson (2009), become the norm for these new digital era enterprises.[7] In the new digital economy, both production and distribution costs substantially diminish and so the proportion of 'free' versus 'paid' product changes dramatically in favor of a 'freemium' model, where a minority of paying customers subsidises a majority of free users. Most of the pioneering business models were first developed in the sphere of the music industry and were based mainly on the recognition that any content, if it becomes popular, gets pirated sooner or later, and that there is no way to counteract unauthorised copying. By recognising that it is expensive and counter-productive to fight illegal reproduction effectively, these business models have approached the matter radically and made their content free. This free availability, in turn, made satellite products that were not so easy to copy all the more likely to sell. Thus, the main revenues for musical bands which hold intellectual property rights and make their content available on-line for free are now generated from merchandise, memorabilia, advertising on behalf of corporate sponsors, events, luxury lifestyle products or tourism.

Although 'freemium' models, where the 'live' extension grows in importance, can and do work in music, no one has yet worked out how the payment for a live option will work for film. Such opportunities and new approaches in relation to film are discussed here in the context of events organised by Power to the Pixel, a company dedicated to supporting film and the wider media in its transition to a digital age, as well as by TH_NK, a London- and Newcastle-based agency specialising in digital innovation, networking and on-line reputation. The inherently borderless, transnational essence of businesses operated over the Internet is yet another disruptive feature that enhances the new business models by permitting access to an unlimited number of global users.

In a virtual infrastructure where creation and maintenance costs are dramatically reduced, concerns over 'piracy' are likely to be undermined and eliminated. New models for film circulation are likely to be built around recognising that those who cannot pay for content ought to be treated as consumers with equal rights and legitimacy, and that it is the content owners who ought to adjust their own operations and accommodate the potential consumers of pirated content.[8]

Film Festivals: Space of Flows

Developments in digital technology profoundly change the way in which film festivals develop their programmes, relate to their audiences and interact with each other. These changes are most palpable in three spheres.

First, many festivals now stream some (or all) of the films on their programmes on-line as well; there has been growth in the number of film festivals that operate entirely on-line, as Marijke de Valck points out in her essay in this volume. Such a change in exhibition practice, however, disturbs the notions of community, togetherness and live-ness around which festivals have traditionally evolved (Harbord 2009).

Second, there are the profound changes to the position of the film festival in the hierarchy of film circulation. In the traditional distributor-dominated set-up, the film festival was outside the distribution chain and seen as pre-cursor to distribution itself: a film would screen at festivals in the hope of striking deals that would get it through to distribution. In the new disintermediated set-up, however, the film festival becomes a key element of the film's circulation. Once it has become a site for the direct exhibition of cinema, a festival also receives the chance to network closer with other festivals, a development that is greatly facilitated and enhanced by the appearance of technological means that enable coordinated streaming of the same content to multiple festivals.

Third, a host of new services has grown up around the transmission of digital submissions to festivals. Content is now streamlined directly to festival programmers around the world and this has allowed them to apply new strategies to festival planning.

Manuel Castells' concept of 'space of flows' is particularly suitable for describing this new world of the film festival. These flows, in Castells' usage, are 'the material arrangements that allow for simultaneity of social practices without territorial contiguity'. The 'space of flows' is 'made of networks of interactions; the goals and task of each network configurate in a different space of flows' (2005 [2001]: 628). Film festivals, alongside financial markets, business services and even cross-border trafficking, can be regarded as space of flows, as all these phenomena are increasingly 'made up of nodes and hubs' and provide 'habitats for the social actors who operate the networks'. The space of flows comprises 'electronic spaces such as websites, spaces of interaction as well as spaces of one-directional communication, be it interactive or not, such as information systems' (2011 [2005]: 629).

Well-established and innovative film festivals have looked to extend the space of flows and capitalise on their privileged access to content by seeking additional platforms for showcasing the wealth of material they receive. The best-known example is perhaps the Sundance Film Festival which has been running its TV Sundance Channel for over a decade now: a cable channel featuring art house, indie and foreign cinema that receives a fairly wide exposure through a number of carriers across North America. This model underwent even further development after its architect, Geoff Gilmore, moved from the Sundance Institute to Tribeca Enterprises (which also runs the eponymous film festival). 'It's not enough any more to do what a festival traditionally does,' says Gilmore (Kay 2010: 14). He now seeks to combine traditional modes of festival exhibition with the use of VOD and specialised television carriers, such as Comcast, Cablevision and Verizon, to release specialist foreign films that, in his estimation, could reach audiences of up to 40 million people. Other new ventures have included the simultaneous release of festival films via VOD technology, first by Sundance Select in January 2011 and then by Tribeca in April 2011. The new technologies allow festivals to deliver alternative, indie and world cinema in a much easier fashion – as one can see by the thriving associations between film festivals and new streaming providers like MUBI and Jaman, both featured in this volume.[9]

There is something like festivals 'direct' – with many festivals starting to make available on-line material also shown at the festival. One such recent example is the Festival Internacional de Cine del Sahara in the refugee camp of Dhakla, Western Sahara. International activists and local audiences participated in the 'live' edition of the festival (confirming the live-ness of the event), while supporters and diasporic audiences from around the world were able to take part and express solidarity via the on-line streaming of the films shown at the physical festival (Simanowitz and Santaollala 2012).

Yet wouldn't moving on-line rescind the all-important togetherness and the live experience that festivals provide? Apparently not. As Gubbins notes in this volume, it may even enhance community building: the two spheres remain closely related – the desire for real time communality seems to grow as more and more social space is co-opted by the on-line world, and the two spheres mutually complement each other. 'An on-line festival is not just for people who can't be there in person,' writes Geoffrey Gilmore. 'The people who are attending the films want to be part of the community and on-line experience as well. Festivals have always been about creating a community, but now they can do this is [in] a number of different ways' (Gilmore 2011).[10]

Digital developments present tremendous opportunities for festivals and filmmakers, a theme developed here by de Valck. In the past, film festivals operated in a complex logistical bubble ordained by distance and time; location and calendar position were of primary importance. New technology helps to overcome such logistical limitations; the filmmakers' burden of shipping screeners and prints to festivals is also taken away. Other dimensions of the traditional film festival also change. Hannah McGill, until recently artistic director of the Edinburgh International Film Festival, talks of a 'last-days-of-the-Raj feeling that increasingly pervades the film festival circuit'. The traditional festival set-up seems no longer sustainable in an era of 'multiple channels of instantaneous digital communication' where 'distribution and exhibition models evolve more rapidly and confoundingly than ever', and where those film festivals that 'remain resolutely committed to old-school forms of presentation' and 'fetishise exclusivity via premiere status, while overlooking advances in technology' are in danger of extinction (McGill 2011: 281).

In this new environment, festivals are gradually beginning to operate in a more or less coordinated manner and to form a network that is enabled by improved technology, easier logistics and, yes, disintermediation; the lessened power of distributors who previously dictated circulation of material and the facilitated direct access to content change the picture substantially. The improved networking of festivals is largely determined by the advancements in technology: nowadays more festivals can spring up without the constraints of overcrowding or direct competition for resources that were previously imposed by spatial and temporal factors; exhibition through the festival circuit comes increasingly to resemble a distribution sequence. The new disintermediated business model also includes wider outreach – as seen in the case of Tribeca's global content initiatives and the extension of the film festival on-line. These developments may also bring an end to the practice of 'festival hopping', as services such as Festival Scope make content available to practitioners and eliminate the need to attend festivals in person. The 'free radical' professionals who had previously hopped from one festival to another no longer enjoy the powerful networking role they once had (Iordanova 2009); new on-line services take over this function.

Festivals that previously competed for premières and new films now realise that they serve different publics and that therefore they can still showcase the same programme, even while simultaneously streaming it in cyberspace to even wider audiences. It is now a frequent occurrence that festivals that share similar themes and scope or have geographical and calendar proximity opt to collaborate.[11] In such a context, playing at festivals (where the charging of screening fees is gradually becoming the norm) becomes equivalent to distribution: one realises more and more that the festival is no longer the venue where distributors could be accessed; the festival itself is the distribution. There is also the networking of festivals that share similar political standings in a global context, as illustrated by the activities of the thriving Southern Film Festivals Platform that includes a range of festivals from what can be termed the Global South (Iordanova 2010b).

Some of these new festival partnerships are actively sought after, while some are entered into by accidental overlaps of thematic or aesthetic spheres of interest. These new linkages are facilitated by enabling technologies such as the digital transmission service offered by Withoutabox, which markets itself as a revolutionary and liberating 'suite of on-line tools' that undermine the old distribution channels and ensure that filmmakers get direct access to festivals.[12] As Alex Fischer notes in another of his contributions to this volume, Withoutabox has supplied radically new and effective means by which filmmakers now interact with film festivals.[13] Its recent pairing with the IMDb under the Amazon umbrella will make a further enhancement of the global circulation of independently-produced films even more likely.

Until recently it was not possible for a professional to be instantly familiar with new content showcased at festivals taking place concurrently in different locations; one could either be at the festival in Toronto or at the festival in Venice. Beyond Withoutabox, however, new initiatives have emerged which link festival practitioners, circulating content and exhibition outlets. The MEDIA-sponsored Paris-based transnational operation Eye on Films uses advanced technology to build networks of festivals, cinemas and distributors, and Festival Scope makes content available on-line for buyers who cannot physically attend festival markets but can still view what is on offer. These services coordinate submissions to festivals and thus become the nodes in a new global network that guarantees a more extensive festival circulation.

The New Cinéphilia

'Repertory cinema has relocated into cyberspace,' proclaimed Ben Slater in a 2007 article intended to highlight the 'new cinéphilia' that has been increasingly in focus since the turn of the new millennium (Rosenbaum and Martin 2003, De Valck and Hagener 2005). Not only mainstream Hollywood, but also rare historical and foreign films can now be downloaded or viewed on-line; such material is also available for free from sites such as YouTube, where full length classics, documentaries or new international and other specialist films that are not officially distributed can be found cut into parts of ten-minute duration for easier and more stable streaming.[14] This represents not only a new way of circulation, but also a radically new viewing experience.[15]

'Yes, I believe you can be a cinéphile even if the majority of your film watching happens outside the cinema,' remarks Mathieu Ravier. Today, technology is leveling the playing field and so making, sharing, watching and talking about films is becoming 'more than ever, accessible to everyone' (Ravier 2011). Some viewers rely on advanced home cinema set-ups while others become members of on-line communities where material is shared via elaborate networks that often span countries and continents.

The Internet not only caters to special interest audiences by making available a wide range of classic and contemporary non-mainstream cinema, it also allows those fans based far from major metropolitan hubs to gain unprecedented access to films that were previously out of reach for them. This is a disruption that makes the film lover's experience more inclusive as it allows access to a wider diversity of material and brings to life a multiplicity of various critical voices. 'As a reaction against the Hollywood hegemony and the chauvinism of the classic art-house canon,' writes Slater, 'young cinéphiles who live in the cinematically less well-traveled regions (South-East Asia, Eastern Europe, the Middle East) are able to reconsider the films of their home countries in a level of depth and detail that visiting programmers and critics can never muster.' This unprecedented level of access allows them to both 'champion ground-breaking young directors, as well as excavate marginalized masters of the past' (Slater 2007: 27).

Writing in this volume, Slater compares his own formative experiences growing up in provincial England of the 1980s with the much broader cinematic exposure that his younger Internet-generation friend, the late Filipino critic Alexis Tioseco (1981-2009), enjoyed from the mid-1990s, even though he was based in the seemingly remote outpost of Manila, from which he edited his on-line magazine, *Criticine*.

Film fans can now discuss cinema in cyberspace at the lively IMDb discussions fora that bring together the critical opinions of viewers from all over the world.[16] Committed cinéphiles grow ever more active in such a context, which brings them together and allows the meeting of those of similar awareness and knowledge. Critics no longer need to be affiliated with established media outlets in order to have their voices heard; they can and do participate in discussions at dedicated sites (such as Twitch or The Evening Class), congregate for ad hoc on-line fora (see, for example Project: New Cinéphilia 2011), or run their own specialist blogs or increasingly respected personal sites (e.g. Chris Fujiwara's Insane Mute). In doing so, they embrace a host of new opportunities that sometimes supply them with alternatively-styled eminence equal to or even superseding the authority of officially sanctioned film critics and criticism.[17]

Two further specific characteristics of the Internet-enabled cinéphiles are worth highlighting: they seem to share a particular appreciation of the international experience and they advocate from a specific activist point of view. The heroes of these new modes of cinema appreciation are often people with particular cosmopolitan credentials who have lived the experience of moving countries and have gained exposure to cinema from various parts of the world – Hengameh Panahi of Celluloid Dreams is an Iranian based in Paris, Efe Cakarel of The Auteurs and MUBI is originally from Turkey, Gaurav Dhillon of Jaman is an Indian-American, Ben Slater, who contributes the essay on cinéphilia here, is British but based in Singapore and Mathieu Ravier is a Frenchman writing out of Sydney.[18]

When reacting to these new modes of viewing and discussing cinema, traditional marketing for film also tends to move into cyberspace. Recommendation algorithms and word-of-mouth publicity via vernacular but vibrant channels play growing roles in the promotion of films. Publicity strategies change profoundly as chat rooms, recommendation engines, Twitter feeds and blog-based film criticism gradually become the make-or-break focus of marketing efforts. The new cinéphilia can push up a small independent feature as easily as it can undermine a multimillion-dollar production.[19]

It is Ravier again who, when writing in the context of the recent MUBI-sponsored Project: New Cinéphilia (2011) identified the new cinéphilia as 'activist'. Concerned over 'the lack of diversity and representation' and that 'the multiplicity of voices behind and around the camera is less reflected in mainstream culture, media and awareness than it could be', he saw diversity on the screen as under threat and felt that it was important to combat and overcome the prevailing 'ignorance about alternatives'. His conclusion? That the new cinéphilia ought to be treated as 'a form of activism or resistance' (Ravier 2011). According to this understanding, cinéphilia has a corrective and counter-cultural role to play by engaging in a rebalancing act aimed at bringing the awareness of truly diverse global cinema to wider audiences.

* * *

Digital disruption not only erodes traditional channels of commercial – theatrical and ancillary – exploitation of cinematic content. It also leads to radical changes in the ways that the film festival circuit operates, in the ways in which film content is disseminated to a worldwide spread of diasporic audiences, as well in the ways in which a new global cinéphilia emerges and manifests itself.

It is a democratising process. Having moved on-line, film becomes liberated from the 'tyranny of geography': the new distribution set-up permits unrestrained availability of distinctive products. The residents of a remote village can now have access to cultural goods just as easily as those based in vibrant metropolitan hubs.

All essays in this volume aim to outline essential features of this new digital dynamics of world cinema. The main chapters survey advancing models and technologies that condition the changes of the global landscape for commercial cinema within the new film economy. They examine emerging circulation environments and report on issues and difficulties that arise in the process of advancing innovation. The case studies and resource materials chart evolving examples (IMDb, Jaman, Withoutabox, MUBI) whose full impacts are still to be assessed.

Some active areas that play a role in these profound changes in global film circulation processes still belong to the grey economy and remain understudied for various reasons. Film festivals, for one, still represent an unregulated global industry that cannot be quantified based on currently available data, yet they nonetheless function as a major form of cinematic exhibition. Then there is the large grey area of diasporic video distribution via eclectic channels such as ethnic grocery stores and makeshift market stalls; there is Internet TV and clandestine cable broadcasts (the latter yet another area where reliable estimates are hard to come by). And then comes the growth of Internet-enabled film streaming taking place outside known and regulated commercial channels. We have made a special effort to acknowledge and make advances into the discussion of these multifarious channels.

Indeed, as per Geoff Gilmore's remark which opens this essay, the Internet *is* changing the ways in which people experience watching movies. In a manner similar to the processes underway in the publishing and music industries, cinema, too, is in the process of moving on-line.

Works Cited

Abbas, Ackbar and John Nguyen Erni (eds) (2005) *Internationalizing Cultural Studies: An Anthology*. Oxford: Blackwell.

Anderson, Chris (2009) *Free: The Future of a Radical Price*. New York: Hyperion.

Bettig, Ronald (2007) 'Hollywood and Intellectual Property', in Paul MacDonald and Janet Wasko (eds) *The Contemporary Hollywood Film Industry*. Oxford: Blackwell, 195-209.

Boudway, Ira (2011) 'The Next Indie Darling, Courtesy of the Crowds', *Business Week*, 30, May, 52.

Broderick, Peter (2008) 'Welcome to the New World of Distribution'. On-line. Available HTTP: http://www.peterbroderick.com/writing/writing/welcometothenewworld.html (20 June 2011).

Burgess, Jean and Joshua Green (2009) *YouTube: Online Video and Participatory Culture*. London: Polity Press.

Castells, Manuel (2005 [2001]) 'Grassrouting the Space of Flows', in Ackbar Abbas and John Nguyen Erni (eds) *Internationalizing Cultural Studies: An Anthology*. Oxford: Blackwell, 627-36.

Cendrowski, Scott (2011) 'Bytes Beat Bricks', *Fortune*, 4 July, 10.

Chan Kim, W. and Renée Mauborgne (2005) *Blue Ocean Strategy: How to Create Uncontested Market Space and Make the Competition Irrelevant*. Boston: Harvard Business Press.

Cineaste (2008) 'Film Criticism in the Age of the Internet, A Critical Symposium', *Cineaste*, 33, 4, 30-47.

Cunningham, Stuart and John Sinclair (eds) (2001) *Floating Lives: The Media and Asian Diasporas*. Lanham, MD: Rowman and Littlefield.

Curtin, Michael and Hemant Shah (eds) (2010) *Reorienting Global Communication: Indian and Chinese Media Beyond Borders*. Urbana and Chicago: University of Illinois Press.

Dargis, Manohla (2010) 'Declaration of Indies: Just Sell It Yourself!' *New York Times*, January 14. On-line. Available HTTP: http://www.nytimes.

com/2010/01/17/movies/17dargis.html?scp=1&sq=declaration%20of%20 indies&st=cse (10 June 2011).

Davis, Darrell William and Emilie Yueh-yu Yeh (2008) *East Asian Screen Industries*, London: BFI.

Davoudi, Salamander (2011) 'UK Cinemas will Fight VOD Plans', *Financial Times*, May 1. On-line. Available HTTP: http://www.ft.com/intl/cms/s/0/74990b68-7423-11e0-b788-00144feabdc0,s01=1.html (10 June 2011).

De Valck, Marijke (2007) *Film Festivals: From European Geopolitics to Global Cinéphilia*. Amsterdam: Amsterdam University Press.

De Valck, Marijke and Malte Hagener (eds) (2005) *Cinéphilia: Movies, Love and Memory*. Amsterdam: Amsterdam University Press.

Dhillon, Gaurav (2010), Unpublished Skype interview conducted by Stuart Cunningham and Jon Silver, 1 April.

Dhillon, Gaurav and Galaria, Faisal (2007) 'Hi-def Independent Films Online with Jaman', Podtech interview conducted by Robert Scoble, *Classic ScobleShow*, 27 June. On-line. Available HTTP: http:// connectedsocialmedia.com/2931/hi-def-independent-films-online-with-jaman/ (12 August, 2011).

Fischer, Alex (2011) 'Film Festival Submission: Case Study'. On-line. Available HTTP: http://www.st-andrews.ac.uk/worldcinema/index.php/resources/ research (28 September 2011).

Garrahan, Matthew (2011) 'Hollywood Studios Agree Pay-TV Deal', *Financial Times*, March 31. On-line. Available HTTP: http://.ft.com/cms/s/0/968f2d0e-5be8-11e0-bb56-00144feab49a.html#axzz1Zel69vPs (20 July 2011).

Gilmore, Geoffrey (2011) 'How the Internet Is Changing the Film Festival Experience', *Future of Film Blog*, 4 April. On-line. Available HTTP: http:// www.tribecafilm.com/tribecaonline/future-of-film/How-the-Internet-is-Changing-the-Film-Festival-Experience.html (23 April 2011).

Goodridge, Mike (2010) 'Small Is Beautiful', *Screen International*, 1722, April, 1.

Harbord, Janet (2009) 'Film Festivals-Time-Event', in Dina Iordanova and Ragan Rhyne (eds) *Film Festival Yearbook 1: The Festival Circuit*. St Andrews: St Andrews Film Studies, 40-6.

Hastings, Reed (2011) Interview conducted by Charlie Rose, *Bloomberg Business Week*, 9 May, 26.

Iordanova, Dina (1999) 'Expanding Universe: From the Ethnic Foodstore to Blockbuster', *Framework: The Journal of Cinema and Media*, 41, Autumn, 54-70.

_____ (2009) 'The Film Festival Circuit', in Dina Iordanova with Ragan Rhyne (eds) *Film Festival Yearbook 1: The Festival Circuit*. St Andrews: St Andrews Film Studies, 23-39.

_____ (2010a) 'Rise of the Fringe: Global Cinema's Long Tail', in Dina Iordanova, David Martin-Jones and Belen Vidal (eds) *Cinema at the Periphery*. Detroit: Wayne State UP, 30-65.

_____ (2010b) 'From the Source: Cinemas of the South', *Film International*, 8, 5, November, 95-9.

Izzo, Phil (2011) 'Top 10 Dying Industries,' *The Wall Street Journal*, 28 March. On-line. Available HTTP: http://blogs.wsj.com/economics/2011/03/28/top-10-dying-industries/ (17 August 2011).

Jenkins, Henry (2006) 'Pop Cosmopolitanism: Mapping Cultural Flows in an Age of Media Convergence', in *Fans, Bloggers and Gamers: Exploring Participatory Culture*. New York: New York University Press, 152-73.

Kay, Jeremy (2010) 'Tribeca Takes on Distribution', *Screen International*, 1722, April,14-15.

Keane, Michael, Anthony Y.H. Fung and Albert Moran (2007) *New Television, Globalisation, and the East Asian Cultural Imagination*. Hong Kong: Hong Kong University Press.

Keen, Andrew (2008) *The Cult of the Amateur: How Blogs, MySpace, YouTube and the Rest of Today's User-Generated Media are Killing our Culture and Economy*. London: Nicholas Brealey Publishing Ltd.

Larkin, Brian (2008) *Signal and Noise: Media, Infrastructure, and Urban Culture in Nigeria*. Durham: Duke University Press.

Lessig, Lawrence (2005) *Free Culture: The Nature and Future of Creativity*. New York: Penguin Books.

_____ (2009) *Remix: Making Art and Commerce Thrive in the Hybrid Economy*. New York: Penguin Books.

Levine, Robert (2011) *Free Ride: How the Internet is Destroying the Culture Business and and How the Culture Business Can Fight Back*. London: Bodley Head.

McGill, Hannah (2011) 'Film Festivals: A View from the Inside', *Screen*, 52, 2, Summer, 280-6.

McMillin, Divya C. (2010) 'The Global Face of Indian Television', in Michael Curtin and Hemant Shah (eds) *Reorienting Global Communication: Indian and Chinese Media Beyond Borders*. Urbana and Chicago: University of Illinois Press, 118-39.

Macnab, Geoffrey (2010) 'Now Appearing in Theatres', *Screen International*, 1724, June, 27.

MUBI (2011) *Project: New Cinéphilia*, MUBI and Edinburgh International Film Festival, May/June. On-line. Available HTTP: http://projectcinéphilia.MUBI.com/ (10 July 2011).

Needham, Col (2011) 'Spotlight on IMDb Founder Col Needham', Edinburgh International Film Festival event, 19 June.

Ravier, Mathieu (2011) 'Cinéphilia as Activism', *Project: New Cinéphilia*, 26 May. On-line. Available HTTP: http://projectcinéphilia.MUBI.com/2011/05/26/cinéphilia-as-activism/ (10 July 2011).

Roddick, Nick (2007) 'Cinema on Demand', *Sight & Sound*, October 2007, 14.

Rosenbaum, Jonathan and Adrian Martin (eds) (2003) *Movie Mutations: The Changing Face of World Cinéphilia*. London: BFI.

Sardar, Ziauddin (2005 [2000]) 'On the Political Economy of a Fake', in Ackbar Abbas and John Nguyen Erni (eds) (2005) *Internationalizing Cultural Studies: An Anthology*. Oxford: Blackwell, 658-63.

Shackleton, Liz (2010) 'The Sky's the Limit', *Screen International*, 1724, June, 6-7.

_____ (2011a) 'Net Worth', *Screen International*, 1734, February, 38-9.

_____ (2011b) 'Internet Pioneers', *Screen International*, 1734, February, 39.

Sight & Sound (2008a) 'Who Needs Critics', *Sight & Sound*, September. On-line. Available HTTP: http://www.bfi.org.uk/sightandsound/feature/49479 (28 September 2011).

_____ (2008b) 'Critics on Critics', *Sight & Sound*, September. On-line. Available HTTP: http://www.bfi.org.uk/sightandsound/feature/49480 (28 September 2011).

Simanowitz, Stefan and Isabel Santaollala (2012), 'A Cinematic Refuge in the Desert: Festival Internacional de Cine del Sahara', in Dina Iordanova and Leshu Torchin (eds) *Film Festival Yearbook 4: Film Festivals and Activism*. St Andrews: St Andrews Film Studies.

Sinclair, John, and Graeme Turner (eds) (2004) *Contemporary World Television*. London: BFI.

Slater, Ben (2007) 'The New Cinéphiles,' *Screen International*, November, 26-7.

Sundaram, Ravi ([2001]2005), 'Recycling Modernity: Pirate Electronic Cultures in India', in Ackbar Abbas and John Nguyen Erni (eds) *Internationalizing Cultural Studies: An Anthology*. Oxford: Blackwell, 43-50.

Tartaglione, Nancy (2010) 'The Wild Man,' *Screen International*, 1724, June, 46.

Vega, Noel (2009) 'Obituary: Alexis Tioseco,' *After Dark*, September. On-line. Available HTTP: http://criticafterdark.blogspot.com/2009/09/alexis-tioseco-1981-2009.html (10 July 2011).

Wiseman, Andreas (2011) 'MUBI to show 4.1 Film Festival Competition Titles', *Screen Daily*, 8 August. On-line. Available HTTP: http://www.screendaily.com/news/digital/MUBI-to-show-41-film-festival-competition-titles/5030649.article (12 September 2011).

Notes

[1]   Kickstarter, the best-known crowdfunding site, which only launched in 2009, has rapidly become one of the main sources of fundraising for independent cinema. It helps filmmakers to crowdsource up to six-figure sums, most commonly for activist projects that are not likely to meet with the approval of institutional backers. By spreading the investment more widely, this funding model lessens the likelihood of interference from investors and studios.

[2]   More recently, commentators have noticed that a certain 'blurring [of] the line between TV and film' also goes the opposite way, as in the case of HBO, which 'has often screened its made-for-HBO features in festivals' (Goodridge 2010).

[3]   Jaman, a Silicon Valley-based enterprise that launched in January 2007, is engaged in the download of and on-line access to feature films. It differs from its competitors in that it promptly licenses content from international cinema and makes it available to global audiences. By assertively putting in place content agreements with a variety of international rights holders to peripheral cinematic content and taking future licensing deals for libraries featuring Hong Kong, Indian, cult and art house titles, Jaman purposefully capitalises on international and independent film that remains in the periphery of distribution. It also works with film festivals, aiming to take exclusive rights for on-line showings of films that are screening at certain festivals (Tribeca, San Francisco IFF, Cinequest), thus fostering a festival distribution circuit and pushing festival exposure towards something that may soon come to resemble a truly global distribution pattern.

[4]   A number of sites make video material available for download, using either BitTorrent, the on-line file sharing system, or other new technologies of peer-casting (iTunes, Babelgum, Joost, Veoh, GONG, to name just a few of the sites discussed in this volume). Many of the download sites comply with geo-blocking restrictions: content from LoveFilm, BBC's iPlayer, Channel 4, Sky Anytime and BTVision, for example, is restricted for use within the United Kingdom.

[5]   Mininova, a P2P BitTorrent site, and once a source for illegal content, legitimised its operations in late 2009 at the behest of the Dutch courts by removing access to over a million torrent files deemed to infringe copyright, offering instead access to the content of only approved and legally compliant uploaders. It has remained a successful P2P site with over 18,000 files available and a download rate of one file every 1.6 seconds. See http://torrentfreak.com/10-alternatives-to-mininova-091126 and http://

www.mininova.org/statistics. (Thanks are due to Steve Blackey for drawing my attention to this.)

6   Reportedly, founder Jamie King's own two-part *Steal This Film* (UK/ Germany, 2006/2007) was produced mainly with crowdsourced finance and then released and distributed via BitTorrent. The service has been signing up a number of other films for P2P release; the site claims that 9.8 million downloads of films had taken place by June 2011.

7   It is important to note, however, that not everybody is as welcoming to the new developments. There are specialist authors – such as Andrew Keen (2008) and Robert Levine (2011) – who have taken a critical stance on these matters; they each offer alternatives to the disruptive developments related to copyright as triggered by the advancement of the 'crowdsourcing' and 'freemium' models.

8   Skype, the revolutionary Internet phone operation, is one of the best-developed examples of such new 'freemium' models: only 10% of its operations are paid for by users, yet this small fraction of paid activity is sufficient to subsidise the vast global operation of the remaining 90% of the

transnational network and ensure it stays free. The sizable free element, which now accounts for a much higher proportion of the usage, is in the core of these new business models (see a number of further examples in Anderson 2009). While not free, other on-line film businesses experiment with affordable models that use tiered-pricing: UK-based Spanner Films, for example, is using an 'honesty box' pay structure and charges clients on a differential sliding scale, depending on their perceived ability to pay for content.

9   MUBI, for example, entered into a collaboration with the Latin American 4+1 Film Festival, which takes place simultaneously in Argentina, Brazil, Colombia, Mexico and Spain, to stream recent hits from other festivals such as Locarno, Cannes, Mar de Plata and Berlin. The films are sourced from different festival competitions and re-mixed for the purposes of competing for a '4+1 Audience Award' (Wiseman 2011).

10   In his opening post at the *Future of Film Blog* which centres its attention on these same developments in the life of film, Gilmore remarks: 'Recent advances in digital technology mean that we have new ways of thinking about what an online festival can be. At Tribeca, we see the online festival as being a way of building out a community; a way of interacting with the Tribeca Film Festival and, perhaps most importantly, a way of interacting with the film festival (especially its filmmakers) – even if you live in New York and are going to the Tribeca Film Festival in person' (Gilmore 2011).

[11] The Sheffield Doc/Fest and the Edinburgh International Film Festival attempted such collaboration by sharing over 10 première documentaries in June 2011.

[12] See Alex Fischer's revealing account that compares the process of submitting work to film festivals via a traditional method and via Withoutabox (Fischer 2011).

[13] The claim of servicing 5,000 festivals (as seen at the Withoutabox home page on the Web; www.withoutabox.com) sets the number of film festivals significantly higher than other estimates, which usually set the figure at about 3,000.

[14] Examples include classical Soviet feature *Aerograd* (Alexander Dovzhenko, USSR, 1935; available to view at: www.archive.org/details/aerograd), an activist documentary *Good Kurds, Bad Kurds* (Kevin McKiernan, U.S., 2000; available to view at: www.youtube.com/watch?v=x33grBe_wjQ), or a contemporary Turkish political thriller that is not likely to receive distribution in the West – *Kurtlar Vadisi Filistin (Valley of the Wolves: Palestine 2011*, Zübeyr Sasmaz, Turkey, 2011, available to view at: www.youtube.com/watch?v=NbWS5d_cAvl). All sites accessed 28 September 2011.

[15] In 2008 Hammer Films rose from the grave and in an attempt to resurrect the name of the classic British gothic horror brand released a new feature film *Beyond the Rave* (Matthias Hoehne, UK, 2008) in just such a way. Twenty five-minute 'webisodes' were delivered via the social networking site MySpace and on YouTube (see www.youtube.com/watch?v=epQytGiyRGo). (Thanks to Steve Blackey for drawing my attention to this.)

[16] The IMDb itself is yet another example of a crowdsourced resource where the majority of information about international cinema has been contributed by volunteers based all over the world. See Alex Fischer's case study on IMDb's origins and evolution in this volume.

[17] The terminal decline of traditional professional film criticism has been discussed extensively in the context of print and on-line publications (Cineaste 2008, Sight and Sound 2009). There is consensus both that print is going electronic and that the distinction between professional and amateur film critics is dissolving. The first such influential indie critic was Harry Knowles of *Ain't It Cool News*, who directly swayed Hollywood's fortunes for a while through Web-based postings made out of his flat in Austin, Texas: a city that is not exactly perceived as a centre of power in film industry circles. Popular print-based critics such as Jonathan Rosenbaum have moved most of their existing writing to Internet sites where they

publish all new writing and from which they communicate directly with readers and fans. More recently, a host of new cinéphile bloggers (Girish Shambu, Noel Vega) have turned into the new masters of film discussions in cyberspace, bringing the cinema of the periphery more and more into focus. Geographical borders and distance no longer matter as, indeed, 'the cinéphile community has become such a small world today linked by the Internet' as Noel Vega remarks at his blog *Critic after Dark* (2009). Such situations raise serious questions about the precariousness of critical work and the repercussions of various 'free culture' models, issues raised by Keen (2008) and Levine (2011).

18 The chances to increase the diversity and reach out to non-Western cinéphiles expand far beyond the professional circles. For example, critic Jonathan Rosenbaum, who now writes mainly for his own site, speaks of a Persian teacher based in a remote Iranian town as one of his most influential readers; he describes his correspondence with this distant cinéphile (who would otherwise not likely have access to the *Chicago Reader* for which Rosenbaum wrote for over 20 years) as one of the most satisfying experiences to have come along with this new Internet-based mode of interactive critical writing (Jonathan Rosenbaum, talk at the University of St Andrews, Scotland, October 2009).

19 Mainstream distributors are growing conscious of the reputation of films in the domain of Internet conversations, paying specific attention to the buzz a film generates on social networking sites like Facebook and monitoring postings to millions of blogs, with the assistance of services such as Blogpulse and Technorati, which track tens of millions of blogs.

On-line Film Distribution: Its History and Global Complexion

Stuart Cunningham and Jon Silver

On-line distribution of film and related screen content is an emergent element in the dynamically changing landscape of screen culture. Will on-line distribution have an impact on the film industry to the extent that peer-to-peer downloading has transformed the music industry? Does on-line distribution offer new affordances to rest of the world, independent (indie) and amateur cinema? Where in the world are there good examples of the uptake of such affordances?

Our focus here is on-line – that is, screen content delivered and consumed over the Internet and via the Web – which is to be distinguished from most of the major forms of video-on-demand (VOD) delivered by cable, satellite, Internet Protocol Television (IPTV), informal markets/street vendors, or the postal service. This is because we want to concentrate on how film is being distributed in the context of the broader culture of the Internet. We only touch on the new world of on-line-enabled production, disintermediated marketing and crowdsourced financing as they intersect with emergent strategies for the on-line distribution of film.

We follow Ramon Lobato in making a distinction between 'formal' and 'informal' film distribution – the formal lies within the legally sanctioned, formal economy on which distribution data and trends are routinely based, while the informal encompasses grey (secondary markets, household-level peer-to-peer exchange) as well as black markets (Lobato 2009; 2010). In this chapter, we concentrate on the formal market, while also building into our analysis the increasingly dramatic effects on the formal of the informal.

The on-line distribution formal market is small: commercially, North America dominates, with 95% of a very small U.S.$365 million market according to current market estimates. Rest-of-the-world and indie films constitute parts of large catalogues, with very few dedicated legal sites (the outstanding exception is Jaman, which is featured in a case study elsewhere in this book). However, on-line distribution operations related to the rest of the world are growing and feature a wide range of experimental strategies to create a more level playing field for non-Hollywood filmmaking. Our three-year study identified over 300 on-line distribution sites around the world (see appendices 2 and 3). Many are now defunct.

Winds of Change?

For most of the twentieth century, America dominated the world economy and Hollywood dominated the world's cinema screens. It is a baleful truth that 'the majority of European films still do not find their way into the cinemas outside of their home territories' (Cineuropa 2009), but this also holds true for most of the rest of the world because Hollywood's increasingly well-resourced release strategies for its blockbusters consistently roadblock screens available for films from the rest of the world. It is a lock-out, or it seems that way from the other side of the fence.

However, just as in recent decades there has been a transformative change in the world economy and geopolitics – the rise of China and India, the relative decline of the U.S. and Japan, serious challenges to the U.S.'s historic economic hegemony and vast Asian populations of increasing wealth – so, too, are there now different opportunities for filmmakers from the rest of the world to carve out spaces in a digitised world of art and entertainment.

There are early signals of a potential change in the dynamics of world cinema. During the 2000s, in theatrical markets in France, Germany, Italy, Japan and the UK, a general trend was evident that, despite Hollywood's saturation releasing strategies, locally made films were achieving greater commercial success in their home markets (see Table 1, page 33).

Hollywood does not dominate the Indian or Chinese theatrical markets and as prosperous middle classes emerge within these rapidly growing economies, the demand for domestically-produced filmed entertainment will increase. Certainly, some major home-grown media corporations are emerging from within both the Indian and Chinese industries which have the capital, scale and clout that may enable them to compete with Hollywood in the future.

The Hollywood studios have invested heavily in trying to ensure that digital film distribution becomes a sustaining technology; however the 'digital dawn' (Silver and Alpert 2003) has also been a disruptive

Table 1: Local Film Market Shares 2000-2009 (Box-office/Admissions as Percentage)

	2000	2001	2002	2003	2004	2005	2006	2007	2008	2009
France	28.9	39.0	34.0	34.8	38.4	36.8	44.7	36.6	45.4	36.8
Germany	12.5	16.2	11.9	17.5	23.8	17.1	25.8	18.9	26.2	27.4
UK	21.0	11.7	15.4	11.9	12.4	33.0	19.0	28.0	31.0	16.5
Italy	17.5	19.4	21.8	22.0	20.3	24.7	26.2	33.0	29.3	24.4
Spain	10.0	18.0	14.0	15.8	13.4	17.0	15.4	13.5	13.3	16.0
Japan	31.8	39.0	27.0	33.0	37.5	41.3	53.2	47.7	59.5	56.9
South Korea	-	-	45.2	49.7	54.2	55.0	64.2	50.8	42.1	48.8
China	-	-	-	-	55.0	60.0	55.0	45.9	39.0	56.6
India	-	-	-	-	-	92.5	86.0	76.5	90.5	92.0
Russia	-	-	-	-	12.0	27.7	23.3	26.3	25.5	23.9

Source: Compiled by the authors from the annual *Focus. World Film Market Trends* reports published by the European Audiovisual Observatory for the years 2001-2010.

technology, as it has been in the music industry, and has created distinct opportunities for non-Hollywood filmmakers to find new audiences on-line. This will be the main concern of our investigation.

The tale of the first decade of on-line distribution is one of two markets – a burgeoning, ubiquitous informal market of illegal downloading of films and TV programmes, and a slowly emerging but still very small, formal market for selling films legally via the Internet. This has resulted in three waves of firms seeking to develop sustainable business models and has resulted, for the most part, in widespread failure and many casualties – firms large and small, some well-financed and others poorly capitalised, from the U.S. and from the rest of the world.

There has been intense experimentation in the establishment of viable on-line distribution business models both by and in competition with the dominant Hollywood players. The 'burn rate' of venture capital and other investment in on-line distribution has been very high for over a decade and affords a classic case study of the rapid fires of 'creative destruction' in a highly volatile but high-stakes game, because no one doubts that digital distribution will, eventually, dominate both formal exhibition and household consumption in most territories. Almost inevitably, there is a concentration of innovation, in both platforms and business models, in the dominant U.S. hothouse, which means that international and indie on-line distribution either need to establish links with the major on-line distribution (e.g. iTunes, Hulu, Amazon, Netflix) through content aggregators that supply indie product to those majors, or by using their platforms (e.g. CreateSpace, Amazon Instant Video and IndieFlix). One index of the inevitable synergies, and also complexities, that exist in on-line distribution between Hollywood and the rest of the world is that both case studies of premium rest of the world and indie affordance highlighted in this chapter (Jaman and Amazon-owned companies) operate out of the U.S., while simultaneously competing with Hollywood for space to innovate and grow in on-line distribution.

The first commercial sale of a feature film on-demand via the Internet was offered by U.S. firm SightSound in 1999, and that same year another U.S. website, CinemaNow, launched the first commercial on-line movie download service and the first made-for-the-Internet movie, *Quantum Project* (Eugenio Zanetti, U.S., 2000), which premiered on-line in 2000 on SightSound (see Appendix 1).

Whilst the U.S. was quick off the mark, innovations in on-line distribution were also emerging in Asia and Europe. The first non-American websites into this space were Korea's Cinero, a VOD website also launched in 1999, and Afilmcinado, a 'sparsely stocked alternative' German site with 'horribly slow downloads even with a broadband connection' (Stables 2000), which went live the following year. Exploding Cinema was an on-line short film festival run by the Rotterdam International Film Festival in 2001. That same year, a group of 34 French producers formed a company to collaborate and develop an on-line VOD platform from which to distribute their movies – UniversCine. This was still part of early dotcom era e-commerce, when most consumers used Web 1.0 via copper telephone lines.

A decade later, despite the rapidly increasing diffusion of broadband around the world and of better compression software, on-line distribution remains an emergent market, the annual value of which was estimated to be U.S.$284 million in the U.S. market and only U.S.$88.4 million in Europe (Loeffler 2010a). Appendix 1 in the Resources section is a digest of the milestones in this short but eventful journey. It shows that there has been considerable global diversity of innovation in this space from the pioneering days of on-line distribution and prior to the emergence of U.S.-based market leaders of significant size and scale – Netflix, Apple iTunes, Hulu, Amazon and YouTube.

On-line Distribution by Region

Europe

To appreciate the barriers to development faced by independent on-line movie services employing Web browser-based delivery of films in Europe, one must add the powerful mix of public service broadcasters, telecommunication players and uneven broadband penetration to the established mix of direct-to-home-satellite, cable and emerging Internet Protocol Television (IPTV) services, and the fact that video piracy has migrated on-line. There are a number of on-line distribution sites in Europe's largest VOD markets, such as LoveFilm (UK and Germany), Glowria (France – films delivered on-line via Netbox), MaxDome (Germany) and Film Is Now (Italy), that do show 'local' films, and some have quite large catalogues. To survive commercially, however, and to attract a critical mass of customers and then hold them, their catalogues are mostly dominated by mainstream Hollywood box-office driven hits.

In the formal markets of Europe, on-line distribution is, at this stage, a peripheral supplement and has been greatly affected by the global financial crisis. In 2009, 29 standalone transactional on-line movie services in Europe closed their doors and *Screen Digest* reported that transactional on-line movie spending in Western Europe (rental and download-to-own) totalled €64.9 million (U.S.$88.46 million), up 85% from 2008, but equal to less than half the size of the U.S. market of €209 million (U.S.$284 million); 81% of all European on-line movie spending occurred in France, Germany and the UK (Loeffler 2010a).

In Western Europe, satellite platforms that preceded the diffusion of cable attract the majority of high-spending customers who want Pay TV and a VOD service, whilst in poorer Eastern European markets, where satellite and cable services are less predominant, IPTV set-top boxes lead VOD development (Broughton 2009).

Despite Europe being a potentially lucrative site for the consumption of diverse film content, on-line distribution retail is not a profitable market. This is partly because of the high up-front distribution guarantees that the major Hollywood studios demand for their product, and partly because large media device manufacturers such as Apple (iPod/iPad/iTunes), Sony (Playstation Network) and Microsoft (Xbox Live Marketplace), and even larger libraries like Netflix in the U.S., are using digital downloads like a retailer's loss-leader: selling them at below cost download prices or using them as a free value-add to the core business (e.g. Netflix's free watch instantly for its DVD-by-mail subscribers). The only growth in the on-line distribution market came from these large firms, which enabled the major studios to command higher prices for their movie packages. In these market conditions, the industry shakeout intensified because smaller, standalone on-line distribution websites did not have sufficient financial resources to sustain an on-going business and most will not survive if this scenario continues and venture capital finance to the sector dries up in the wake of the major financial downturn in Europe and North America.

Table 2: VOD Platform Competition to On-line Distribution in Europe

European region	Countries	IPTV	Cable	Satellite	Total
Nordic	Denmark	4	2	2	8
	Norway	6	2	2	10
	Sweden	3	1	2	6
	Finland	3	0	2	5
UK/Ireland	UK	2	1	1	4
	Ireland	1	1	1	1
France/ Benelux	France	5	1	1	7
	Belgium	1	1	0	2
Germany/ The Alps	Netherlands	2	1	0	3
	Germany	2	3	1	6
	Austria	1	1	0	2
	Switzerland	2	1	0	3
Iberian peninsula	Spain	0	8	0	8
	Portugal	2	1	1	4
Mediterranean	Italy	4	0	1	5
	Greece	2	0	0	2
Eastern Europe	Estonia	1	0	0	1
	Poland	2	1	3	6
	Slovenia	2	0	0	2
	Czech Republic	3	0	0	3
	Slovakia	2	0	0	2
	Hungary	2	0	0	2
	Romania	0	0	2	2

Source: Richard Broughton (2009) 'Video-on-Demand Yet to Develop', *Screen Digest*, January 2009, 13-20.

European innovators

Despite the financial downturn throughout Europe between 2008 and 2010, there were some notable success stories in France, Denmark and Spain that presented innovative approaches to the dissemination of European film culture and to the preservation of its heritage in the on-line distribution landscape.

UniversCine – France

One of the most interesting European innovators in the on-line distribution landscape for independent films, both from a filmmaker and an audience perspective, was UniversCine, a VOD platform initiated in France in 2001, during the earliest pioneering years of the on-line distribution sector. It was a collaborative vision founded by a group of 34 independent producers who wanted to develop an on-line platform that would eventually enable them to control the VOD exploitation of their films. UniversCine's goal was 'to transmit and broadcast cinematographic culture, experiment with new means of distribution and consumption of films and examine content, audiences and the means of renewing the relationship between the public and independent cinema' (Leffler 2007).

Today about 50 producer-shareholders, who together represent nearly 40% of films produced in France each year and nearly 20% of films released in theatres, own UniversCine. The company seeks to 'establish an open model, unifying and collaborative operation of independent films on VOD to become a leading player in this sector'.[1] The on-line distribution site launched in 2007 with 250 independently produced films available at a rental fee of €4.99 for 48 hours of unlimited viewing (Leffler 2007). As a content aggregator and distributor it has since amassed a library of over 1,400 titles, mostly European independent films, which are now available to download from a website which is both stylish and easy to search and navigate. Films are supported by informative editorial content about each film and the filmmakers, and there are also opportunities for users to post comments. French content now equates to about 40% of the catalogue.

A European Audiovisual Observatory (EAO) survey showed that in June 2009, UniversCine had become one of the eight largest French suppliers of content alongside major players CanalPlay, Virgin Mega, Club Video (SFR), Orange, TF1 Vision and two smaller players, Arte VOD and France Televisions (Lange 2009). UniversCine's plan is to evolve into a pan-European federation with new locally-managed VOD platforms in Belgium, Switzerland, Ireland, Spain, Germany and Finland.

Movieurope (FIDD) – Denmark

A second European innovator in on-line distribution, founded in Denmark, is FIDD (Filmmakers' Independent Digital Distribution), another collaboration-based distribution company which has eliminated the middleman and seeks to optimise the earning potential of independent films through its VOD portal. The company's mission is to become a leader in the digital distribution of European films. Founded in 2005, FIDD is 50% owned by 'hardcore capitalist investors' and 50% by United FIDD (160 plus European filmmakers from 17 EU nations, comprising 40 Danish and 30 Swedish companies, 15-20 Norwegian, Finnish and Icelandic film producers, and various other European players). Involvement with FIDD is open, joining costs nothing, and the deal is non-exclusive, so the producer is not prohibited from also placing their film elsewhere on the Web. Founder and CEO Niels Jensen states that the philosophy of the company is one share, one vote and that he sees the upper limit for the number of producer participants being between 1,000 and 1,200 into the future. FIDD's financing comes from three sources – investors, revenues from VOD subscriptions and from the European Commission's MEDIA programme (Jensen 2010). Its strategy is to establish a Scandinavian base and then expand into the Baltic and, eventually, throughout Europe. Jensen says that a key difference between UniversCine and Movieurope is that 'UniversCine is an inwards project; they collect films from around Europe to be shown in France, we collect films around Europe to be shown worldwide' (Jensen 2010). In late 2010, 87% of Movieurope's Web traffic was Danish.[2]

Movieurope is an impressive on-line movie portal, elegant and simple to use, easy to search and navigate, and it provides 22 themed, genre-based channels and four volume-based movie packages as monthly subscriptions featuring a library of over 1,200 titles. FIDD chose the subscription VOD pricing model in preference to a pay-as-you go rental or download-to-own fee because, as Jensen explained, typically charging fees of €3-5 per movie stream or download tended to encourage people to focus on mainstream films and choose blockbusters, because they knew the brand, while FIDD felt that it was difficult to value documentaries or short films in a VOD model. Consequently it opted for a subscription model and segmented the market, offering different price points for different packages containing varying quantities of films available on a monthly basis and themed either by genre (thriller, comedy, drama, romance, horror, kids, shorts, docs, fitness, erotica, etc.) or by the quantity of available films (platinum, gold, silver, bronze).

Movieurope engages marketing partners who target their own customer bases and receive 20% of the revenues that they generate. Jensen says that there are no costs deducted from the selling price and that it is a more cost-effective proposition to distribute non-mainstream films via VOD than to launch them theatrically. There is full economic transparency as revenues flow back to producers according to an agreed formula that allocates points for each film in a producer's catalogue on the site – based on criteria such as admissions, budget, production year and duration – and then multiplies those points by the number of views. FIDD has also opened a German office and was offering a catalogue of 1,400 titles by late-2010. A multilingual site in 10 European languages is also being planned.

Table 3: Examples of Movieurope Subscription VOD Pricing (November 2010)

Platinum Package	1276 movies 199 Kroner per month = 27 EUROS
Gold Package	400 movies 99 Kroner per month = 8 EUROS
Bronze Package	100 movies 59 Kroner per month = 8 EUROS
Scandinavia Package	200 movies 29 Kroner per month = 4 EUROS
Comedy Package	20 movies 39 Kroner per month = 5 EUROS
3 Film Package	3 movies 15 Kroner per month = 5 EUROS

Filmotech – Spain

A third European site that stands out in the on-line distribution landscape for providing legal movie content is Spain's Filmotech, which was initiated in 2006 by EGEDA (Entidad de gestion de derechos de los productores audiovisuales/Audio-Visual Producer's Rights Management Association), and is an organisation set up to represent the interests of producers of audio visual content in Spain and Latin America. It launched as a legal on-line movie platform in 2007 for independent content 'whose films cannot be considered as premium or that simply do not have access to the platforms' (Benzal and Vilches undated). Its goal was to enable audiovisual producers in Spain to make the best of the digital shift and to offer users a legal platform. Filmotech has established a similar on-line operation catering for Dutch cinema in the Netherlands.

Filmotech offers over 1,300 titles it describes as 'the best in Spanish cinema', constituting both back catalogue and current, as well as independent films from other parts of the world. Films stream in real time on any platform with any Web browser, and the site also contains rich editorial content in the form of articles, film reviews, news and information about films currently in cinemas. Producers are provided with 65% of net revenues generated from on-line movie rentals.

Europa Film Treasures – Denmark

A European website particularly worthy of note for its cultural heritage role is Europa Film Treasures, which preserves 'the treasures of our European cinematographic heritage' in an on-line archive and makes them available via a VOD site in five languages (English, French, Spanish, Italian and German). A simple Choose-Discover-Watch click button menu allows users to stream European productions from the pioneering era of filmmaking through to the present day, which have been selected and curated from the prestigious collections of 37 different film archives from around Europe.

Two other smaller but interesting European sites, typical of many below-the-radar innovations occurring in the on-line space are Filmklik, which offers a small library of 370 films available for streaming on demand to consumers in Hungary (Cineuropa 2007), and Europe's Finest, a VOD platform that offers a small library of 60 'European film classics' as cinema-on-demand to art house cinemas.

The Asia-Pacific

The Asian region features the two most populous nations (China and India) as well as the most wired nation (Korea) on earth. India has very low household broadband penetration but extremely high domestic cinema engagement. Informal market substitution effects are countered with market innovation, not state intervention. The distribution company Moser Baer, for example, drastically lowered unit prices of DVDs as a way of dealing with cheap pirated content and from 2007 this altered the DVD market (Baxter 2009). There is, as you would expect, a plethora of pirate download sites via portals, social networking sites, film blogs and torrent sites. There are also, however, several legal sites, mostly belonging to the major studios: Rajshri, ErosEntertainment and BigFlix (which is part of the huge distribution concern Reliance). The key point about these sites, though, be they formal or informal, is that they are accessed principally from outside India by non-resident Indians and by other South Asian expat communities desperate for the rich content that is largely unavailable in any other way. Most action around the on-line distribution of Indian cinema is from outside India, both from a consumption point of view and, indeed, in some ways from a distribution point of view. This is another powerful overlay of the story of the globalisation of Indian cinema in general, and a useful synergy for Indian-based distributors for whom on-line distribution (that is, to overseas non-resident Indians and others) and domestic release do not conflict.

Whereas the informal market in India is as much about Indian film as Hollywood, in China it is mostly about Hollywood, but also encompasses film and television from Europe, Japan and South Korea. China has the biggest broadband user-base in the world. Warner Brothers research in China showed that 80% of Web users had watched video content in the last six months of 2008 (Landreth 2008), a statistic replicated worldwide (Rick 2009). There is low consumption of Chinese cinema, and the informal market is huge – about 93% of movies sold in China are pirated (Cavernelis 2008). The informal on-line economy is also huge and dates from at least 10 years ago when, in 2000, e-Donkey was launched as a peer-to-peer file sharing forum. That was followed closely by BT (Bit Torrent) China in 2003 and the two big YouTube imitators, Tudou in 2005 and Youku in 2006. By 2008 there were at least 300 sites offering video to a voracious public.

A number of on-line distribution sites have emerged in China (see

Appendix 2 and 3 in the Resources section) but they cater mostly to big studio mainstream films. The really innovative thinking in China seems to be occurring in television rather than film (The Economist 2010). Additionally, the on-line screen culture of China has provided an unprecedented platform for personal expression and the flowering of vernacular creativity which will, in time, influence the quality and domestic impact of Chinese cinema. Meanwhile, in Korea pay TV reaches 95% of households, with cable, satellite and Internet Protocol Television (IPTV) dominating the local market; so VOD via those platforms is well-developed even while the on-line distribution market is very small. Japan provides half of Asia's VOD revenues and has a range of robust domestic cable, satellite and IPTV services, so once again distribution on-line is still a small ancillary market. We found no legal on-line movies stores in the Philippines, although there were a number of portals leading to informal Tagalog-language movie download websites.

In Australia, the local on-line distribution market is underdeveloped for two key reasons: the slow emergence of compelling on-line movie services and the use of strict caps on broadband usage which restricts data-heavy on-line video consumption (Loeffler 2010b). Only a few major on-line distribution sites exist – such as the pioneering Big Pond Movies which launched in 2006 as a Netflix imitator, initially offering an on-line DVD rental service with home delivery, together with a streaming service providing download-to-PC rentals on-demand. Since 2006, Australia has hosted one of the world's eight iTunes stores offering movies to rent and download to own. Telstra, the largest Australian telecommunications company, introduced T-Box, a new digital set top box providing IPTV direct to the home television and unmetered broadband for customers of its subsidiary Big Pond Movies. Cable operator Foxtel offers a free value-add streaming service to its subscribers called Foxtel Download. Games consoles Xbox 360 and PlayStation began offering movies-on-demand in 2009 and 2010. Internet Protocol Television operators also entered the Australian market – TiVo partnered initially with TV's Seven Network, then in 2009 with Blockbuster, and finally with a new on-line platform, Hybrid TV's Caspa-on-Demand. Fetch TV launched in 2010 and QuickFlix, another Netflix copycat site, announced that it would launch an on-line movies-on-demand service in 2011. The major sites are all dominated by Hollywood product. Australian content accounts for only 1-3% of some sites, a fact which closely mirrors the usual ratio of box-office takings of Australian films versus Hollywood and international films in the local market.

Innovators in the Asia-Pacific

No real innovation in the on-line distribution of feature films is evident in Asia. In Australia, with mainstream content widely available on more established on-line distribution sites and other VOD platforms and with large minimum guarantees demanded by Hollywood distributors for their product, the newer entrants into the on-line distribution space are being forced into thinking innovatively about how to differentiate their services. This is beneficial to both local Australian films and to films and TV content from the rest of the world.

QuickFlix - Australia

Like Netflix, QuickFlix historically delivered DVDs ordered on-line by customers to their homes by mail. In 2011 it plans to launch an on-line distribution service whose reach will extend beyond the mainstream to the benefit of Australian independents. QuickFlix CTO and Director of Product Development, Tim Parsons, says his company has

> a very large library of 43,000 titles [...] we know from our database what each of our customers rent and from their feedback what they like [...] we might say, so let's do a film festival that's sponsored by Sony and Red Bull, and so then we generate 20 emerging (Australian) producers and directors that have come out and we curate them and then we have several film critics who will, you know put it together as a whole package. We aggregate it together and then put that out to our audience at a sponsored festival. That's the kind of thing QuickFlix can do. (Parsons 2010)

Caspa-on-Demand - Australia

Hybrid TV has established a team dedicated to securing Australian content that will be packaged as on-line festival programmes and targeted to specific on-line audience segments. In promotional partnerships with consumer branded products relevant to the profiles of those audiences, leading media consultant Simon Curry says that Caspa intends to aggressively market suitable local content to local audiences (Curry 2010).

Table 4: VOD Platform Competition to On-line
Distribution in Asia-Pacific

Asia/Pacific Region	Country	IPTV	Cable	Satellite	Total
Australasia	Australia	3	3	2	8
	New Zealand	0	1	1	2
North Asia	China	1	13	0	14
	Hong Kong	1	1	0	2
	Japan	5	2	1	8
	South Korea	3	7	1	13
South Asia	Singapore	1	1	0	2
	India	0	3	2	5

Source: *Screen Digest*, January 2009, 19. Australian statistics updated to include two IPTV entrants in 2010 – Fetch TV and Hybrid TV/Caspa-on-Demand.

Africa

The first legal movies-on-demand service in Africa was launched in 2010: AfricaFilms provides a legal downloading service targeting Africans living abroad and world cinema buffs (Ruigrok 2010). It is a portal dedicated to African film and TV and charges U.S.$4-5 for a 48-hour rental. It offers content owners a non-exclusive contract with a 50-50 revenue split and is totally transparent, allowing producers to securely log-on to the site to check sales, which they then invoice to the company for payment. The non-exclusive rights deal covers the world but enables producers to withdraw the film from the site on a territory-by-territory basis as they sell the distribution rights to their films around the world. Content owners can also take advantage of an offer to develop their own branded VOD store at the site using a template and the AfricaFilms platform. Responding to the social, geographic and economic realities of Africa, the company has also launched a mobile cinema business. Franchisees take their motorcycle mobile video store to villages within their region to exhibit films for as little as U.S.$0.60.

The African Film Library is a beta movies-on-demand rental service with a curated library of over 600 African films. Backed by South

African TV channel M-Net, the site promises a high quality experience and a wide range of films from across the continent. M-Net appears to be modelled on France's CanalPlay, which also backs the Africa Magic TV channel. The African Movie Channel (AMC) is a UK-based VOD channel offered through Tiscali TV, which caters for African diasporas. There are a number of informal portals and movie download sites catering for Nollywood movies and other African cinemas, such as Izogn, Ayitinou, Ghana Cinema, Nollywood Movies, Vibe Ghana, Video On-line Nigeria and African Movies (see Appendix 2).

Latin and South America

Our survey of several film producers' associations throughout South and Latin America yielded only a handful of legal on-line movie-on-demand services on that continent. Brazil and Chile appear to be ahead of other markets, with Saraiva in Brazil and Bazuca and Cinépata in Chile, while INCAA (the Argentine State Film Board) plans to launch a VOD service in 2010-2011. The on-line distribution market in South America appears to be embryonic.

North America

While the focus of this book is the contemporary dynamics of non-Hollywood cinema, much of the experimentation in on-line film distribution has been conducted by, and in geographically proximate competition with, the Majors. Hollywood has been driven to undertake such expensive and mostly unsuccessful experiments by the hugely successful meeting of global demand for cinema through informal peer-to-peer platforms. The lessons learned from this history, largely of failure, are of benefit to those who are attempting to level the playing field for international and independent filmmakers globally (including those whose business may be dedicated to the rest of the world but is actually based in North America, such as Jaman). To consider 'North America', though, is not only to consider Hollywood, but also what may eventually become major challengers to the dominance of the Majors, such as Apple's iTunes and Amazon's integrated services to independents, wherever they may be in the world (see the Amazon case study in this chapter).

All firms entering the on-line distribution space during its first decade were confronted with the harsh realities of trying to establish a sustainable business within a volatile, complex and emerging technological environment. Although some of the barriers they faced have receded, many remain. In the pre-broadband era, the principal factors undermining the first wave of on-line distribution websites were that audiences suffered lengthy download times due to copper wire telephone dial-up connections and primitive compression software for large video files. Large flat-panel computer monitors were not yet available, so the viewing experience on small monitors was poor and there were only clunky methods of sending film content direct to television sets. There was a lack of high-quality film entertainment available on-line – most were B-movies or older content in the public domain (Cunningham, Silver and McDonnell 2010). Added to this mix was the rapid shift of emphasis of 'ripped' film content to on-line and informal markets following the Napster-led P2P 'creative destruction' of the music business and the fact that software was available to digitise content and upload DVDs. Almost any film content could be accessed illegally, anonymously and freely, with just a few clicks of a mouse.

Hollywood's failures

As a strategic response to the threat of video piracy and the 'napsterization of films on-line', and to try to exploit the opportunities presented by on-line distribution, Hollywood itself quickly moved on-line (Graham 2002). Sony, Warner, Universal, Paramount and MGM launched MovieLink, an on-line video rental store offering films for digital download for a 24-hour period at premium prices equal to bricks-and-mortar video store rental rates. Fox and Disney announced a similar co-venture called Movies, but it attracted the attention of the U.S. Justice Department on anti-trust grounds after the MovieLink launch, which involved five other major studios, and the project was abandoned. Disney went ahead alone with MovieBeam, a digital set top box providing Disney content via the Internet to televisions in the home. Despite the availability of 'premium' content and the gradual diffusion of broadband Internet within the U.S., a critical mass of on-line audiences failed to develop, uninspired by the major studios' offerings, particularly at price-points matching video rental stores. Both sites were sold in 2006 at prices well below the level of investment made by the studios.

There were even attempts to use the BitTorrent platform. In2Movies was an on-line distribution joint venture in Germany, Austria and Switzerland by Warner Brothers and Arbato Mobile (a division of Bertelsmann) that used legal delivery of Warner Brothers movies and

TV programmes via a BitTorrent P2P network, which was established in 2006 but closed in 2008 due to intensive competition in the German market (Screen Digest 2008).

Hollywood failed to make any on-line impact with legal downloading services over a five to seven-year period during which the seven Majors, together with Steven Spielberg's aborted Pop, lost combined investments of well over U.S.$100 million. The company had planned to produce short films featuring A-list Hollywood talent but failed because it was ahead of the market. In commentary on Pop's demise, *Business Week* noted: 'Too few folks are sufficiently wired to get superfast broadband connections to watch Hollywood's Internet fare, and therefore too few people are willing to pay anything for it' (Grover 2000).

Undermining Hollywood's attempts to dominate on-line distribution were two key factors: firstly, that the core cinema-going audience, aged under 25, was both the heaviest Internet user group and the age group most likely to engage in informal downloading; and secondly, that rapid upgrades to technological affordances (faster broadband and better compression software) benefited file sharing P2P sites more rapidly than legal on-line distribution businesses.

Independent casualties in North America

A number of well-financed firms that attracted heavy user traffic still failed in the on-line distribution space – Vongo was a short-lived on-line film download rental service with a small premium content library that was backed by Liberty Media's Starz Entertainment. Veoh, an Internet TV service that also offered both films-on-demand and user-generated content and had former Disney Chairman Michael Eisner on its board, burned through U.S.$70 million before filing for bankruptcy in 2010 (Richmond 2010). Veoh's CEO Dmitry Shapiro stated that his company's business model was unsustainable – despite its delivering 240 million video streams per month to 28 million unique users – because it only delivered monthly revenues of U.S.$1 million (Rayburn 2010). Another high profile failure was JOOST, a P2P TV platform that provided films and TV on demand and was self-financed by the founders of Skype from the proceeds of their $2.6 billion sale of Skype to e-Bay (they also raised a further $45 million investment from venture capital firms) (Business Wire 2007). Despite JOOST attracting 3.5 million unique viewers, the outgoing CEO Mike Volpi attributed its failure to copyright owners:

[M]ost of the economics accrue to companies that own the content itself and for the intermediaries there aren't any, that I can think of, profitable business models out there. The challenge is that media companies have approached the sector with more of a self-publishing model, meaning that content comes from their websites, as opposed to through aggregators. (Volpi 2009)

From 2009-2010, six of the 12 most interesting independent film-on-demand services that we were tracking on a watch list also ceased trading (see Table 5).

Table 5: Changes between 2009 and 2010 to On-Demand Sites

Still On-line:	Closed Down:
Create Space in partnership with Withoutabox (both owned by Amazon and linked to IMDb and Box Office Mojo, also both owned by Amazon)	B-Side – now Slated, shifted its focus towards social media (on-line indie content aggregator with supply deals to Amazon VOD, Netflix, Hulu and iTunes)
Jaman (world cinema on-line)	Undergroundfilm (indie film community)
EZTakes and i-Arthouse (same owners – focused on indie releases)	Caachi (on-line self-distribution platform)
Babelgum (web TV platform focused on indie films and shorts)	Dovetail (on-line indie distribution platform)
Indieflix (on-line indie distribution)	Heretic (on-line indie films on demand)
IndieGoGo (on-line marketplace for indie production)	Zoie Films (world's first on-line film festival)

Source: Compiled by the authors based on their tracking of independent film-on-demand websites.

Jaman, a seventh company among the most important websites for independent content and one of the best-known for non-Hollywood cinema, has also faced significant difficulties following the global financial crisis. This despite Jaman performing very well in on-line distribution and considering the level of resources available to it as a smallish start-up when compared to those of Apple or to the combined might of NBC-Universal, Fox and ABC-Disney (Hulu's owners), as shown in Table 6 below. We used available metrics for Jaman *v* iTunes *v* Hulu and devised a formula that enabled us to compare the volume of films downloaded per hour and per minute at each of the three websites. We calculated that Jaman's audiences watched one film per minute of world cinema content (i.e. independent films with little global brand equity) compared to 35 films per minute of premium Hollywood content rented or bought from iTunes, and 58 Hollywood films streamed free per minute from Hulu.

Table 6: Benchmarking Estimates for Jaman *v* iTunes *v* Hulu

Jaman	1,609 films downloaded daily = 67 films per hour **= 1 film watched per minute**
iTunes	50,000+ films sold daily in November 2008 = 2083 films per hour **= 35 films sold or rented per minute**
Hulu	3,469 movies streamed daily = 145 streams per hour **= 2.4 films streamed per minute**

Source: Jaman statistics provided by Gaurav Dhillion, CEO Jaman. iTunes metrics from Lucy Green and Fay Hamilton (2008) 'On-line TV and Video Audience Demand Continues to Grow but Profit Evades Many Players', *The Future of On-line Media Distribution*. Screen Digest event held in London on 11 November 2008. On-line. Available HTTP: http://www.greenfieldscommunications.com/releases/08/081111_SD_On-lineviewing.pdf (14 June 2011). Hulu streaming metrics for Feb 2010 based on Nielsen data published in Nielsen (2010) 'February On-line Video Usage Rises', *Marketing Charts*, February. On-line. Available: HTTP: http://www.marketingcharts.com/television/february-On-line-video-usage-rises-10-12276/nielsen-top-On-line-brands-video-streams-feb-10-mar-2010jpg/ (26 July 2011).[3]

We interviewed Jaman CEO Gaurav Dhillon, who stated that Jaman's two biggest problems were the gaining of Internet rights to a sufficient volume of premium content and the fallout from the global financial crisis and its impact on venture capital availability (Dhillon 2010). (For more on Jaman, see the case study in this book.)

The current state of play

Since 2007, the emerging major players in the on-line distribution space have been led by iTunes, Netflix, Blockbuster (with MovieLink), Amazon VOD and Hulu. The fundamental difference between them and the previous waves is that they have brought with them an existing critical mass of customers to whom they have had the ability to directly market as potential audiences.

In 2010, the renting and selling of movies from Apple's iTunes stores still operated in only eight countries – the U.S., Canada, Australia, New Zealand, France, Germany, Britain and Japan; yet it had been selling 50,000 films per day since 2008 (Green and Hamilton 2008). Netflix placed 10,000 titles from its 90,000 film library on-line in 'Watch Instantly' mode as a free value-added service to its large base of existing Netflix customers who had to use their ID and password to watch those films. In 2010, it transformed its core business model from a monthly subscription for DVDs-delivered to the home, migrating its customers to a U.S.$7.99 monthly subscription service for unlimited movie and TV downloads via Watch Instantly, plus an extra $2 monthly fee for unlimited DVDs delivered to the home. Netflix is clearly focused on preparing its customers for the digital transition and eventual demise of the bricks and mortar video store when VOD replaces DVD optical discs as the second window after cinema release. After Blockbuster was sold by Viacom, the video chain acquired Movielink from the Hollywood studios as a way to enter the world of on-line distribution and sought to pursue a similar long term strategy to Netflix. However, as a late entrant, and in the harsh economic climate from 2008, it became another casualty in the developments related to on-line distribution, filing for Chapter 11 bankruptcy in 2010.

Internet powerhouse Amazon established its Amazon VOD service, which, like Netflix, offers VOD rentals and is geo-blocked and thus available only to U.S. customers. It has a huge customer base, operates a sophisticated customer relationship management system, and has the ability to push promotional offers to customer's email accounts. Amazon is also a known and trusted on-line brand. Then there is Hulu, a joint venture between NBC-Universal, Fox Network and Disney through its

ABC TV network subsidiary. Hulu is an increasingly popular site that provides free, advertising-supported catch-up TV from the three national networks; 85% of its streams are TV shows and 15% are movies at the end of the distribution value chain on free-to-air television. In 2010 it introduced a subscription service, Hulu Plus, but by the end of the year it had reduced the monthly fee from U.S.$9.99 to U.S.$7.99.

Finally, a potentially large player in the on-line distribution feature film rental market is the most recent entrant, YouTube. Faced with litigation from Hollywood for a plethora of ripped content on its site, in 2009 YouTube – the Internet's #1 site for VOD with a 40% plus market share – introduced long-form video content, high definition with 16:9 aspect ratio, and completed a deal with MGM to introduce old movies for VOD (Reuters 2008). In 2010 it initiated a YouTube Video Store, geo-blocked for U.S. users only, which offered film and TV downloads for rental.

In the U.S. the on-demand market is dominated by cable and satellite delivery for a combined total of around 90%. The U.S. market dominates global VOD, earning 95% of annual revenues, which includes transactional VOD, PPV (pay-per-view) sports and PVR rental (Screen Digest 2009).

Table 7: Video-on-demand Competition to On-line Distribution in North America

Country	IPTV	Cable	Satellite	Total
USA	3	8	2	13
Canada	3	4	2	9

Source: Richard Broughton (2009) 'Video-on-Demand Yet to Develop', *Screen Digest*, January 2009, 13-20.

Case Study: Amazon

The dark horse in the on-line distribution arena is e-retailing giant Amazon, which has quietly assembled a group of branded divisions and companies that together have the potential to facilitate on-line distribution for independent filmmakers. The value proposition it offers to aspiring filmmakers is significant if those filmmakers are able to exploit the promotion and marketing potential of attendant social media.

Amazon has built a vertically integrated on-line film production-distribution-exhibition business that can help independent filmmakers from the development stage of their projects through to audiences screening their films on TV (e.g. via a Roku box) or, for exceptional films, distributing them to cinemas. Amazon's branded divisions and subsidiary companies are: Amazon Studios, CreateSpace, LoveFilm, IMDb and Withoutabox (a subsidiary of IMDb also owned by Amazon), which integrate with Amazon's VOD service (recently re-branded as Amazon Instant Video) and Amazon's e-retail fulfillment service. This provides a virtual one-stop shop that enables filmmakers to develop and distribute their content on-line wherever Amazon reaches – and that is as close to global as the Web gets. Amazon also owns Box Office Mojo – one of the Internet's highest profile movie box-office databases.

Amazon Studios

Amazon Studios launched in 2010. It provides aspiring writers and producers with the opportunity to upload their scripts or feature-length films to the new website (and gives Amazon an 18-month exclusive option on each project). And, like a reality TV contest, it combines audience voting and feedback from on-line fans, together with monthly contests for best film and best script as judged by a panel of industry experts. The winners are entered into an annual competition with a U.S.$100,000 prize for best screenplay and a U.S.$1 million prize for best film; further bonuses are paid upon the film's theatrical release and if it achieves pre-determined box-office benchmarks (Fernandez 2010).

Amazon Studios' business goal is to develop theatrical films from the winning entries (Cohen 2010) and to facilitate this end it negotiated a first-look deal with Warner Brothers; with an agreement that if Warner Brothers decides to pick up a project, Amazon will become a co-producer. On the surface, this may appear to be a website that reinforces Hollywood's dominance; however, it reframes film development by providing aspiring filmmakers with a rare opportunity to receive both professional feedback on scripts and films, as well as using on-line community tools to gain immediate and on-going audience responses from the early stages of development all the way through to the fine-tuning of a work-in-progress film. The Amazon Studio platform enables filmmakers to market test their films and to see how re-worked scenes or alternative endings actually play to a real audience. Of course crowdsourced feedback may not suit every filmmaker, but it does give them an opportunity to engage a wider audience, or the gatekeepers to a wider audience, from an early stage, building interest and desire for the final cut.

Amazon is targeting unknown filmmakers, seeking out user-generated content that has commercial potential. It is an open platform, available to filmmakers anywhere in the world. Amazon Studios is run by Roy Price, a former Hollywood talent agent whose father ran Universal and Columbia Pictures. So it has the expertise and contacts to professionally develop and produce projects from aspiring filmmakers. And for those producers unable to get a development deal with the new studio, Amazon provides a range of other self-distribution options through its subsidiary companies.

Create Space (Previously CustomFlix)

CreateSpace is a self-distribution platform with no physical inventory – all its films are digital files that can be streamed or purchased as download-to-own. Producers provide finished art for a DVD label and sleeve and, after an on-line transaction, a DVD is burned, inserted into a case and shipped via Amazon's usual fulfillment service. The film then appears in Amazon VOD's catalogue.

DVD prices are set by the filmmaker. The deal with CreateSpace enables producers to retain copyright through a non-exclusive license and incorporates a fixed revenue-sharing split that begins from the first sale. The DVD also appears on Amazon and the filmmakers qualify for a listing on IMDb. CreateSpace also provides filmmakers with their own customised e-store and offers a range of fee-based on-line marketing services to facilitate development of an audience on-line.

Withoutabox

Withoutabox is a free platform where filmmakers can identify the most appropriate festivals for their film. It lists over 5,000 festivals worldwide, from major events like Sundance, to regional festivals and thousands of small or niche festivals (see the case study in this volume). Over 800 festivals receive submissions electronically via Withoutabox, so it is a virtual one-stop shop for festival entry. Filmmakers pay only the published festival entry fee for any festival they select. The festivals each pay a fee for representation on Withoutabox and this income maintains the core system.

Acquired by IMDb in 2008, Withoutabox is now integrated via hotlinks to CreateSpace and IMDb. The shared mission of CreateSpace and Withoutabox is 'connecting filmmakers profitably to their worldwide audience' (Withoutabox 2010). Once the filmmaker has established an account with Withoutabox for their film, the site automatically offers an IMDb listing for the film and the ability to promote it by leveraging IMDb's range of free promotional services. Withoutabox and IMDb also provide a range of free and fee-based value-adding marketing services in the form of an EPK (electronic press kit).

IMDb

IMDb is a cinema or TV lover's dream website. You can rapidly find in-depth information on almost any film, TV programme, actor or crewmember from any era and from almost every country. The site is widely regarded as the most comprehensive film database freely available on the Web and a modestly priced IMDb Pro monthly subscription service exists to cater for industry professionals. It attracts 57 million visitors a month and enables filmmakers to upload trailers, clips and TV spots to promote their films (Withoutabox 2010). It also offers IMDb Video – a popular streaming platform that allows the upload of the full movie to be streamed free on the site, should that be an attractive option for any new filmmaker wishing to raise their industry profile.

An IMDb listing is an important part of any filmmaker's public profile, but only films that have been publicly screened at recognised film festivals, that have had a theatrical release, or that have been publicly broadcast, are eligible for inclusion on the database. It is because the Create Space or Withoutabox platforms include, as part of the submission process, the automatic availability of an IMDb listing that they are so important for new and independent filmmakers. (See also the IMDB case study in this volume.)

LoveFilm

In January 2011, Amazon acquired LoveFilm, Europe's largest Web-based film subscription service that emulated the Netflix business model by offering DVD rentals delivered by post, plus an expanding VOD streaming service in some European countries.

The addition of LoveFilm to the mix appears to be one of the final pieces in the emerging Amazon strategic jigsaw puzzle. Amazon can now 'play' at both ends of the market. In production, it facilitates the emergence of new filmmakers (via Amazon Studios) by providing platforms for low cost independent productions to engage in cost-effective DIY distribution and marketing (via CreateSpace, Withoutabox and IMDb). And at the top end of the market, Amazon retails Hollywood movies and theatrically released independent films (via Amazon Instant Video in the U.S. market, LoveFilm in Europe, and it sells DVDs globally via Amazon).

Appendix 4 in the resources section displays the publicly available distribution deal terms illustrating how producers can monetise their films on a range of large and small platforms – iTunes, Hulu, Netflix, Amazon Instant Video (formerly Amazon VOD), CreateSpace, IndieFlix and SnagFilms.

Final Thoughts: The Interdependence of the Informal and the Formal

We have stressed throughout that formal on-line distribution is, to date, a marginal business enterprise. For most of its history the size of audiovisual files has made file compression and bandwidth critical threshold factors in on-line distribution's development. Furthermore, restrictive caps on household broadband plans are a financial disincentive to consumers to use downloaded movies and TV programmes as a regular substitute for TV viewing. For those seeking to make on-line distribution work, there are diseconomies of scale: the more successful the enterprise becomes, the more costly it is to provide the service. The formal market on-line is actually more mainstream than that which exists in cable, satellite and DVD niche retail in major territories. VOD rights are already tied-up in existing distribution contracts, so small start-ups can't get global rights for films and can't afford the large minimum guarantees demanded by Hollywood for major studio movies. There are numerous close substitutes for on-line distribution: cable, IPTV-catch up, DVD and satellite.

Still, it is arguable that informal, peer-to-peer file sharing of film on BitTorrent and similar platforms is the most significant impediment to the growth of cash-flows from formal on-line distribution. This is the only on-line market which has reached, and for some considerable period of time, a 'critical mass'. Clearly, pervasive free downloading and P2P filesharing forms a major part of film culture built around on-line distribution. Nevertheless, there is a lack of credible evidence as to what downloading actually costs copyright owners. A succession of industry-funded reports has made highly publicised claims that vast sums have been lost to piracy. Many of these studies appear to be based on questionable extrapolations of consumer behaviour and assumptions that downloaded copies can be directly translated into foregone sales. Free downloading and P2P filesharing needs to be analysed in its own right, as well as in its complex relations to off-line piracy. We also need to analyse: the way it operates as another avenue of Hollywood distribution, which may actually further entrench Hollywood's dominance; the way in which it forces change in the formal economy and engenders state action; and the extent to which it has to be factored into the business models of on-line distribution companies.

Well-established, free downloading in major world markets has caused Hollywood to experiment with its release 'windows', using day-and-date more often to forestall knock-offs. This has benefited audiences as well. And audiences similarly benefit when DVD vendors attempt to lower prices to raise sales. State action can force change. For example, 2008-9 brought a massive state-led restructure and shakeout of the on-line distribution scene in China, which had grown chaotically. One of the more enterprising on-line distribution business ideas we heard in the course of our research was to track popular films on Torrent sites and offer deals to the rights holders of those films for sufficiently low point-of-sale prices to attract those who want to watch but also want to be legal. The informal drives the need for continuing innovation in the formal.

There are also informal production strategies, with crowdsourced financing and storylining, storyboarding and even actual on-line production. These are innovations arising directly from informal on-line consumption cultures, and the last word should go to those who are grasping the opportunities that digital and on-line are offering – in production, distribution and audience reception. The production sector has been significantly democratised by digital technology and software has become affordable for independents virtually worldwide: from computer software that facilitates script development (story engines like Dramatica and script formatting programs like Final Draft) to on-line screenplay coverage (Screenwriter); from production management software (Movie Magic) to high definition digital cameras (the Red) and post-production software (Avid, Final Cut Pro). Today, anyone owning a high-end mobile phone can make a short film and upload it to YouTube within minutes.

And there are innovative distribution-cum-exhibition initiatives. RAIN is a network of Brazilian digital cinemas launched in 2002 which beams its films by satellite to 453 digital cinemas. It has exhibition alliances in the UK and India and also operates 26 art house digital cinemas in the United States. RAIN implemented a Theatrical-on-Demand (TOD) business model that lists its film inventory on-line, thus giving its audience members the ability to interactively propose what they would like to see, when they want to see it, and in which cinemas within the network. RAIN's novel TOD will allow moviegoers, grouped in on-line YouRAIN Internet film clubs, to recommend what films play when and where over its digital cinema network. Virtual cinema club members can also refer wish-lists to friends and, by exploiting YouRAIN's social networking system, let other people know what films they're 'attending'.

A well-publicised example of crowdfunding is the British film *The Age of Stupid* (Franny Armstrong, UK, 2009), which raised £450,000 of production finance by selling quasi 'shares' in the form of donations of between £500 and £35,000, to 223 individual and groups of investors who supported the climate change message of the film. It attracted worldwide media attention, partly due to its message, but also due to its innovative 'Indie Screenings' distribution model, whereby anyone could buy a license to screen the film, charge whatever ticket price they wished and keep the profits from the screening. Indie Screenings returned more than £110,000 to the producers from 1420 screenings: 'its white label software will let any filmmaker anywhere in the world distribute their film via local screenings, DVD, download and pay-per-view' (www.indiescreenings.net).

Russian-born, Los Angeles-based producer-director Dmitri Trakovsky self-financed his documentary *Meeting Andrei Tarkovsky* (U.S., 2008) about the famous Russian writer-director, but launched a determined on-line campaign to promote the film and its screenings across the world via Facebook and Twitter. He leveraged those platforms to raise money that allowed him to self-distribute a DVD release to people who paid in-advance for the DVD via Amazon and PayPal.

In a highly innovative twist on crowdfunding, three enterprising British teenagers still studying at school came up with an idea to raise one million pounds to make their film adaptation of Jules Verne's little known novel *Clovis Dardentor*. They developed a website called Buyacredit that enables anyone to buy a producer's end credit on the film for £10. By April 2009, they had raised £105,000 and had attracted not only hefty donations from some famous British celebrities and many ordinary investors, but also a swathe of publicity in the national press for their yet-to-be-made film (Pidd 2009).

Acknowledgments

Thanks to Paul Taylor and Jing Zhao for their research assistance.

Works Cited

Agence France Press (2007) 'Independent Film Makers Win On-line Stage', *The Age*, 29 October. On-line. Available HTTP: http://news.theage.com.au/technology/independent-film-makers-win-On-line-stage-20071029-16rz.html (14 June 2011).

Baxter, Richard (2009) 'Video Market Monitor: India', *Screen Digest*, September. On-line. Available HTTP: http://www.screendigest.com/reports/09videomarketmonitorindia/pdf/SD-09-09-VideoMarketMonitorIndia/view.html (14 June 2011).

Benzal, Miguel Ángel Benzal and Laura Vilches (undated), 'EGEDA's Answers to the Consultation Launched by the European Commission in the Framework of Its Communication to the European Parliament, the Council, the European Economic and Social Committee and the Committee of the Regions on Europeana – Next Steps'. On-line. Available HTTP: http://ec.europa.eu/information_society/activities/digital_libraries/doc/consultations/2replies/egeda.pdf (14 June 2011).

Block, Dana (2009) 'Jaman Launches Facebook Connect to Unite Film Lovers around the World', *Social Media Portal*, 9 February. On-line. Available HTTP: http://www.socialmediaportal.com/PressReleases/2009/02/Jaman-Launches-Facebook-Connect-to-Unite-Film-Lovers-Around-the-World.aspx?ReturnUrl=%2FSearch%2FDefault.aspx%3FTag%3DOn-line%2Bcommunity%26Pg%3D1%26Sz%3D50 (14 June 2011).

Broughton, Richard (2009) 'Video-on-Demand Yet to Develop', *Screen Digest*, January, 13-20.

Business of Cinema (2009) 'Jaman Rolls Out International Operations', *Business of Cinema*, 14 January. On-line. Available HTTP: http://www.businessofcinema.com/news.php?newsid=11523&page=44 (14 June 2011)

Business Wire (2007) 'Joost Closes $45 Million in Financing', *Business Wire*, 10 May. On-line. Available HTTP: http://www.businesswire.com/portal/site/home/permalink/?ndmViewId=news_view&newsId=20070509006451&newsLang=en (14 June 2011).

Business Wire (2008) 'Jaman Expands Library To Include Original Internet Series from 60 Frames'. *Business Wire*, 8 December. On-line. Available HTTP: http://www.businesswire.com/news/home/20081208005364/en/Jaman-Expands-Library-Include-Original-Internet-Series (8 September 2011).

Cavernelis, Dennis (2008) 'Studio Breaks Rules to Fight On-line Piracy', *Los Angeles Times*, 11 November. On-line. Available HTTP: http://articles. latimes.com/2008/nov/04/business/fi-warner4 (12 November 2008).

Cineuropa (2007) 'New Ways of Distribution in Europe – Mobile, Internet. The New Challenges of VOD', *Cineuropa*, 19 September. On-line. Available HTTP: http://cineuropa.org/dossier.aspx?lang=en&treeID=1368&docume ntID=81263 (14 June 2011).

Cineuropa (2009) 'Distribution and Exhibition. European Distributors: Up Next!', *Cineuropa*, 17 September. On-line. Available HTTP: http://cineuropa. org/dossier.aspx?lang=en&treeID=1369&documentID=112822 (14 June 2011).

Cohen, David S. (2010) 'Amazon.com Goes into the Development Business', *Variety*, 16 November. On-line. Available HTTP: http://www.variety.com/ article/VR1118027595?refCatId=13 (14 June 2011).

Cunningham, Stuart, Jon Silver and John McDonnell (2010) 'Rates of Change: On-line Distribution as Disruptive Technology in the Film Industry', *Media International Australia*, 136, August, 119-132.

Curry, Simon (2010) Telephone interview with Simon Curry, Founding Partner Galbraith & Co. Media Advisors, conducted by Jon Silver, 15 October.

Dhillon, Gaurav (2010), Unpublished Skype interview conducted by Stuart Cunningham and Jon Silver, 1 April.

Dhillon, Gaurav and Galaria, Faisal (2007) 'Hi-def Independent Films Online with Jaman', Podtech interview conducted by Robert Scoble, *Classic ScobleShow*, 27 June. On-line. Available HTTP: http:// connectedsocialmedia.com/2931/hi-def-independent-films-online-with-jaman/ (12 August, 2011).

EAO (2007) 'Video on Demand in Europe', A Report by NPA Conseil, Commissioned by the European AudioVisual Observatory and the Direction du développement des médias (DDM – France). *European Audiovisual Observatory*, Strasbourg.

The Economist (2010) 'China's Got Viewers: Despite Government Meddling and Rampant Piracy, Commercial Television Is Surging in the Middle Kingdom', *The Economist*, 18 November. On-line. Available HTTP: http://www. economist.com/node/17522454 (14 June 2011).

Fernandez, Jay A. (2010) 'Amazon.com Brings Moviemaking to the Masses with Amazon Studios Launch', *Hollywood Reporter*, 16 November. On-line. Available HTTP: http://www.hollywoodreporter.com/blogs/risky-business/amazoncom-brings-moviemaking-masses-amazon-45925 (14 June 2011).

Frater, Patrick (2008) 'NDTV Lumiere Pacts with Jaman; Deal Covers Streaming, Downloading of 30 Films', *Daily Variety*, 13 August. On-line. Available HTTP: http://www.variety.com/article/VR1117990535.html?categoryid=19&cs=1 (14 June 2011)

Goldstein, Gregg (2007) 'Jammin with Jaman.com', *Hollywood Reporter*, October 1. On-line. Available HTTP: http://www.hollywoodreporter.com/news/jammin-jamancom-151369 (12 August, 2011).

Graham, Jefferson (2002) 'Studios Aim to Squash Movie Piracy', *USA Today*, 11 November. On-line. Available HTTP: http://www.usatoday.com/life/movies/news/2002-11-11-movielink_x.htm (14 June 2011).

Green, Lucy and Fay Hamilton (2008) 'On-line TV and Video Audience Demand Continues to Grow but Profit Evades Many Players', *The Future of On-line Media Distribution*. Screen Digest event held in London on 11 November 2008. On-line. Available HTTP: http://www.greenfieldscommunications.com/releases/08/081111_SD_On-lineviewing.pdf (14 June 2011).

Grover, Ronald (2000) 'What Burst Pop.com's Bubble?', *Business Week*, 25 September. On-line. Available HTTP: http://www.businessweek.com/2000/00_39/b3700102.htm (26 July 2011).

Jaafar, Ali (2009) 'Jaman Logs Site in U.K.'. *Daily Variety*, 14 January. On-line. Available HTTP: http://www.variety.com/article/VR1117998549.html?categoryid=20&ref=ra&cs=1 (14 June 2011)

Jaman (2008) 'Jaman Delivers Award Winning Film *Punching at the Sun* to Movie Lovers around the Globe', Jaman press release at the Sundance Film Festival, 22 January. On-line. Available HTTP: http://www.jaman.com/m/news/releases/01_22_08.html (14 June 2011).

Jensen, Niels Albaek (2010) 'Video On Demand Distribution in Europe – Case Study: Movieurope.com. Interview with Niels Albaek Jensen, Founder & Managing Director, FIDD', *Cineuropa*, 19 July. On-line. Available HTTP: http://cineuropa.org/dossier.aspx?lang=en&treeID=1308&documentID=148726 (14 June 2011).

Jobs, Steve (2010) 'Apple Special Event September 10th, 2010 – Watch Apple CEO Steve Jobs unveil the new iPod line-up, Apple TV, and iTunes 10'. On-line. Available HTTP: http://www.apple.com/apple-events/september-2010/ (26 July 2011).

Landreth, Jonathan (2008) 'Warners Sets VOD in China', *Hollywood Reporter*, 5 November. On-line. Available HTTP: http://www.allbusiness.com/media-telecommunications/movies-sound-recording/11689404-1.html (14 June 2011).

Lange, Andre (2009) 'A First Census of Audiovisual On-demand Services in Europe', *Observing Audiovisual On-demand Services in the European Union: Market and Regulatory Issues*, Brussels, 3 November. On-line. Available HTTP: http://ec.europa.eu/avpolicy/docs/other_actions/eao/census.pdf (14 June 2011).

Leffler, Rebecca (2007) 'French VOD Site UniversCine Going Live', *Hollywood Reporter*, 18 April. On-line. Available HTTP: http://www.hollywoodreporter.com/news/french-vod-site-universcine-going-134335 (14 June 2011).

Lobato, Ramon (2009) '*Subcinema: Mapping Informal Film Distribution*', PhD thesis, School of Culture and Communication, University of Melbourne.

____ (2010) 'Creative Industries and Informal Economies', *International Journal of Cultural Studies*, 13, 4, 337-54.

Loeffler, Tania (2010a) 'On-line Film Spending near Doubled', *Screen Digest*, 463, April, 105. This article is also partially available on-line. Available HTTP: http://www.screendigest.com/reports/100421c/10_04_On-line_film_spending_near_doubled/view.html (2 September 2011).

____ (2010b) 'Australia Ready for On-line Movies', *Screen Digest*, 6 July. On-line. Available HTTP: http://www.screendigest.com/reports/201066c/10_07_australia_ready_for_On-line_movies/view.html (14 June 2011).

Nielsen (2010a) 'February On-line Video Usage Rises', *Marketing Charts*, February. On-line. Available: HTTP: http://www.marketingcharts.com/television/february-On-line-video-usage-rises-10-12276/nielsen-top-On-line-brands-video-streams-feb-10-mar-2010jpg/ (26 July 2011).

____ (2010b) 'Top On-line Brands Ranked by Video Streams', *Marketing Charts*, February. On-line. Available HTTP: http://www.marketingcharts.com/television/february-On-line-video-usage-rises-10-12276/nielsen-top-On-line-brands-video-streams-feb-10-mar-2010jpg/ (14 June 2011).

Parsons, Tim (2010), Telephone interview with Tim Parsons, Chief Technology Officer and Director of Product Development, QuickFlix, conducted by Jon Silver, 5 October.

Pidd, Helen (2009) 'Teenagers' Credit Note Approach to Fund £1 Million Film of Clovis Dardentor', *The Guardian*, 14 April. On-line. Available HTTP: http://www.guardian.co.uk/film/2009/apr/14/clovis-dardentor-film-funding (14 June 2011).

Rayburn, Dan (2010) 'Veoh Should Be a Reminder That Execution & Focus Are More Important Than Vision', *Business Insider*, 13 February. On-line. Available HTTP: http://www.businessinsider.com/Veoh-bust-should-be-a-reminder-that-execution-and-focus-are-more-important-than-vision-2010-2 (14 June 2011).

Reuters (2008) 'YouTube to Post Full-length MGM Films', *Reuters*, 10 November. On-line. Available HTTP: http://www.reuters.com/article/idUSTRE4A90KO20081110 (14 June 2011).

Richmond, Will (2010) 'Veoh Throws In the Towel After $70 Million Invested', *VideoNuze*, 12 February. On-line. Available HTTP: http://www.videonuze.com/blogs/?2010-02-12/Veoh-Throws-in-the-Towel-After-70-Million-Invested/&id=2433 (14 June 2011).

Rick, Christophor (2009) '80% of Internet Users Watch On-line Video, Worldwide'. *ReelSEO*, 6 May. On-line. Available HTTP: http://www.reelseo.com/80-Internet-users-watch-On-line-video-worldwide/ (14 June 2011)

Ruigrok, Inge (2010) 'African Video on Demand Portal Takes on Film Piracy', *The Power of Culture*, June. On-line. Available HTTP: http://www.krachtvancultuur.nl/en/current/2010/june/africa-films (14 June 2011).

Screen Digest (2008) 'In2movies store to close', *Screen Digest*, 4 June. On-line. Available HTTP: http://www.screendigest.com/news/bi-040608-sj2/view.html (16 August, 2011).

Silver, Jon and Alpert, A. (2003) 'Digital Dawn: A Revolution in Movie Distribution?', *Business Horizons*, 46, 5, September-October, 57-66.

Stables, Kate (2000) 'Cyber Cinema: September 2000', *The Guardian*, 1 September. On-line. Available HTTP: www.guardian.co.uk/film/2000/sep/01/cybercinema (14 June 2011).

Volpi, Mike (2009) 'Interview: Mike Volpi: Broadcasters' own VOD plans killed Joost'. Interview by Robert Andrews. *Paid content*, 6 July. On-line. Available HTTP: http://paidcontent.co.uk/article/419-interview-mike-volpi-broadcasters-own-vod-plans-killed-Joost/ (14 June 2011).

Ward, Audrey (2009) 'Jaman Partners with Cinetic to Expand Catalogue', *Screen Daily*, 17 February. On-line. Available HTTP: http://www.screendaily.com/jaman-partners-with-cinetic-to-expand-catalogue/4043336.article (14 June 2011).

Withoutabox (2010) 'Frequently Asked Questions', *Withoutabox*. On-line. Available HTTP: https://www.withoutabox.com/index.php?cmd=faq.filmmaker (26 July 2011).

Wood, Jennifer M. (2008) 'Jaman Launches Movie Channel for the World', *Movie Maker,* 15 May. On-line. Available HTTP: http://www.moviemaker.com/blog/item/jaman_launches_movie_channel_for_the_world_20080515/ (14 June 2011).

Woodson, Alex (2008) 'Jaman Plucks Spurlock Pics', *Hollywood Reporter,* 24 April. On-line. Available HTTP: http://www.hollywoodreporter.com/news/jaman-plucks-spurlock-pics-110146 (12 August, 2011).

Notes

[1]   The Universcine website (www.universcine.com) may not download easily in some Web browsers but Google Web Cache enables readers to see the site: http://webcache.googleusercontent.com/search?hl=en&gs_sm=e&gs_upl=2875l4640l0l4828l11l7l0l0l0l0l0l0ll0l0&q=cache:cyRVW-PcYsEJ:http://www.universcine.com/+universcine&ct=clnk www.universcine.com (16 August, 2011).

[2]   A snapshot of Movieurope's Internet traffic is provided at Server Insiders – a website that specialises in review and analysis of Internet domains. See: HTTP: http://www.serverinsiders.com/domain/movieurope-com.html (16 August, 2011).

[3]   Figures for Jaman are based upon 1,761,854 films downloaded over 1095 days from 2007-2010 = 1,609 daily; figures for iTunes reflect both rentals and download-to-own; figures for Hulu are based on 647,560 streams of TV and feature film content over 28 days in February 2010 = 23,127 streams daily (all content) of which an estimated 15% are movies, i.e. 3,469 films. Hulu's mix was 85% = TV shows and 15% = films.

Digital Revolution:
Active Audiences and Fragmented Consumption[1]

Michael Gubbins

We now live in an age of ubiquitous entertainment: in a couple of decades most of the developed world has gone from controlled and scheduled access to film, music and television to a multi-channel multi-linear and mobile access, increasingly on-demand.

The seeds of a demand-driven digital revolution have been sown in a number of ways:

- A radical change in consumer attitudes, precipitated by the widening of choice to unprecedented amounts of content.
- A continuous stream of technological innovations, built on the back of an exponential rise in digitised content and an ever-improving broadband communications infrastructure.
- Record availability of data and market intelligence about audiences and taste, often freely given in return for access to targeted content.
- A huge increase in choice and access to not just new film, but also to a far greater range of specialist international film and to an increasingly large digitised back catalogue.
- An emerging audiovisual culture where equipment is cheap and widely available, from mobile phones to video cameras.
- The rise of social networks, allowing the aggregation of communities of interest that transcend national borders and ensuring a constant and largely unmediated commentary on content.

The argument of this chapter is that these developments have changed the relationship between audiences and content. The changes can be contradictory and confusing; digital change has fragmented audience demand and yet strengthened certain linear, communal forms of consumption. Multiplex cinemas, peak-time television and live music, for example, have all fared relatively well, despite the recent economic downturn. That is not the paradox it seems; while, as we shall see, the huge increase in choice has tended to dissipate demand and disperse audiences, with consequences at both a business and cultural level, the Internet can also aggregate audiences and social networks can amplify demand.

The benefits of scale that result from taking advantage of this environment are clear; Hollywood can afford to ensure that its products are always visible. There are, however, examples of considerable independent success, a good one being the phenomenal success of Swedish thriller writer Stieg Larsson's *Millennium* trilogy of books. They created a buzz that rapidly spread on-line, meaning that the books became international bestsellers, spawning three Swedish films,[2] which earned more than U.S.$215 million worldwide and were then sold to the U.S. for remakes.

It is argued here that this wealth of content choices, accessible on-demand on multiple platforms and devices, has created what can be characterised as an 'active audience'. This concept does not imply a homogenous change in consumption patterns or taste, but it does imply that the multimedia access to content on-demand has fundamentally changed the relationship between audience and content.

This is already having an effect, if only initially, by eroding the economic foundations of the existing film industry. Theoretically there are opportunities for more positive change, not least in the increase in access to content that was previously limited largely by the impositions of a film industry weighed down by rights issues, the costs of distribution and practices such as release windows. There is, for example, the potential to dramatically redefine the cultural diversity of cinema, not just through the narrow definition of who makes a film, but also by altering the interaction between product and audience. This focus on consumption rather than supply has long been a recurrent theme for film.

Back in 2002, Alan Parker, then chairman of the UK Film Council, suggested that a sustainable film industry could only be achieved by focusing on reaching audiences: 'In a successful industry, distribution pulls production behind it. Distribution pull, not production push' (Parker 2002: 10). The current state of digital change may not be what he had in mind, but there is no question that the digital has refocused attention on a demand-driven globalised economy and on access to not only new content, but to a vast, digitised back catalogue.

Unquestionably, there is and will be far greater availability of film than at any time in history, with illegal counterfeiting and file-sharing sites servicing any demand that industry fails to fulfil. A new industry is growing to feed this demand, with an estimated 700 VOD services in Europe alone running alongside specialist satellite broadcast services and powerful 'catch-up' services, electronic sell-through, streaming, etc. (Hartman 2011). Advocates have even posited the idea of an emerging, hybrid, 'transmedia' art form, tuning into a hypothesised demand for interactive and non-linear content. It is based on the idea that the wide range of platforms and media, from videogames to conventional cinema, offers different entry points to a single, if decentralised, narrative.

The potential for new artforms is exciting, but they are predicated on an interpretation of digital development that is far from clear. We are in the early stages of a change in consumer behaviour that will revolutionise film: in the short term by undermining the business model on which the industry has been based and in the long term by changing the relationship between audience and content.

The rate of change and its effect on film are not yet clear. Digital distribution has an obvious theoretical potential to increase the reach of non-Hollywood film, which has always been held back by the economic viability of producing and transporting large numbers of prints.

The ability to aggregate audiences beyond national borders may improve the economics of specialised film, and yet the very act of efficiently servicing existing cinema fans may make it harder to reach new audiences and to broaden mainstream interest. Similarly, in taking on piracy in the interests of supporting the creative industry, it is possible that the potential reach of cinema could be severely curtailed. Invisibility could become more of a danger than piracy.

This study suggests that we are still in the process of change and that film has struggled to come to terms with a changed digital environment, and yet the future of film is far from clear, particularly for non-Hollywood film. This sets a challenge for government policy makers and businesses.

Digital Revolution and the Dynamics of Cinema

What is perhaps most remarkable about this vastly increased choice is how little positive influence it has exerted so far, with a big gap between the theoretical increase in choice and the delivery of commercially-viable content or new digital art forms.

The slow progress is partly because the traditional analogue business has been seen as remarkably resilient, continuing to provide the lion's share of revenues and hence being something to be protected: cinema receipts, if not always attendances, have held steady around much of the world; DVD is certainly in decline, but a combination of lower prices, Blu-ray quality and permanence has ensured that we have not seen the free fall that some predicted; and the linear formats of television (see below) have been highly resistant to change.

A study from Deloitte in 2010 estimated that 90% of television was still viewed within the daily programme schedule, and even suggested that consumers exaggerated how much they used video recorders and on-line services. BSkyB revealed that even when its Sky Plus service is used to record programmes, 60% are watched within a day of the initial screening (The Economist 2009).

New forms of multi-platform, transmedia art have thus far failed to produce the kind of breakthrough works that have punctuated the history of film and television. In part, the failure has been about a shortage of funding – as a result of the lack of a clear business model and because national funding set-ups are generally tied into specific single-media channels, such as film, television and the like.

The reality is that the initial impact of digital change in film has been largely negative, fracturing traditional business models without throwing up many immediately viable alternatives, at least on the same scale.

Digitisation and Democratisation

If the immediate effect of the digital revolution on the dynamics of cinema, in artistic and commercial terms, has failed to live up to expectations, it is partly because the benchmark by which progress has been judged has been so skewed. The disappointment has been exaggerated by the ascendancy of two dominant but opposing discourses.

The first is that current technology trends are no more than the 'digitisation' of the existing business; just another big step in a series of evolutionary changes in the history of cinema, such as sound and colour. This perspective acknowledges the disruptive nature of digital change in the short term, but sees the next few years in terms of assimilation and mainstreaming and suggests that digital technologies will eventually replace revenues lost from physical products, such as DVDs.

In other words, digital developments are essentially replacements or upgrades to existing processes. Much digital innovation fits that picture; the installation of digital equipment in cinemas and the introduction of 3D, for example, can, to an extent, be seen as the latest in a line of improvements to the theatrical experience: comfortable multiplex buildings, improved screens and Dolby Surround sound have all have played a big part in the renovation of the cinema industry in most of the world after the nadir of the mid-1980s. From this perspective, the last few years have been difficult because digital revenues remain only a fraction of even the reduced revenues from DVD and theatrical sources. In part, this is because of an assumption that the home entertainment and multiplex-fuelled boom of the 1990s and 2000s represented the natural size of an organic film industry; however, as this chapter argues, there is no clarity yet on the nature, never mind the size, of a digital industry fit for the on-demand age.

The sense that the Internet is a Wild West to be tamed has been typified by the fight to impose upon it the same intellectual property rules that have prevailed in the physical business, and in the view that piracy is the fundamental barrier preventing recovery. That idea will be severely tested in both the courts and by consumer behaviour.

The second opposing argument is that digital represents a wholesale change in consumer attitudes and even taste, based on interactivity and a democratisation of the process of film-making. This view often takes a teleological view of progress, from the industrial and commercial exploitation of entertainment towards (or back to) a democratic oral tradition. This thinking often dovetails with broader arguments about the supposed erosion of Internet freedom, through anti-piracy laws and the like. For example, Tim Berners-Lee, often credited with being the father of the Web, has condemned any law which deprives the user of an on-line connection: 'It's such an empowering thing to be connected at high speed and without borders that it is becoming a human right' (Cellan-Jones 2011).

This perspective has been challenged by the relatively slow rate of progress of digital change, which certainly remains on the creative and business margins, with only patchy signs of the flowering of distinctive digital forms of art, or even of a mass desire for greater active participation in the creative process from audiences. Digital change is following a pattern described in 2006 by Danish Web consultant Jakob Neilsen as 'participation inequality' – or the 90:9:1 rule – in which the on-line world is divided between 90% of 'lurkers' who never contribute, 9% of users who contribute a little and 1% of users who really contribute to content (Nielsen 2006).

The idea has been further developed by technology analyst Forrester Research, which has produced what it calls a 'social technographics ladder' to describe levels of audience activity. At the bottom of the scale are a small and decreasing number of 'inactives' who, out of disinclination or because a lack of skills or resources, are not involved in any form of engagement with the Internet. The majority are 'spectators' who read on-line content, watch video, look at ratings and so on, but do not themselves contribute further.

At the top are the 23% of 'creators' who publish, upload and generally contribute content; the research suggests that this number seemed to reach a plateau in 2010. These top-level contributors are, of course, still extremely significant and the 13 million hours of content uploaded to YouTube is one useful testament to the scale of this activity (Bernoff and Anderson 2010).

It is, however, difficult to build a business model based on the highest level of participation, as the many crowdsourcing and crowdfunding projects, which I discuss further below, have discovered. Identifying and mobilising this minority is an emerging skill. Without access to the Hollywood studios' resources, the independent industry at every level generally falls back on intuition, experience, box office-data and downright guesswork, all of which have serious limitations in their application to future business.

There are many potential influences that might change this participation deficit, including more intuitive software and hardware, higher broadband speeds and an injection of capital into projects from the public and private sectors. There is little evidence at this stage, however, that participation is a driving force in digital change; instead, what has emerged are active audiences who demand access to existing content at a time, place and price of their choosing.

The Hype Curve

The cliché that digital business is overestimated in the short term and underestimated in the long term largely holds true. A closer look at the way that mainstream journalism has covered digital change reveals that the evolution of technology is perceived as a rollercoaster of hype and rejection.

Technology analyst Gartner has developed a convincing model to describe the evolution of technology businesses, which it terms the 'hype curve' or 'hype cycle' (Gartner 2011). A technology trigger generates considerable hype, eventually reaching what the analyst calls the 'peak of inflated expectations', before a crash of disappointment drops expectations into a 'trough of disillusionment'. In time, consumers come to appreciate the value of a product without it being oversold, and the viable services it offers eventually reach the mainstream and a 'plateau of productivity'.

This analysis puts audience demand at the heart of business models but leaves considerable room for doubt about the final scale of acceptance of any given technology, and about the overall effect of digital change on the dynamics of world cinema as a whole. Many factors are involved in that final outcome, including competition between formats and platforms, the resilience of previously dominant formats such as DVD, and the competition for time from other entertainment forms, such as television and games. What is also not clear is how far this changed environment will influence consumer taste. That is an area where there remains a considerable degree of unpredictable art alongside the emerging science of data tracking. We may now know who the audiences are, but not necessarily exactly what they want.

Fragmentation and Marginalisation

The story of digital change for film has thus far largely been one of fragmentation: a single model for film, however unequal, has fractured. This fragmentation takes many forms. There is the demographic split in attitudes to content and technology between younger audiences, who have grown up with freely available on-line access to content, and the rest. The evidence for a distinct Net Generation should not, however, be overstated; the fastest growing demographic among the 575.4 million Facebook users worldwide, for example, is the over-55s, and 37.5% of users in the U.S. in November 2010 were over 35 years old (Comscore 2011).

There has also been the fragmentation of business models, which has disrupted a linear value chain from producer to exhibitor and opened up new means of distribution, which have in turn cannibalised or undermined existing revenue streams.

And then there is the fragmentation that comes from the far greater range of choice, as evidenced by the explosion of digital and on-line channels. Ironically, it is those routes to market with the most limited choice, such as cinemas and peak family viewing times on television, which have fared best in the current turbulent period.

While there is far more access to European film on specialist television and VOD services, these tend to become educated ghettos. While, for example, the UK Film Council measured 3.4 billion viewings of feature films in all forms of television in 2009, the screening of art house and foreign-language film has dropped alarmingly at peak times (UK Film Council 2010). Another forthcoming study for the UK Film Council (see Gubbins 2011b) contrasts the five million UK audience for *The Incredibles* (Brad Bird, U.S., 2004) during Christmas 2009 – which made it the thirteenth most watched programme of the season – with the 23.5 million who made up the biggest ever audience for a television movie, *Live And Let Die* (Guy Hamilton, UK, 1973) in Christmas 1980 (Phillips 1997).

The dispersion of content across a wide number of channels, catch-up services and on-line platforms, reduces the audience for film on any single channel and reduces its attractiveness to advertisers. The taste-making curatorial role of mainstream television has disappeared in much of the world, with even nationally-funded films pushed to the edge of the schedules. The creation of a film culture and, particularly, the discovery of new specialist film become difficult when film is pushed to the edges of the schedules or onto specialist channels.

Critics and Curators

One of the immediate effects of digital change has been the decentralisation of critical comment and recommendation; however, this trend is often overstated. Personal recommendation has always been a key factor influencing a spectator's choice of film. What has changed is that word of mouth has been amplified by the Internet. Importantly, the verdict of peers and, indeed, critics is now instantly available through mobile phones and social media, such as Twitter.

The much-vaunted decline of the critic also owes at least as much to the economic difficulties of traditional media as to any decisive shift in consumer habits. Many newspapers with crashing circulations have seen film criticism as a luxury to be axed or marginalised, and even the film trade papers have cut the number and size of reviews as their advertising revenues have fallen.

The immediate decline of the critic may not be the result of consumer rejection, but it may help to accelerate the redefinition of the line between critic and consumer. Word of mouth, amplified by mobile phones, Twitter and Facebook has become a serious force in deciding the fates of films. This is becoming an era of more personalised services and recommendations, as shown by the iTunes Genius feature, or by the instant, aggregated opinion of Rotten Tomatoes. Again, this new world is not evolving in a simple linear fashion driven only by forward-thinking companies and new technologies. It is being driven by the vagaries of consumer acceptance and, as a result, there are far more failures than success stories in the field, though services such as German sites Moviepilot and Myfilmstation have been successful in some countries. The once powerful News Corp-owned My Space social network found that mobilising the audience is tough, even with scale on your side, and announced big cutbacks in 2011. Even Apple's iTunes has struggled to create its customary momentum for its new Ping service.

Yet there is evidence that younger audiences are less interested in the views of traditional critics. For Hollywood, the opinion of particular professional critics has become all but irrelevant and some films can perform well despite pretty much universal critical loathing. This may be welcome on one level, but the shift of power from critic to audience is a challenge to marketers. The opinions of consumers, amplified by mobile phones and social networks, are difficult to control – so far, trying to build a word-of-mouth campaign is proving more art than science. For independent film, critical opinion retains much of its power.

At film markets such as Cannes and Berlin, reviews can make the difference between being sold to a particular territory or not. The mainstream media, however, retains considerable influence. One of the tricks of the new marketing world is to find existing brands trusted by the kind of audiences a film desires to reach. It is now commonplace, for example, to see that the review quoted on the poster for a female-oriented film is sourced from a woman's magazine rather than a newspaper critic.

Art house film and 'quality' newspapers and magazines have long been natural bedfellows, not least because there is a significant audience crossover. Some digital trends may actually strengthen that relationship: the migration of publications on-line, for example, has added an international readership to news brands and has created the need for visual content, which film-makers are well-placed to help fill with trailers, free content and special deals on DVDs and downloads.

The fact that newspaper critics survive at all is evidence that a section of the audience actively seeks a guide to navigate the bewildering range of new and archived content. The unwanted 'gatekeeper' for some is an essential 'curator' for others; this has been an essential factor in the growth of film festivals and art house cinemas.

Monitoring the Audience – Data and Metadata

Among the most significant digital developments is the creation of data and metadata which allows far greater understanding of audience demand, as well as providing for a more effective means of categorisation and archiving (Wactlar and Christel 2002).

The lack of clarity in understanding and exploiting consumer demand has been a significant part of the development of film. William Goldman famously suggested that in film you had to remember that 'nobody knows anything' (Goldman 1983: 39). What one does with the knowledge one acquires is, of course, scientific only insofar as it identifies demand and builds communities – knowing who you are reaching does not negate the challenge of finding the right product.

One of the fast-emerging trends that had not been foreseen is the potential value of metadata – essentially the data about the data we produce; each part of the filmmaking process produces information which has potential value to someone. The cast list, for example, has helped spawn services such as the Internet Movie Database (IMDb). Experiments are now taking place in an attempt to discover other areas of value, including locations of shoots, the clothes worn by the cast and the music in a scene. This information has the potential to be turned into consumer value. For example, one could click on the clothes in a scene and be taken directly to a place to purchase them; or on a snippet of the soundtrack and be taken to iTunes; or on a location and be redirected to a holiday company. The idea has already been tested in a limited way: UK comedy *Chalet Girl* (2011), for example, experimented with interactive trailers promoting ski companies (see Chalet Girl 2011).

The potential for mining and exploiting existing value might open up new revenue streams, which could be essential given the diminishing returns of a relationship between producer and audience that is based on product sales within clear windows. The passive accumulation of data on existing audiences is, of course, important. For example, examining patterns in consumer behavior, such as on-line purchasing of cinema tickets or downloading habits, allows a more efficient targeting of services. This is as important to independents as it is to Hollywood, and powerful free or low-cost tools are increasingly available to businesses, even if the skills to use them remain in short supply.

Another concept that may prove to be more important, however, is the 'superfan'. The now defunct UK Film Council's Innovation Fund was involved in supporting innovative projects to find and engage superfans through what it called 'activity seeding'; the provision of social media mechanisms that encourage already interested audiences to become active supporters.

Cinema

Despite the physical limitations of screen times and spaces, the theatrical business has worked hard in recent years to increase choice and improve the consumer experience. Digital production technologies and digital distribution have opened up promising new areas, mostly in the latest generation of 3D films.

The record-breaking success of *Avatar* (James Cameron, U.S./UK, 2009), which took close to U.S.$3 billion worldwide, and two other U.S.$1 billion films from 2010 – *Toy Story 3* (Lee Unkrich, U.S.) and *Alice in Wonderland* (Tim Burton, U.S.) – points to digital 3D's considerable commercial potential, although doubts have also started to emerge. *Kung Fu Panda 2* (Jennifer Yuh, U.S., 2011), for example, took less than its 2D predecessor in its opening U.S. weekend – as did several other relative underperformers that year (Box Office Mojo 2011). The success of the mainstream as a premium revenue earner is important to specialist cinema: it creates the economic basis for the installation of 3D screens and increases the expectations of audiences who will help support the work of auteurs that embrace the format, such as Werner Herzog, Wim Wenders and Martin Scorsese. Some 113 films were available at Cannes in 2011, almost double the previous year

There are also reasons for confidence in alternative non-cinema content, such as live music. In March, 2011, a Royal Opera House production of *Carmen* was transmitted live by satellite in 3D from London to 1,500 cinemas worldwide and premium ticket prices were charged for the screening. Similarly, a concert film by rock group Iron Maiden, *Iron Maiden: Flight 666* (Sam Dunn and Scot McFadyen, U.S., 2009), opened on 500 screens in 42 countries, with more than 100,000 consumers watching mostly one-day-only screenings (EMI 2009).

The growth of gaming, the continuing expansion of live music and forthcoming major sporting events, including the 2012 Olympics, all point to an area of potential growth; the potential of the 'event' to become a critical factor in the success of digital cinema is explored further below. These changes can be seen as an extension of previous theatrical innovations such as Cinerama and Imax, but the question here is whether digital cinema represents something more – an extension of choice and an opportunity to extend the reach of specialist cinema.

Specialist Cinema and Cinema-on-Demand

While exhibitors have been willing to invest in projection equipment to screen 3D films and even alternative content such as opera, there are few who have made the commitment on the basis of increased access to specialist or art house film. One of the unfulfilled promises of digital change is that it would lead to a greater range of content and open up new markets for specialist film. Yet the link between wider choice and digital cinema has only become a reality where there has been state intervention, such as with the UK's Digital Screen Network, which paid for digital installations in return for an agreement to show a quota of UK, classic and world cinema. The independent production industry, which lacks the financial muscle of Hollywood, has been reticent about making such a leap of faith – it wants digital screens before making the digital jump, and this has led to a degree of paralysis in the market. Investment in digital cinema has been driven by Hollywood's 3D strategy.

There are financial, political and legal factors holding back the development of an indie boom at cinemas. Some are theoretically short-term, such as the 'virtual print fee' payment model through which distributors contribute to the payment for digital cinema conversion, which effectively replicates the existing cost base; or the lack of a digital delivery satellite infrastructure, which means that most digital copies cost just the same to get to the theatres as conventional prints. And then there is the thorny issue of the Digital Cinema Initiative's (DCI) standard for digital copies, which has caused controversy as being unnecessarily expensive for smaller cinemas (see Gubbins 2011a: 55-60). The economics of cinema still militate against specialist content.

One of the under-explored promises of digital cinema is that it will give customers a say in what is shown. Cinema-on-demand is a simple concept and, given the spare capacity in most cinemas for much of the week, it looks like sound business logic to allow a self-selecting audience to guarantee ticket sales for a film they have chosen themselves.

There is even an example of cinema-on-demand in action in the Brazilian market. MovieMobz, a service set up by digital entrepreneur Fabio Lima using the country's pioneering RAIN network, has been running with some success since 2005. It is not clear how far this model can be replicated in Europe, although there have been some limited experiments, such as the MEDIA programme-supported Europe's Finest.

Third-party websites have also been trying to bridge the gap between cinema-goers and programmers. Moviepilot, for example, is a German movie recommendation service which in 2010 launched a service called Support Your Local Cinema, which provided a direct link between selections made through its on-line service and cinemas.

The business model for most cinemas is still based on revenues from first-run films and with an emphasis on the opening weekend (another obsession of the scarcity model). Therefore, unless there is a radical restructuring of business, on-demand screenings will struggle to be more than a marginal addition to exhibitor revenues in the mainstream market. The big distributor will fight to retain its ability to call the shots.

Events

One of the clearest benefits deriving from the vast increase in access due to digital change has been, paradoxically, that it has driven audiences to seek out those events and occasions which seem to offer a unique or authentic experience. In what at first appears to be a paradox of digital change, but is in reality a product of it, the importance in many entertainment fields of those twin terms – 'event' and 'experience' – has grown. The Internet has dramatically increased choice and fragmented the user experience, creating unprecedented means for non-linear consumption, but this has also served to heighten the desire for the unique and authentic. In the sport and music industries, for example, where there has been an exponential increase in both on-line content and dedicated television channels, the growth areas have been in the live fields.

There are also very interesting signs that the communal screening of film in a public setting may be moving beyond the cinema. There are already interesting experiments in areas such as 'pop-up cinema', in which venues are co-opted for specific film events. One striking example is a UK initiative called Secret Cinema, where an audience is gathered on-line and through social networks to film 'happenings'. More than 12,000 people attended a screening of *La battaglia di Algeri* (*The Battle of Algiers*, Gillo Pontecorvo, Italy/Algeria, 1966) under London's Waterloo Station in 2011 (Farmer 2011).

The main events in film, of course, are festivals. The major festivals with big markets, such as Cannes and Berlin, provide the means for films to progress to international distribution, but the potential for festivals to become distributors in their own right has been on the agenda now for a couple of years, with some practical experiments from festivals such as Sundance, Tribeca and the International Film Festival Rotterdam.

The festival as distributor is one of those ideas that looks stronger on paper than in reality, but the idea puts festivals in direct competition with distributors – and that potential rivalry is already the cause of some tension. Distributors are now routinely demanding screening fees from festivals, believing that the balance of benefits from festival appearances has shifted (Peranson 2008). Of course, with festivals we return again to the core theme of fragmentation.

Festival funding itself can be a highly political process, as the sniping between Venice and Rome demonstrated when the Rome Film Festival was launched in 2006. Like every other area of film, festivals are looking at how to reinvent themselves for a digital age. This process is likely to be accelerated by a number of trends: reduced public funding and sponsorship in the aftermath of the economic downturn, pressure on the sales and distribution sectors and competition in a crowded festival calendar.

The idea has much to recommend it. At Cannes, for example, the world's press reviews the key competition films and breakout market titles. If those films were to be distributed on-line or through digital cinemas while the buzz was still strong, financial returns could be very great, but months later, when those titles are eventually released, the momentum has been lost.

There have been attempts to supply a virtual event experience on-line to mirror the real-world experience. There have been music concerts in the virtual world Second Life, and exclusive interactive game launches on Facebook, for example, but the audience is not easily manipulated and, while social networking is now widely considered an essential part of the marketing of a film, there are few of the hoped-for examples of breakout hits that succeed in riding the wave of social network posts and tweets.

New Forms of Distribution

The means by which content is accessed is far more than a technical issue; it plays a key role in shaping attitudes to and expectations of the content it delivers. The big change in mainstream music culture, which turned an industry on its head, came with the iPod, which created an intuitive and user-friendly means to play mp3s, then already a decade-old audio compression format. The ability to store and play music on mobile devices created demand that had initially been serviced largely by a wealth of illegal sites while the music industry dithered. The initial culture of digital music was strongly defined by both software and hardware.

Since the beginning of the century, other distribution developments have created new forms of content acquisition which have changed music still further and will have a considerable effect on film. They include the BitTorrent file-sharing protocol (2001), which created a simple and very fast means through which to share content; YouTube (2005), which created the means to show user-created content, but also demonstrated the potential for a streamed service; and Facebook (2004) and Twitter (2006), which became tools for sharing links to, and comment on, content. In each case, a technical trigger created demand that then exerted influence on the way that content was consumed.

Downloads

Once the inevitability of digital change kicked in and the potential for savings became clear, downloads naturally became the focus of the film industry. With electronic margins at 60-70%, compared with 20-30% for optical discs, it is no surprise that change has been high on the agenda.

The failure so far to deliver on that promise derives from a number of factors:

- The fact that piracy and file-sharing takes a significant percentage of the download market – *Avatar*, for example was illegally downloaded 16.8 million times in 2010 according to file-sharing service TorrentFreak, despite expectations that the 3D theatrical format would reduce theft.[25]
- Fears of the effect on physical revenues, including theatrical release and supermarket DVD sales.

- Concern about the deals demanded by dominant delivery services, such as iTunes.
- Worries about consumer resistance, in terms of download speed, price and, significantly, file sizes, which require the consumer to store content, often, ironically, on physical formats such as DVD.

The performance of films in the download market is patchy, although there are signs of growth. Warner Bros revealed at the Screen Digest PEVE Digital Entertainment conference in London in 2010 that releasing its films on Blu-ray Disc, DVD, VOD and as downloads was having a significant effect. It said that Clint Eastwood's *Gran Torino* (U.S./ Germany, 2008), for example, earned U.S.$60 million from VOD and downloads, against a total box office take of U.S.$148 million (Screen Digest 2010); however, these are figures which are rarely revealed.

Apple, which only introduced its movie download and rental service in 2009, has quickly come to dominate both markets, not only because of the muscle of the iTunes brand, but also through attractive devices such as the iPad. These are huge advantages, but Apple will face tough competition in the future film market from the telecom giants, technology companies, retailers and ambitious on-line giants, including Amazon and Google.

Specialist independent film has remained largely on the margins of iTunes, and of the download business in general, for commercial reasons deriving from the complicated tangle of territorial rights agreements. Government film subsidy, which is largely based on theatrical release, has also removed some of the incentives and the drive to innovate. A more competitive download market is emerging and there are other players trying to establish a strong download business, including the DVD on-line rental service LoveFilm and its new owner Amazon, as well as satellite and cable TV and telecoms companies. Some film distributors have tried to set up their own download services, Curzon Artificial Eye's Curzon on Demand is one, but they are expensive both to build and to service, and have yet to have a proven impact.

Streaming, Subscription and the Decline of Ownership

Increasing broadband speeds in most of the world, the advent of Internet-enabled television and the wider consumer acceptance of high-definition mobile devices are quickly opening up a strong market for streamed content. There are distinct advantages in watching streamed content rather than downloading, not least because the size of files means that downloading eats up space and costs money in storage. Streaming seems to be the most viable basis for VOD services in the future, not least because it does not require a major change in consumer culture. YouTube has already prepared the ground for mass market streaming, and streamed content to television will quickly feel like simply another television service. Services such as MUBI, On-line Film, Reframe and IndieFlix have created a means for independent specialist film to reach audiences with streamed content. And YouTube has attempted to take a lead in this area with its Screening Room, which has hosted full-length features since Wayne Wang's *The Princess of Nebraska* (U.S., 2007).

The missing link for audiences has to some extent been plugged, with many televisions now Internet-enabled, allowing streaming straight to the screen. As is so often the case in this examination, however, technical potential runs into problems when it comes to establishing a business and legal framework to make services financially viable.

That the music industry has been struggling with these issues can be seen in services such as Spotify, Pandora and Last FM entering the mainstream and increasingly getting financial support from concerned major labels. Such services allow unlimited access to content streamed to the desktop, laptop, mobile phone or Internet-enabled television. Who needs to own albums and singles when there is access to millions of tracks through a subscription fee? Spotify passed 10 million users in 2010, with access to around 10 million songs for free with advertising breaks, or advertisement-free for a subscription fee.

The advent of cloud computing adds a new level to the discussion. It is possible to imagine every song being available to anyone worldwide through any device – and similarly, by extension, all films. The technical barriers to this vision are fast disappearing; turning it into a revenue stream, however, remains the obsession of industry.

Spotify and similar services are delivering important revenues, but not at the level of the analogue world. A report from the International Federation of the Phonographic Industry (IFPI) puts stark numbers to the problem: between 2004 and 2010 the digital market in music grew 1,000%, but revenues for the industry as a whole in the same period fell 31% (IFPI 2011). Film is facing the same set of issues.

Internet Protocol TV (IPTV) and Video-on-Demand (VOD)

On-demand services have been growing fast, with The European Audiovisual Observatory counting close to 700 VOD sites in Europe in its 2010 Focus report (European Audiovisual Observatory 2010). VOD now describes a confusing array of services, from the near video-on-demand of films offered on a rolling start pay-to-view basis by satellite channels to streamed video subscription services.

The countless channels available include many in highly specialist areas with, typically for digital advances, pornography accounting for a large part of the change. The big problem for this VOD explosion is that more channels are not necessarily better for audiences, who are themselves constrained by time and do not necessarily possess the desire or the technical capability to search for content.

The explosion of channels includes a huge number of what the industry disparagingly refers to as 'bottom feeders', those hoping to make profit from smaller independents in something like the self-publication sector in book publishing.

Some more established players, such as Babelgum and Jaman, may find a strong niche, but the VOD market is still strongly weighted towards established brands – notably Apple, but also telecoms companies, television stations and channels, on-line rental companies such as LoveFilm and Netflix, and the technology giants. They have the advantage of devices, brand recognition and, increasingly, access to television.

These bigger brands will want the same control over content that they had in the analogue world. Outside of the Hollywood Studios, it is difficult to drive a deal with these dominating names. For example, European film, still locked in its confused maze of rights and windows, is finding that on-demand services do not necessarily offer advantages.

One of the few brands to have established a foothold (albeit with the strong support of the European Commission's MEDIA project) is art house subscription service MUBI (formerly The Auteurs), which demonstrates both the potentials and the pitfalls of the emerging VOD landscape. It has put itself in a relatively strong position by establishing a relationship with Sony, which has included a place for MUBI on the PS3 games console menu. This gives it access to millions of televisions and the distinct advantage of being embedded in existing set-top boxes. The site is well-designed, intuitive and has a clear focus on great European film. It has built up a strong community with insightful contributions from members.

Yet the confusion over rights is an ever-present restriction on the fulfillment of what might once have been something like a one-stop shop for those who love European art film. The service is severely restricted in what it is able to show from country to country, despite the global reach afforded it by Sony and its website.

Mobile

The mobile market may be particularly significant given that in 2010 there were an estimated five billion cellphone users worldwide. By 2014, 92% of mobile devices in Western Europe will be able to access the Internet through 3G technologies (Morgan Stanley 2009: 26). Mobile broadband is among the fastest growing areas of the broadband market in Europe, with Finland, Austria and Portugal leading the way with penetration rates of dedicated mobile broadband cards above 15% by 2010 (European Commission 2010: 5).

And mobile content has already inspired experiments in filmmaking. In 2009, UK director Sally Potter's *Rage* claimed to be the first major film to be distributed for free exclusively through a mobile phone (see Rage 2009). Downloadable in seven parts, *Rage* boasted a cast including Jude Law, Steve Buscemi and Eddie Izzard. The innovative UK-based Pure Grass Films, which has been working with successful media companies such as Endemol, has also enjoyed some success in the mobile field with films such as *When Evil Calls* (Johannes Roberts, UK, 2006). Fox Mobile is among the big corporations now experimenting with the idea of 'mobisodes' aimed at younger markets, with the marketing-led *Honey and Joy* (Drew Antzis and Tamara Bick, U.S., 2011).

New mobile creative forms may emerge most quickly in Asia, home to the world's fastest mobile and Web networks – or even in Africa, where the lack of theatres and DVD players is helping to stimulate a leap towards mobile technology. South African company DV8 has been strong in this area and the Nollywood industry in Nigeria is also experimenting.

Mobile is set to become an area of exponential growth, driven by consumer demand for new players, although the size of the market and the speed of adoption are not yet clear, particularly given the current economic climate.

Curation, Recommendation and Social Networking

The early narrative of digital change was of a democratising trend away from 'gatekeepers' restricting choice. There has been one attempt to help the problem of navigating through the chaos of VOD with the setting up of search services that can locate content on multiple platforms. The UK Film Council's Find Any Film was a pioneer in this respect. The link between user taste and VOD, particularly when coupled with social networking through services such as Twitter and Facebook, looks like an interesting option.

Social networking, in its many guises, is perhaps the most significant trend of recent years and remains a great, if still elusive, hope. The ability and desire to congregate with like-minded people on-line offers the most direct means of engaging with the active audience. It is important to understand, however, that the network is the people, not the technology provider.

Putting up a Facebook page and hoping for a response will achieve little. A common mistake is to see social networking as a shortcut rather than a time-consuming, but potentially rewarding venture demanding new kinds of skills. Effective on-line networking begins with understanding the medium and how it is being used. Assumptions about on-line behaviour, for example, are often based on false perceptions – not least that social networking is something only for the young. Community building is now supported by intuitive tools which aid sharing of content and interact with audiences; Twitter is the most hyped, but there are also a wealth of other social tools for tagging, mapping and analysing audience behaviour.

For the initiated expert, understanding this world opens up a wealth of possibilities: Liesl Copland, an agent at William Morris Endeavour Global, claims that the 'only talk back session ever to touch the supply chain logic in the movie industry was the focus group. But now that activity is happening in a new layer that the Internet has provided... Our TVs, our computers and our phones are learning us' (IndieWIRE 2009).

New Business Models

It has become clear in recent years that there will be no single business model to replace the one that has been the foundation of the physical goods market. The radical open-source wing of film-making has been growing in confidence in recent years. Although many filmmakers and radicals appear on platforms together, they are a disparate group. What unites them is a sense that the Web should not operate in the same way as the analogue world.

The digital debate that took up much of the early part of the digital revolution was about the so-called Long Tail and the potential of making money from giving away much of what we had previously believed to be core assets.

Predictably, Chris Anderson, the celebrated author of *The Long Tail: Why the Future of Business Is Selling Less of More* (2006), has again been at the forefront of the discussion with his book *Free: The Future of a Radical Price* (2009). He proposes a re-evaluation of pricing, which he suggests is currently based on old-world economics. We have to accept that the Internet has created open and free access to intellectual property and the task of making money is to build on the increased exposure that creates for film-makers, writers or artists.

The idea has since suffered a backlash, particularly given the paucity of examples of mainstream success stories and a growing sense that the digital age is pushing profit away from producers and towards platforms and hardware providers. In some ways the debate has moved into even more difficult territory.

Advertising Support and Subscription

The pre-roll advertisement, which provides funding for free content on YouTube, news media websites and the like, has now become commonplace. Accepting advertising to access free content is also the basic model for music sites such as Spotify (see below).

Advertising is playing a more prominent role in audiovisual content, and YouTube and Amazon are prominent among those exploiting the opportunities, but the evidence for consumer acceptance is not yet clear and variations, such as skippable 'true view' ads introduced by Google and others in 2010, have already become available. Advertising is also part of an opt-out subscription model, pioneered again in music by sites such as Spotify, which offers the consumer a chance to watch free content with ads or to pay a subscription fee for an ad-free model. The advent of Internet-enabled television should significantly boost the free market.

There is uncomfortable pressure on filmmakers and artists to take a hit on the development of new free platforms by agreeing to poor deals and exclusivity. Some independent services are trying to create fairer deals. German service On-line Film, for example, allows independent documentary makers to reach audiences through a streaming and download platform using the BitTorrent P2P file sharing protocol to exchange files and does not use digital rights management.

It is an approach also being employed by a number of younger independent producers who feel locked out of the traditional process. It is clear, though, that there needs to be a broader debate about how to ensure producers retain a greater portion of digital rights. There are now plenty of examples of artists going straight to the audience with free content, hoping to create revenue elsewhere.

Brand Support

The involvement of commercial brands in filmmaking has long been a controversial subject. The focus has traditionally and primarily been on product placement, but the relationship between brand and filmmaking goes further. In some cases, brands have actually driven the entire project, as in the case of *Somers Town* (Shane Meadows, UK, 2008), which was controversially backed by Eurostar (Cox 2008). Some brands see support for art as a kind of social capital that can strengthen its image and thus they perceive filmed content as an effective means of communicating the kind of brand image that traditional marketing cannot convey. In some ways it is a logical extension of the changed nature of audience engagement – brands are looking to tap into and share a relationship between content-makers and audience. Advertising has long understood the power that imagery exerts, with many directors making money from television and cinema campaigns.

Among recent partnerships, sportswear business PUMA backed Jeremy Gilley's documentary *The Day after Peace* (UK, 2008), and in 2010 announced an extension of its support to the BRITDOC Foundation (Pumavision 2010). Similarly, mobile phone giant Orange, which has long promoted itself through film, co-funded the French Happy Fannie production *Faits divers paranormaux* (*Supernatural Oddities*, Jean-Christophe Establet, France, 2010), which included strong transmedia elements (Orange and Happy Fannie 2010).

Although the trend lost a little momentum after the global economic downturn of 2010 and 2011, the experience of the music industry suggests that this form of brand-content relationship will grow. Brand-music partnerships have become an essential part of the economics of the business, with advertising now becoming a prime way to launch music and with new forms of showcasing emerging, such as Universal and SEAT's On Track television programme (Shields 2010). The relationship between brand and content is likely to become an increasingly important part of film finance and, although it raises questions about commercial influence over content, there is a sense that brands have a vital interest in maintaining the integrity of the relationship between artist and audience.

Crowdfunding

Crowdfunding has achieved some degree of industry credibility, thanks in part to the success of what might be called activist cinema. Perhaps the strongest recent example in Europe has been The Age of Stupid (Franny Armstrong, UK, 2009), a campaigning drama about global warming starring Pete Postlethwaite, directed by Franny Armstrong and produced by Lizzie Gillett.

The project managed to raise more than 1 million from a few hundred investors. Its use of social media and interaction with supporters is an object lesson in audience collaboration. The inspiration for such projects tends to be political; one clear example being the game-changing on-line campaign to elect Barack Obama as U.S. President in 2008. They work where there is a sense of political impotence in mainstream democratic decision-making and where supporting a film is a tangible form of protest.

The question is whether the approach is really more about financing a political campaign through film than supporting a film with a political objective. Does it represent a new form of political action or a potential new business model?

The history of crowdfunding as a means for audiences to commercially support specialist content is mixed at best, and early experiments in crowdfunded music found it easier to raise money from venture capitalists than audiences. High-profile Dutch music start-up Sellaband, for example, filed for bankruptcy in 2010, three and a half years after launch and two years after a 3.5 million injection of venture capital. (Its subsequent acquisition by German investors suggests some longer-term confidence.)

A number of platforms for crowdfunding have shown some signs of promise in partly or fully funding micro-budget films, including U.S.

site Kickstarter and European sites like Touscoprod and People for Cinema. Among the bigger successes was the 52,000 raised through Touscoprod for Gilles Marchand's *L'Autre monde* (*Black Hole*, France/Belgium, 2010), which was selected out of competition at Cannes in 2010 (Touscoprod 2011). The International Film Festival Rotterdam funded two short films in 2010 through its crowdfunding project, Cinema Reloaded – Argentinian filmmaker Alexis Dos Santos' *Random Strangers* (UK/Netherlands/Argentina, 2011) and Malaysian director Yuhang Ho's *No One Is Illegal* (Netherlands, 2011). There are, however, problems that have not yet been overcome: the lack of fundraising skills, legal complexities over the rights and status of donors and the lack of understanding of the commitment necessary from filmmakers to make crowdfunding work.

There is, therefore, no convincing evidence at this stage that crowdfunding will by itself deliver a viable business model for larger-budget films hoping for significant returns for the producer; or indeed for funders looking for more than altruistic support or political commitment for their money, particularly given the legal complexities of rights and returns. There are signs, however, that crowdfunding may come to form part of the financing of a film, rather than the whole. In 2011, Matthew Lessner's film *The Woods* (U.S.), whose budget was supplemented by more than U.S.$11,000 in crowdfunding, became the first Kickstarter-supported project to be accepted at the Sundance Film Festival (McGregor 2010).

Fully funding film may not be the point. Experience is demonstrating that the key to crowdfunding is not to take the money and run, but rather to create a dialogue with audiences and a shared sense of ownership. This requires commitment from filmmakers.

Voluntary Payments and Creative Commons

Faith in the altruism of consumers has been severely tested over the last few years, despite some high-profile experiments in voluntary payments, particularly in music.

UK rock band Radiohead's free download release of their album *In Rainbows* in 2007 was among the best-known attempts to try a pay-what-you-want approach and a great deal of hype earned it some success. Yet a report from analyst ComScore (disputed by the band) suggests that around 62% of downloaders paid nothing (Comscore

2007), although that leaves a sizeable group of contributors who may have contributed as much as U.S.$3 million (2.3 million). Still, the band did not repeat the exercise for the 2011 release of its *King of Limbs* album. It is also important to remember that Radiohead was able to draw on an existing fan-base built the traditional way, through studio releases.

There have been few successf stories in film to match that kind of radicalism, although Jamie King's VODO service, launched in 2009 and billed as 'free-to-share films available through BitTorrent', has actively seized the potential of P2P networks used for illegal file-sharing to distribute content very widely for free, hoping that even a small percentage of voluntary donations from a large audience will make a significant impact. The site claims that 9.8 million downloads of films had taken place by June 2011. Founder Jamie King said the inspiration for VODO was his own experience in raising U.S.$30,000 (23,000) from donors for his own *Steal This Film: The League of Noble Peers* (UK/Germany, 2006), which was released and distributed through BitTorrent; $30,000 is not a great sum, but is more, he provocatively points out, than a lot of producers see for more conventional releases. The service has been signing up a number of films for P2P release, with the top-rated download – *Pioneer One* (Bracey Smith, U.S., 2010) – topping three million downloads (according to data captured from the Vodo website, www.vodo.net/toplists, on 26 July 2011). Most of these experiments are based on the widest possible access to content with non-exclusive deals.

Retaining rights ownership – even if only to give them away to the audience – is fundamental to these digital ambitions and the use of Creative Commons (CC) licensing has been widely explored in many industries as a practical means to create a flexible rights industry.

Advocates see CC as a way to overcome the narrow restrictions of the existing rights systems, allowing rights holders to strike a balance between supporting creative production and invisibility. Like the free software and open-source movements, the aims are cooperative and community-minded but the means are voluntary. Creative Commons attempts to offer creators a best-of-both-worlds way to protect their work, while encouraging certain uses by declaring 'some rights reserved'. There are now more than 130 million Creative Commons licensed works around the world – a six-fold increase on the number in 2005.

New Forms of Narrative

The idea that digital change will create new Net-native forms of art has a basis in history; film itself has always evolved in part from pioneering directors exploring the potential of innovations in production, post-production and exhibition equipment; the latest incarnation of 3D demonstrates this.

According to Liz Rosenthal, founder of influential digital consultancy Power to the Pixel:

> Maybe there will be a time in the not-so-distant future when it becomes irrelevant to define a project as cross-media, as it will be universally expected that a story should be experienced across multiple platforms and we will simply focus once more on storytelling. (Gubbins and Rosenthal 2011: 7)

While the Internet is beginning, as we shall see, to open up a variety of innovative ideas and works, its contribution so far has been more in creating new means to distribute and talk about content than in creating influential works. It has been a much bigger influence on games, which have found a means to create multiplayer, interactive content with global influence. Alternate reality game pioneer Jane McGonigal's suggests that by the time the average U.S. teenager reaches 21, they may have spent as much as 10,000 hours gaming – about what they spend in school (McGonigal 2010). It is perhaps natural, then, that some advocates see the growth of new art forms based on the kinds of interaction we see in gaming or in on-line social networking, and the concept of 'gameification' has entered the debate in digital film circles. This thinking suggests that the dynamics of cinema will fundamentally change, with a changed relationship between filmmaker and audience opening up discussions about the primacy of the text over the reader.

Interactive Content

The audience-driven narrative is nothing new. There were numerous (failed) experiments in choose-your-own-ending films during the 1950s, with intermittent attempts to revive the idea since, including the 2010 Israeli film *Turbulence* (Nitzan Ben-Shaul) (Blum 2010).

The idea of film as a lived experience is, however, exciting a number of filmmakers, particularly those using cross-media or transmedia techniques. Many come from the gaming culture, where the power to change narrative is second nature. The fusion of games and film is one that is much talked about but rarely explored beyond the cross-promotional marketing of the game of the film, or the film of the game. Pulling the two together into a consistent narrative is a different matter, but a number of filmmakers are now experimenting with live-action games, where audiences do not decide on the ending of the film itself but rather play real-life games associated with the narrative of the film – live-action role-playing games (LARP). Examples include:

- Lance Weiler's *Pandemic 1.0,* which uses geolocation technology and social gaming to create a story universe in which audiences around the world are invited to become active players in the tale of survivors of the outbreak of a devastating global disease.
- Swede Martin Elricsson's The Company P's long-running cross-media project called *The Truth About Marika*, which turned the audience into a willing and, controversially, unknowing participant in a fictional story of a missing person.
- Kat Cizek's Canadian project *High Rise – Out Of My Window* is an experimental documentary in which audiences virtually 'enter' high-rise blocks in cities around the world to unlock the real stories of those living in them.
- And John Chu's *The League of Extraordinary Dancers* (*LXD*) used the Internet to find dance talent to be used as the basis of a Web series that became a hit on Hulu and established a multi-million following on YouTube.

User-generated Content

One of the most exciting elements of the digital age is the ubiquity of equipment for audiovisual production. As with all consumer electronics, every year costs come down and power goes up and, thanks to the open-source software movement and the development of new social media tools, there is unprecedented support for content creation and distribution.

Filmmaking is already becoming more like music – something you do as well as consume – and a punk sensibility has kicked in with a carefree attitude to copyright infringement or content borrowing.

Culturally, video is becoming central to a Net-native generation, whether through mobile messaging, Skype, social network video or other means.

Perhaps the banality of much of the output so far explains the widespread indifference to this trend from the film business. It has become routine – and complacently self-serving – to dismiss the change as mere amateurism.

Technology analyst Forrester estimates that in the first-quarter of 2010, 23% of U.S. Internet users were 'social media creators' uploading some form of content (although it suggests the trend may have reached a plateau) (Anderson et al. 2010).

In any case, 'user-generated content' is a lazy way of describing a wide range of activity. The term is perhaps most applicable to the communications that vast numbers of us make through texting. There is a layer of keen amateurs who use new technology to post pieces of content for their peers either for work or pleasure. Again these can sometimes unexpectedly reach huge audiences. There are, however, projects that we might call 'social cinema', which aggregate user-generated content to ambitious and culturally interesting final products. *Life in a Day* (Kevin MacDonald, U.S., 2011), for example, brings together thousands of personal video diaries to create a cinematic record of a single day. Directed by Kevin MacDonald and co-produced by Ridley Scott, it launched at the Sundance Film Festival in 2011 (Partridge 2010). Similarly, the ARTE-backed *Gaza-Sderot* (2008, France/Germany/Israel), created a unique documentary work by putting cameras in the hands of Palestinians in Gaza and Israelis in Sderot, resulting in a rolling Web resource that was edited to become an award-winning documentary feature (see Gaza Sderot 2008). Then there is a layer of what perhaps should more accurately be described as undiscovered talent seeking recognition rather than 'users'. And again there have been some phenomenal successes: Dane Boedigheimer's *Annoying Orange* (U.S., 2009) video series on YouTube has been seen close to 450 million times. Real film talent has been emerging from the user-generated content era. One of the biggest emerging talents of 2009 was South African-Canadian filmmaker Neill Blomkamp, whose low-budget *District 9* (U.S./New Zealand/Canada/South Africa, 2009) was a huge global hit; he was first noticed thanks to a six-minute viral video. Making user-generated content of this kind pay for its provider has been difficult. Yahoo Video pulled out of the market when it stopped its uploading service in December 2010.

Transmedia Discipline

The potential for new creative forms evolving from cinema, but entering new transmedia fields, is stunted by an enthusiasm on the part of advocates that often runs beyond their skills to deliver. Michael Monello, co-producer of one of the progenitors of the cross-media approach to filmmaking, *The Blair Witch Project* (Daniel Myrick and Eduardo Sánchez, U.S., 1999), warned the 2010 Power to the Pixel conference in London that many of today's would-be digital pioneers displayed an unrealistic approach to business. He told the conference's Think Tank that there was a lack of discipline among the would-be creators of a new cross-media future: 'We all see the potential and we all want to go to the moon' (Gubbins and Rosenthal 2011: 12). While business models change, the essential economic laws remain the same: production and marketing costs need to be in line with the price point of the potential audience. This lack of discipline is a by-product of a digital world, which has developed at such high speed that business thinking has struggled to keep up. One of the essential foundations of any new business model is an understanding of true costs rather than theoretical ones. The Web seems to offer free access to global markets and that drove much early enthusiasm, but the costs in terms of time, skills acquisition, technical materials and upgrades, quickly add up. In this sense it mirrors a creative issue for film. The cost of film in the camera acted as an often valuable restraint, forcing tight structuring and economy of effort. You had one shot at getting it right. Without these constraints, it is easy to lose discipline.

On-line business is still business, and its potential can only be reached when industrial process and commercial exploitation are in tune with consumer demand. Digital developments make radical business models possible because they can reduce production and distribution costs and create the means to engage audiences, but in this new world a degree of business discipline and the right content remain essential if new sustainable models are to be found.

Conclusion: The Active Audience

The digital revolution is in some ways still in its infancy and this makes predictions of future progress difficult. The advance of new technologies, for example, shows few signs of slowing; Moore's Law, which predicts that computing power will roughly double every 18 months, holds true.

In the last two years alone there have been significant hardware and software advances, including the iPhone, iPad, Internet slabs, eReaders, Twitter, Google Chrome and Windows 7.

What's more, we are on the brink of even more highly significant developments, including Internet-enabled television, next-generation multimedia search engines, 3D TV and 'cloud' computing, through which audiovisual content is stored remotely rather than on local hard disks. All of these innovations are supported by the continuing increase in broadband speeds, which are seen in most of the world as a key driver of economic progress.

Importantly, the key components of digital change are already in place, even if specific technological advances, such as 3D television, face a struggle to make an early impact because of reduced consumer spending in the current economic climate. According to data captured from the Innternet World Stats website (www.internetworldstats.com/stats4.htm) on 26 June 2011, internet penetration in Europe is now well above 50% (and above 90% in parts of Scandinavia). That equates to an average rise of more than 350% in the last 10 years. In Asia the rise is even greater, with the same report calculating a 622% rise over the decade. South Korea leads the world in broadband household penetration (97.6%) and speeds (Euromonitor 2011). Broadband access has also progressed at an astonishing rate, opening up new forms of global communication and entertainment. As soon as faster speeds and bigger pipes are created, consumers find new uses for them – both legitimate and illegal.

The argument here was that these developments are changing the relationship between audience and content, yet some of these changes prove to be contradictory and confusing. It was argued that the newly-found wealth of content choices, accessible on demand on multiple platforms and devices, relies on an 'active audience' and implies a fundamentally changed relationship between audience and content. In doubt is how consumers will respond to these technology triggers, particularly as the last decade has shown that audiences will find value that was not always intended (mobile telephone manufacturers, for example, did not see texting as a service that would change consumer culture).

Film is not heading on a clear path of progress to a single destination; the digital shift described here is not simply a set of evolutionary changes that the cinematic product is undergoing but, rather, represents a new environment in which film is going to have to find its place. New forms of engagement with audiences and even the development of fresh art forms represent genuine potential, but they will be subject to the laws of economics; in a world with fierce and growing competition for consumer time, not all consumer demands can be satisfied. Many of the most exciting ideas that promise to transform the dynamics of cinema may simply prove not to be economically viable, particularly given the strain on public finances, which have been so essential to independent cinema. The effect of digital change on cinema will be reliant, then, on the realpolitik of the industrial and economic environment; and yet the experience of other industries is that there are unstoppable tides in consumer behaviour that will have to be addressed.

Staying still is not an option.

Works Cited

Anderson, Chris (2006) *The Long Tail: Why the Future of Business Is Selling Less of More*. New York: Hyperion.

_____ (2009) *Free: The Future of a Radical Price*. New York: Hyperion.

Anderson, Jacqueline, Josh Bernoff, Reineke Reitsma and Erica Sorensen (2010) 'A Global Update of Social Technographics', *Forrester*, 28 September. On-line. Available HTTP: http://www.forrester.com/rb/Research/global_update_of_social_technographics%26%23174%3B/q/id/57523/t/2 (17 June 2011).

Bernoff, Josh and Jacqueline Anderson (2010) 'Social Technographics Defined', *Forrester*, 2 August. On-line. Available HTTP: http://www.forrester.com/empowered/ladder2010 (17 June 2011).

Blum, Brian (2010) 'A Tech Revolution That Lets You Choose the Movie's Plot', *Israel 21C*, 28 November. On-line. Available HTTP: http://www.israel21c.org/201011288556/technology/a-tech-revolution-that-lets-you-choose-the-movies-plot (17 June 2011).

Box Office Mojo (2011) 'Kung Fu Panda', *Box Office Mojo*. On-line. Available HTTP: http://www.boxofficemojo.com/movies/?id=kungfupanda2.htm (9 September 2011).

Cellan-Jones, Rory (2011) 'Web Creator's Net Neutrality Fear', *BBC News*, 19 April. On-line. Available HTTP: http://www.bbc.co.uk/news/technology-13126777 (26 July 2011).

Chalet Girl (2011) *Chalet Girl Website*. On-line. Available HTTP: http//chaletgirl.findanyfilm.com (accessed 29 November 2011).

Comscore (2007) 'For Radiohead Fans, Does "Free" + "Download" = "Freeload"?', *Comscore* Press Release, November. On-line. Available HTTP: http://www.comscore.com/Press_Events/Press_Releases/2007/11/Radiohead_Downloads (17 June 2011).

Comscore (2011) 2010 *Europe Digital Year in Review*, February. On-line. Available HTTP: http://www.tendencias21.net/attachment/256786 (26 July 2011).

Cox, David (2008) 'Cinema Sells Its Soul', *The Guardian*, 26 August. On-line. Available HTTP: http://www.guardian.co.uk/film/2008/aug/26/somers.town (17 June 2011).

Deloitte (2010) *Media Predictions 2010*. London: Deloitte Touche Tomatsu. On-line. Available HTTP: http://www.deloitte.com/assets/Dcom-Global/ Local%20Assets/Documents/TMT/Predictions%202010%20PDFs/Media_ predictions_2010.pdf (26 July 2011).

Economist, The (2009) 'The Lazy Medium', *The Economist*, April 29. On-line. Available HTTP: http://www.economist.com/node/15980817 (9 September 2011).

EMI (2009) 'Iron Maiden: Flight 666 cinema milestone', *EMI Website*, 11 May. On-line. Available HTTP: http://www.emimusic.com/news/2009/iron-maiden-flight-666-cinema-milestone/ (25 November 2011).

Euromonitor (2011), 'Global Digital Divide Persists but Is Narrowing', *Euromonitor Global Market Research Blog*, 11 February. On-line. Available HTTP: http://blog.euromonitor.com/2011/02/global-digital-divide-persists-but-is-narrowing-1.html (17 June).

Europe's Information Society (2010) 'Digital Agenda: Broadband Speeds Increasing but Europe Must Do More', Europe's Information Society. Thematic Portal, 25 November. On-line. Available HTTP: http://ec.europa. eu/information_society/newsroom/cf/itemlongdetail.cfm?item_id=6502 (8 August 2011).

European Audiovisual Observatory (2010) *Focus 2010. World Film Market Trends*. On-line. Available HTTP: http://www.obs.coe.int/On-line_publication/ reports/focus2010.pdf (17 June 2011).

European Commission (2010) *Progress Report on the Single European Electronic Communications Market*. On-line. Available HTTP: http://ec.europa.eu/ information_society/policy/ecomm/doc/implementation_enforcement/ annualreports/15threport/comm_en.pdf (2 September 2011).

Farmer, Lucy (2011) 'Fun in the Dark', *More Intelligent Life*. On-line. Available HTTP: http://moreintelligentlife.com/content/arts/lucy-farmer/fun-dark (26 July 2011).

Gartner (2011) 'Gartner Hype Cycle', *Gartner Website*. On-line. Available HTTP: http://www.gartner.com/technology/research/methodologies/hype-cycle. jsp (9 September 2011).

Gaza Sderot (2008) *Gaza Sderot* Website. On-line. Available HTTP: http://gaza-sderot.arte.tv (Accessed 25 November 2011).

Goldman, William (1983) *Adventures in the Screen Trade*. Abacus.

Gubbins, Michael (2011a) 'Digital Revolution: Engaging Audiences', *Cine-Regio*. On-line. Available for download on request HTTP: http://www.cineregio. org/press_media/digital_revolution_/ (17 June 2011).

Gubbins, Michael (2011b) 'Lost Demographics', *movieScope*, 22, May/June 2011. On-line. Available HTTP: http://www.moviescopemag.com/24-fps/ industryinsider/lost-demographics/ (25 November 2011).

Gubbins, Michael and Liz Rosenthal (2011) 'Power to the Pixel', Think Tank Report. On-line. Available HTTP: http://thepixelreport.org/wp-content/ uploads/2011/03/ThinkTank2011hiqual.pdf (17 June 2011).

Hartman, Florence (2011), *The Digital Transition: Films, TV, Video: Perspectives from Europe*. On-line. Available HTTP: http://is.jrc.ec.europa.eu/ pages/ISG/documents/FHSEVILLA_2011_Digital_transition_final.pdf (2 September 2011).

IFPI (2011) *IFPI Digital Music Report 2011*. On-line. Available HTTP: http://www. ifpi.org/content/library/DMR2011.pdf (19 August 2011).

IndieWIRE (2009) 'Liesl Copland: "Dear Theater Owners, Fear Not – You Are Not Going Anywhere"', *IndieWIRE*, 13 September. On-line. Available HTTP: http://www.indiewire.com/article/liesl_copland_dear_theater_owners_ fear_not_-_you_are_not_going_anywhere/P0/ (26 July 2011).

McGonigal, Jane (2010) 'Gaming Can Make a Better World', Transcript of speech, *Dotsub*. On-line. Available HTTP: http://dotsub.com/view/87e58675-24ba-408b-abbe-97718a3b17b5/viewTranscript/eng (17 June 2011).

McGregor, Michael (2010) 'Hello Sundance: *The Woods* to Premiere at Sundance', *Kick Starter*, 2 December. On-line. Available HTTP: http://www. kickstarter.com/blog/hello-sundance-the-woods-to-premiere-at-sundance (26 July 2011).

Morgan Stanley (2009) 'The Mobile Internet Report', *Morgan Stanley*. On-line. Available HTTP: http://www.morganstanley.com/institutional/techresearch/ pdfs/2SETUP_12142009_RI.pdf (2 September 2011).

Nielsen, Jakob (2006) 'Participation Inequality: Encouraging More Users to Contribute', *Useit*, 9 October. On-line. Available HTTP: http://www.useit. com/alertbox/participation_inequality.html (17 June 2011).

Orange and Happy Fannie (2010) 'Orange and Happy Fannie Launch Faits Divers Paranormaux, a New Transmedia Experience', Orange and Happy Fannie Press Release, 23 March. On-line. Available HTTP: http://www. orange.com/en_EN/press/press_releases/att00014809/CP_Orange_ HappyFanie_EN.pdf (26 July 2011).

Parker, Alan (2002) 'Building a Sustainable UK Film Industry: A Presentation to the UK Film Industry', *UK Film Council*, 5 November. On-line. Available HTTP: http://www.ukfilmcouncil.org.uk/media/pdf/q/r/BaSFI.pdf (17 June 2011).

Partridge, Tim (2010) 'Life in a Day', *Google Blog*, 7 June. On-line. Available HTTP: http://googleblog.blogspot.com/2010/07/life-in-day.html (17 June 2011).

Peranson, Mark (2008) 'First You Get the Power, Then You Get the Money: Two Models of Film Festivals', *Cineaste*, 33, 3, 37-43

Phillips, William (1997) 'The Myth of TV's Golden Oldies', *Journal of the Royal Television Society*, 28 December. On-line. Available HTTP: http://www.thefreelibrary.com/MYTH+OF+TV'S+GOLDEN+OLDIES.-a060659639 (25 November 2011).

Pumavision (2010) 'PUMA.Creative and Channel 4 Britdoc Foundation Launches New Initiative to Support Documentary Films', September. On-line. Available HTTP: http://vision.puma.com/us/en/tag/film/ (17 June 2011).

Rage (2009) *Rage Website*. On-line. Available HTTP: http://www.babelgum.com/rage (accessed 29 November 2011).

Screen Digest (2010) 'Live from PEVE. Digital Entertainment 2010: Digital and 3D Top of the Agenda'. On-line. Available HTTP: http://www.screendigest.com/events/peve/news/live_from_peve_2010.pdf (17 June 2011).

Shields, Ronan (2010) 'Car Brands Turn to Digital Media to Promote Their Latest Models', *Marketing Week*, 28 July. On-line. Available HTTP: http://www.marketingweek.co.uk/sectors/automotives/car-brands-turn-to-digital-media-to-promote-their-latest-models/3016364.article (17 June 2011).

Touscoprod (2011), 'Black Hole', *Touscoprod Website*. On-line. Available HTTP: http://www.touscoprod.com/project/produce?id=61 (9 September 2011).

UK Film Council (2010) *Statistical Yearbook 2010*. On-line. Available HTTP: http://sy10.ukfilmcouncil.ry.com/pdf/Chapter11-FilmOnUKTV.pdf (26 July 2011).

Wactlar, Howard D. and Michael G. Christel (2002), 'Digital Video Archives: Managing Through Metadata'. On-line. Available HTTP: http://www.clir.org/pubs/reports/pub106/video.html (17 June 2011).

Notes

1   This chapter is based, in part, on the author's 2011 report for Cine-Regio, 'Digital Revolution: Engaging Audiences', which is available for download on request from http://www.cineregio.org/press_media/digital_revolution_/.

2   *Män som hatar kvinnor (The Girl With The Dragon Tattoo*, Niels Arden Oplev, Sweden/Denmark/Germany/Norway, 2009), *Luftslottet som sprängdes (The Girl Who Kicked The Hornet's Nest*, Daniel Alfredson, Sweden/Denmark/Germany, 2009) and *Flickan som lekte med elden (The Girl Who Played With Fire*, Daniel Alfredson, Sweden/Denmark/Germany, 2009).

Internet-enabled Dissemination: Managing Uncertainty in the Film Value Chain

Michael Franklin

In its illegal form, Internet-enabled dissemination of film poses an existential threat to the film industry. In its legal form, it presents an exceptional challenge that pushes traditional industry set-ups into radical reorganisation. Digital distribution has an impact on every aspect of the film industry: it determines not just what films audiences see and how they see them, but also how films are developed, produced and sold. Driven by an economic necessity for multiple, diversified revenue streams, the last decade saw the development of innovative new forms of storytelling across multiple formats and platforms. It is interesting to undertake a holistic examination of the relationships between companies from different sectors of the industry relevant to the escalating shift toward Internet-enabled film dissemination.

The opportunities that Internet-enabled film dissemination provides to audiences, to incumbent distribution companies and to new entrants in the technology field are well documented in industry literature (Finney 2010; OECD 2011). These were also the areas that first experienced the radical changes brought about by the application of Internet-enabled tools. International audiences benefit from the availability of far more diverse content at relatively low transactional cost or effort via services like MUBI, Jaman and Babelgum (Kern 2009). Distributors can now take advantage of a proliferation of exhibition windows, such as the multiplicity of video-on-demand (VOD) channels and paid downloads and more engaging and interactive methods to sell films, such as viral videos and social media (Ulin 2009). However, the benefits of digital distribution have not yet outweighed revenues lost due to Internet piracy and competition from other digital entertainment options, amongst other causes (House of Lords 2010; UKFC 2010; Block 2011).

Digital disruption is understood as the conflict caused by the juxtaposition of exponential rates of change in technology on the one hand and incremental rates of change in society, economics, politics and law on the other. In the creative industries, the disruption is exemplified by challenges to all entertainment companies that are built around analogue products: their models prove unable to cope with the economic properties of information goods in the digital age – including simultaneous consumption, often illegally, at no cost and frequently facilitated by Internet piracy (Downes 2009). The development of new business models that address the problems caused by digital disruption deserve serious academic attention.

Relationships between different film companies are becoming more dynamic and complex in the digital age. Filmmakers engage with Internet-enabled technologies for disseminating film and this results in changes in the types of films produced and in what ways films are made available to audiences. This chain of cause and effect has been little studied but merits serious consideration. In particular, the cohesive application of new models across industry sectors, such as production and distribution, requires critical appraisal. In this context, considering the changes driven by Internet-enabled models as new responses to uncertainty may prove to be useful.

The Film Value Chain and On-line Distribution: Understanding the Problem

At present, the independent film industry is adopting Internet-enabled tools in an attempt to create sustainable businesses. Internet mavens have proclaimed the *prima facie* logic of a global distribution system that allows filmmakers direct access to the maximum potential audience, but without the revenue cuts taken by intermediary sales agents, distributors and exhibitors (Hardy 2010). The reality is, however, much more complex and slower paced than this perceived wisdom suggests. New models have not yet coalesced. A survey of the Internet-driven dynamics of world cinema should consider the interrelations between new technology, new business models and current business interests. One of the most useful analytical tools to address and frame this issue is the concept of the Film Value Chain (Bloore 2009), especially in its relation to the management of uncertainty.

The Film Value Chain (FVC) – where the life of a film is analysed through progressive stages, such as development, financing, production, sales, distribution and exhibition – is the traditional structural-organisational model used to study the independent industry outside Hollywood (Bloore 2009; Finney 2010). It is also the representational framework that practitioners refer to when assessing and responding to uncertainty. Whilst there are many types, levels and definitions of uncertainty in the film industry (Miller and Shamsie 1999), the central type of uncertainty upon which almost all others revolves is consumer demand uncertainty.

In short, the Film Value Chain segments the attendant negative and positive attributes of uncertainty – what traditionally might be labelled risk and reward – over the life cycle of a film. Richard Caves (2000) details the segmentation process from a contract theory approach.[1] He adapts the prominence of asymmetrical information in contract theory discourse to examine the symmetrical lack of information in creative industries: the 'nobody knows' property. Caves looks at how different types of contract seek to deal with structural characteristics of the film business, like the large sunk costs when 'nobody knows' how the film will perform. The option contract – a time-limited right to convert a piece of intellectual property into a film – is a key example. It is used at the development and production stages of the FVC. Looking at the management of uncertainty in the Film Value Chain by means other than contracts, by digital tools for example, is also helpful as legal regulation is often reactive to technological advances. The focus in this analysis is on the management of consumer demand uncertainty.

At each stage of the FVC, different parties are involved in a variety of formulations, and these stages correspond to degrees of separation from consumer demand. For example, development (preparing a script to be filmed) is funded, in part, by the production company, before being re-funded on the first day of principal photography (the start of the film's production period). This arrangement means that the producers shoulder a relatively small financial burden per project. The producers bear the uncertainty of whether the particular script will get made into a film and whether they will recoup their investment (although it is worth bearing in mind that any income must also cover the costs of projects in development which never go into production).

The outcome of the development process – the first uncertainty in the Film Value Chain – is predicated on whether or not investors believe there is a market demand for the film. Investors estimate such demand by relying, in part, on the information supplied by international sales agents about demand from distributors. Distributors, in turn, gauge likely demand based on information built up from exhibitors and from the ancillary window vendors in their respective territories. (It is only the exhibitors and vendors who sell directly to the audience and thus have first-hand knowledge about real demand.) Understanding the potential audience, however indirect the route to acquiring this understanding may be, is crucial to managing uncertainty in the Film Value Chain.

Producers generally do not fund production, but rather source sales or distribution advances and combine them with tax credits and public and private finance. In exchange for external funding, producers give up rights to future revenues and this deprives them of the ability to exploit the film in the range of windows and global territories that the Internet and digital technologies have opened up. Without taking on a substantial portion of the financial cost of production, and thereby directly bearing consumer demand uncertainty, the producers forfeit potential rewards that may improve their company's sustainability.

Even where producers traditionally retain rights to 50% of net profits, the combination of the low likelihood of commercial success, the number of participants charging costs against film revenues and the need to recoup equity investments means that even in the case of a hit, returns are extremely unlikely (Finney 2010).

A substantial decline in DVD revenues (partially attributable to piracy and digital disruption) together with the global financial crisis has made attracting production finance even more difficult (House of Lords 2010). This has placed added pressure on producers and directors to adopt the common practice of deferring their fees, which are usually part of the production budget, in order to reduce the cost of the film.

Although the Film Value Chain has an effective organisational logic, the terms of trade in respect to producers are deemed punitive by their representative body, the Producer's Alliance for Cinema and TV (Pact 2010). In terms of UK business performance, for example, the outcome is often unfavourable. Organising the industry in this way has left UK production companies thinly capitalised and often illiquid (UKFC/NorthernAlliance 2009). The UK Film Council undertook an examination of the finances of the British companies behind the 200 most successful films in the 2006-2008 period. This showed that independent production companies without recognised talent attached (such as those part-owned by prominent directors) or with business models integrated across one or more Film Value Chain sectors, tend for the most part to have insolvent balance sheets (on average these companies showed net liabilities of £40,000) (UKFC/NorthernAlliance 2009).

The study also found that corporate finance problems stretch across the FVC. Although on average British distributors have positive net assets, they also generate retained losses (over £100,000 on average for independents and over £800,000 for integrated models). Sales companies have even greater retained losses and across the sales sector companies struggle to operate successfully (UKFC/ NorthernAlliance 2009).

Based on these financial characteristics, it can be argued that the FVC is failing. Although it might reasonably be asked from whose perspective or by what specific measure, it is nevertheless clear that significant industrial problems exist. PACT has seized upon these issues and argued for change in the mechanisms that provide public support for film. These proposals include the recoupment of public investment and the UK tax credit as producer's equity (PACT 2010).

Given that the traditional Film Value Chain is perceived as untenable and the conception of producer as sales agent and distributor overly simplistic, it is informative to analyse some new hybrid models that are currently being tested, and to examine the change from the traditional Film Value Chain to an emerging replacement through the lens of convention(s) theory (Biggart and Beamish 2003). Convention(s) Theory, or the economic sociology of conventions, is:

> [A]n approach to the sociological understanding of economic organisation and dynamics [...] [that explains] economic order as the product of socially knowledgeable actors working within collective understandings. These understandings are based on shared templates for interpreting and planning courses of action in mutually comprehensible ways that involve social accountability. (Biggart and Beamish 2003: 444)

New Models and How to Think about Them

Practitioners in the film industry such as producers, investors, sales agents and distributors generally do not have sufficient information to make objectively rational decisions by, for example, attributing probability to some event (De Vany 2004; Vogel 2010). Instead the common practice is to rely on routines and rules of thumb in order to allow economic actions to take place (Hodgson 1997; Biggart and Beamish 2003; Feldman and Pentland 2003). People outside the industry may struggle to analyse these operations by way of traditional economic theory, but within the industry they make sense through reference to certain coordination devices. In effect, a commonly devised shared language substitutes for the lack of any reliable formula for operation – an impossibility when uncertainty over cause and effect predominates (Stirling 2003; De Vany 2004).

It can therefore be argued that the Film Value Chain model depends on conventions, where action is only rational between certain practitioners and is enabled through the use of evaluative frameworks that coordinate action and enable filmmakers to operate under uncertainty (Biggart and Beamish 2003; Eymard-Duvernay et al. 2005). Such evaluative frameworks include budgets, financial plans, recoupment charts and sales estimates. Sales agents estimate how much a film will sell for to distributors in each territory around the world. These figures allow for coordinated action across segments of the FVC. Producers use these figures (the 'ask' and 'take' prices) in conjunction with the reputation of the particular sales company as securities to raise production finance from commercial investors. The sales companies themselves have a detailed knowledge of what combination of totals they must hit in each territory in order to make their portfolio and therefore company profitable.

Internet-enabled film dissemination changes the context of these evaluative frameworks and increases their number. Crowdfunding contributions or social media tracking data become important reference points for managing questions of uncertainty.[2] Twitter, for example, can be regarded as a proxy for word of mouth.[3] Hence, observing consumer demand as expressed by the volume of chatter that takes place on the Twitter grapevine has been shown to function as a more reliable predictor of box-office returns than market-based models (Asur and Huberman 2010).

Data extracted from monitoring activity on social networks can potentially inform a distributor's prints and advertising campaigns. French distributor Wild Bunch have strategically shifted their marketing spend on-line because of the efficiencies that highly targeted digital tools provide. The company has been able to distribute 15 films in 2011, compared to 10 in previous years, by acquiring low-budget genre content that can become profitable through niche and viral marketing (Keslassy 2011).

In exhibition, the Brazilian cinema company MovieMobz offers good evidence for the adoption of digital tools to manage uncertainty. A physical cinema-on-demand model operates in 69 Brazilian cities by pre-selling tickets on-line to a wide variety of content. The service is fully integrated with social media so potential consumers drive demand themselves in order to ensure local showings are booked (Launchlab 2008). In 2008 average screen occupancy at Movie Mobz screenings was 32%, a substantial improvement on traditional independent cinema occupancy rates of 8-10% (Launchlab 2008). Where a film is not yet available, and tickets are not yet on sale, a 'want to see' button is used to provide evidence of demand.

Producers in Europe have also pursued this functionality; the forthcoming Finnish film *Iron Sky* (Timo Vuorensola, Finland/Germany/Canada/Australia, 2011) uses an application built on Google Maps to show the global geographic demand for its film, which on 20 June 2011 stood at 32,466 requests (Iron Sky 2011). Whilst not directly connected to exhibitors and distributors in these territories, this 'demand it' service can be used by the producers to manage uncertainty: either as a new sales tool to drive demand from the market, or to enable direct delivery to consumers. On-line audience engagement applies across the FVC, not just at the distribution stage. *Iron Sky* has already raised €767,550 production finance via crowdsourcing and is aiming to achieve €1.2 million through such sources, equal to 16% of the €7.5 million total budget (Vuorensola 2011).

Recognising and interpreting new evaluative frameworks is becoming integral to managing uncertainty and reformulating the Film Value Chain for the digital age. To put it simply, digital tools allow producers to react to consumer demand uncertainty in two ways. Firstly, by engaging with the potential audience earlier and to a greater degree; through interactive media and extended content producers create greater demand and thus increase revenues. Secondly, in order to claim a larger share of revenues, filmmakers pro-actively pursue disintermediation by circumventing some segment(s) of the traditional Film Value Chain model via the Internet. The success of this second strategy often relies on the success of the first. The removal of the traditional sales agent, distributor or exhibitor, which typically funds and executes all marketing activities, means that their marketing role and resources must be replaced (Cones 1997).

Under the traditional Film Value Chain framework, the UK film industry struggled to achieve sustainability. Internet-enabled piracy and digital competition now present additional challenges; however, the same technology also provides the potential to develop innovative responses to reshape the Film Value Chain. Therefore, both as an industrial mode of operation and as a representational framework for understanding the management of uncertainty in the film business, the Film Value Chain is under threat. We need empirical evidence of Internet-enabled responses to the broken Film Value Chain, as well as an analytical assessment of both the data itself and the methodological approaches used to analyse it.

Case Study: Creative Scotland and *Skeletons* (2010)

Investments by Scottish Screen/Creative Scotland in 2010-11 provide an illustrative case study of new digital marketing models tested to adapt the FVC. The film *Skeletons* (Nick Whitfield, UK, 2010), the low-budget (£500,000) directorial debut of Nick Whitfield, was co-produced by Scottish company Edge City Films (Welsh 2011). It achieved a distribution deal with Soda Pictures as part of that company's New British Cinema Quarterly (NBCQ) slate, a programme that launches films in 15 partner venues (NBCQ 2010). The film then won a major prize, the Michael Powell Award, at the Edinburgh International Film Festival in June 2010 (NBCQ 2010). The theatrical release in July 2010 benefited from £10,000 of Scottish Screen Market Development investment, helping Edge City Films to support the touring release (Scottish Screen 2010).

A social media campaign using additional video and audio content provided an Internet-based complement to live events and Q&A screenings (Skeletons The Movie Facebook Page). The campaign directly targeted local and regional on-line and social media; it provided short code links to venues' on-line box-office homepages and maintained on-going conversations with fans and influencers (Skeletons The Movie Twitter Feed). The aim was to increase attendance at each venue on the film's tour.

Information available to the producers was imperfect as details of all showings were not known; however, the available knowledge of dates, venues and relative capacity enables producers to grasp and respond to demand uncertainty in a new way. Traditionally, the producers' response to demand uncertainty could only be indirect. The producer would concentrate on the initial sale of the film to a distributor who would then take full control of marketing to the consumer. The use of new tools for coordinating and evaluating action – for example, matching the number of tickets sold per screen against social media and on-line marketing metrics – constitute emerging ways of managing uncertainty.

In this instance, a new entrant to the sector (the production company) responded to the popularity of certain elements of creative content delivered through its social media campaign by focusing marketing attention on those particular elements.[4] The campaign also used Twitter to target key influencers on each screening, such as venues themselves, regional media bloggers or screen agencies. By doing so over the course of the film's theatrical run, the campaign aimed to maximise the chance of sell-out screenings and thus trigger re-bookings of the film for further screenings that would bring in even greater revenues. Although it is impossible to deal in counterfactuals and to know how the film would have fared without such activity, it is nonetheless fair to say that more than 125 screenings at over 56 venues indicates an appreciable level of success when compared with the initial 15 NBCQ partner cinemas.

The *Skeletons* case study brings some important issues to the fore. One is the distinction between monitoring (recording surface level outputs) and measurement (application of analysis to link engagements to tangible business goals) (Anderson 2011). Despite driving potential audiences to venue ticket homepages, digital systems were not integrated and thus the conversion to purchase could not be reliably measured. The campaign often generated awareness in social media during or soon after a screening and this meant that potential newly-recruited customers could not be converted and instead missed out as the touring release moved on. This lag-on effect is a common trend in the release of films generally (Goel et al. 2010), but one that has significant impact when a touring theatrical run is employed. Closer consideration of the lag-on effect in the planning of similar campaigns could improve revenue potential. A complementary day-and-date digital release of the film could capitalise on the demand of consumers unable to attend the theatre and may further strengthen the distribution strategy.

It is commonplace for multiple partners to be involved with an independent film, even during the distribution phase: media buyers, PR companies and digital agencies all regularly work together. The involvement of producers at the distribution stage adds new value by virtue of the detailed consumer information that can be built-up and leveraged over the entire life-cycle of the film. Producers can use consumer data in a targeted manner to test and produce additional creative (narrative or extra-diegetic) content to support the release.

Complex Models and Managing Uncertainty: Understanding the Variety of Activity Linked to On-line Distribution

Crowdfunding and social media marketing campaigns might not equate to the mainstream understanding of film dissemination via the Internet, yet the multiple implications of Internet-enabled dissemination for roles and companies across the traditional FVC are important. The ways in which companies adapt to environmental realities in this complex, dynamic system have knock-on and feedback effects. It is crucial to be mindful of the aims and effects of new models if we are to get a representative view of cinema in the digital age.

As far as distribution is concerned, new digital marketing initiatives by producers can become crucial elements in the pursuit of the economic viability of niche products (Anderson 2006). The more choice that is available to the consumer via the Long Tail, the more important marketing becomes to help consumers find a specific film (Brynjolfsson et al. 2006). New titles are released faster than the rate at which consumers discover them. In a distribution model where the distributor is selling less of more, the burden of faciliating discovery may be pushed to the producer. Digital media provide the logical tool for achieving this (Tan and Netessine 2010). Research in the music industry has shown that the influence of blogs on sales is stronger in the Long Tail than in the mainstream and purchases are frequently mediated by blog posts and content sampling (Dewan and Ramaprasad 2007).

Distributors traditionally operate on scale; Internet distribution may allow them to take on more niche product and make it profitable by aggregating dispersed audiences. However, such a success depends on obtaining appropriate rights in a sufficient number of territories – a complex practice when digital rights (often covering all known and unknown means of distribution) are bundled with a great deal of other rights and are strictly divided by jurisdictional territories (Finney 2010). The problems in exploiting rights for digital distribution – which is transnational by default as a result of traditional jurisdictionally (territorially) based contracts – are also retrospective. A great deal of existing content remains unexploited in multiple territories in multiple windows because the licensor of the bundled rights has not found it to be worth their time. This is of great detriment to the producer. New digital tools employ geo-blocking technologies which can make films available in certain nations but not others, so these unexplored opportunities can be explored at low cost; however, if the producers wish to pursue this, the problem of retaining such rights whilst obtaining investment to make the film still remains. If the traditional economic practice of buying content at low enough prices to cross-collateralise the hits against the losses retains precedence, then the prices obtained by producers will remain undermined. This influences how films are financed, which films are made and, ultimately, what choice is presented to the audience.

Innovative applications of technology have the potential to deliver positive impact across all sectors. This can be achieved by integrating the aims and activities of companies traditionally separated by function across segments of the FVC. A good example is Distrify – a video player widget with direct purchase options (cinema ticket, VOD, DVD) and social media analytics embedded within it (Green and Gerard 2011). This tool can facilitate the marketing and digital delivery of a film, but also provides a wealth of data about likely audience members as an output, which can feed into development and production of future projects.

Producers and distributors can use such services to increase revenues and minimise the share lost to third parties in the digital space, such as content aggregators. Ultimately distribution may include multi-territory on-line services – the traditional conception of Internet-enabled dissemination of film – but the key components of the film life-cycle likely to facilitate this will also be Internet-enabled, and will allow complex interactions between business activities traditionally separated out along the Film Value Chain.

This is certainly a challenge. It is difficult, for example, to completely align the distributor's interest in boosting the performance of their overall portfolio with the producer's vested interest in an individual project when the industry's stable Paretian characteristics are considered (De Vany 2004).[5] Even if the Long Tail proves a sustainable alternative to the blockbuster-dominated model, entrenched beliefs will need to be altered.[6] Therefore thinking of new models either as amalgamations of different sectors of the Film Value Chain, or as straight replacements to it, is perhaps inadequate. Circumventing traditional Film Value Chain structures with new models and replacing them with exactly the same resources offered by their predecessors may not be possible. As already noted, *Iron Sky* aims to crowdfund 16% of its production budget and may well save on distributors' prints and advertising costs by virtue of the consequent on-line engagement, but traditional finance is still required.

What can be learnt from this hybrid approach is that in assessing how new models are applied, it is prudent to carefully consider exactly what ends they serve and for which parties. Examination of different VOD platforms illustrates this point. There is a salient difference in the goals and deal terms of services like Jaman, which operates to deliver a selection of films unlikely to secure traditional distribution to global audiences, as compared with other services which are perceived as tools offered to filmmakers as part of a viable film exploitation strategy (Thompson 2011). Jaman provides the rights holder with 30% of revenues (Keegan 2007), whereas Flicklaunch or Distrify return a standard 70% of revenues; Distribber simply charges a flat fee (Thompson 2011).

Jaman and MUBI offer professionally curated exhibition windows, with either a social community built in (Jaman) or integrated with external social networks (MUBI). Flicklaunch and Distrify, however, are not themselves destination sites, but rather sales points within video players with an existing on-line audience. (Distribber is slightly different, essentially operating as an extra intermediary, offering paid access to existent on-line exhibition windows – iTunes, Amazon and Netflix, which are like walled gardens, curated by price or recommendation algorithms.) Each type of service is optimised for its own purposes and in the overall ecosystem of Internet-disseminated film they each attempt to make the industry more successful in different ways.

There are many possible digital models that could reformulate the failing Film Value Chain. Understanding the models and assessing their success requires an understanding not only of how well they achieve their aims, but also of their consequences for other elements of the traditional FVC. Thinking about the management of uncertainty and changes to the conventions of the film business provides one productive way to do this.

Works Cited

Anderson, Chris (2006) *The Long Tail: Why the Future of Business Is Selling Less of More*. New York: Hyperion.

Anderson, Hugh (2011) 'Measuring Social Media', *Measurement Matters*. On-line. Available HTTP: http://blog.forthmetrics.com/2011/06/02/measuring-social-media/ (6 June 2011).

Asur, Sitaram and Bernardo Huberman (2010) *Predicting the Future with Social Media*. HP Labs White Paper. Palo Alto: Social Computing Labs, HP Labs.

Biggart, Nicole and Thomas Beamish (2003) 'The Economic Sociology of Conventions: Habit, Custom, Practice, and Routine in Market Order', *Annual Review of Sociology*, 29, 443–64. On-line. Available HTTP: https://

sociology.ucdavis.edu/people/tdbeamis/pdf/biggart-beamish_the-econ-soc-of-conventions_annual-review-of-sociology.pdf (6 June 2011).

Block, Alex (2011) 'Harvey Weinstein: VOD, Internet Still Need Time to Mature', *The Hollywood Reporter*. On-line. Available HTTP: http://www.hollywoodreporter.com/news/harvey-weinstein-vod-Internet-still-194911? (6 June 2011).

Bloore, Peter (2009) *Re-defining the Independent Film Value Chain*. London: UK Film Council. On-line. Available HTTP: http://www.ukfilmcouncil.org.uk/media/pdf/h/b/Film_Value_Chain_Paper.pdf (6 June 2011).

Brynjolfsson, Erik, Yu Jeffrey Hu, Michael D. Smith (2006) 'From Niches to Riches: Anatomy of the Long Tail', *Sloan Management Review*, 47, 4, Summer, 67-71. On-line. Available HTTP: http://digital.mit.edu/research/papers/riches_niches_274.pdf (26 October 2011).

Caves, Richard (2000) *Creative Industries: Contracts between Art and Commerce*. Cambridge: Harvard University Press.

_____ (2003) 'Contracts Between Art and Commerce', *The Journal of Economic Perspectives*, 17, 2, 73-83.

Cones, John (1997) *The Feature Film Distribution Deal: A Critical Analysis of the Single Most Important Film Industry Agreement*. Carbondale: Southern Illinois University Press.

De Vany, Arthur (2004) *Hollywood Economics: How Extreme Uncertainty Shapes the Film Industry*. London: Routledge.

Dewan, Sanjeev and Jui Ramaprasad (2007) 'Impact of Blogging on Music Sales: the Long Tail Effect.' *Workshop on Information Systems*. On-line. Available HTTP: http://www.citi.uconn.edu/cist07/1b.pdf (12 June 2011).

Downes, Larry (2009) *The Laws of Disruption: Harnessing the New Forces That Govern Life and Business in the Digital Age*. New York: Basic Books.

Eymard-Duvernay, François, Olivier Favereau, André Orléan, Robert Salais and Laurent Thévenot (2005) 'Pluralist Integration in the Economic and Social Sciences: The Economy of Coventions.' *Post-Autistic Economics Review*, 34. On-line. Available HTTP: http://www.paecon.net/PAEReview/heterodoxeconomics/Thevenot34.htm (6 June 2011).

Facebook Developers (2011) *Like Button*. On-line. Available HTTP http://developers.facebook.com/docs/reference/plugins/like/ (12 June 2011).

Feldman, Martha and Brian Pentland (2003) 'Reconceptualisising Organisational Routines as a Source of Flexibility and Change', *Administrative Science Quarterly*, 48, 1, 94-118.

Finney, Angus (2010) *The International Film Business: A Market Guide Beyond Hollywood*. London: Taylor and Francis.

Goel, Sharad, Jake Hoffman, Sebastien Lahaie, David Pennock and Duncan Watts (2010) 'Predicting Customer Behaviour with Web Search', *Proceedings of the National Academy of Sciences of the United States of America*. Yahoo Research / Princeton University. On-line. Available HTTP: http://www.pnas.org/content/early/2010/09/20/1005962107 (12 June 2011).

Green, Andy and Peter Gerard (2011) 'Distrify.com/about', *Distrify*. On-line. Available HTTP: http://distrify.com/about (6 June 2011).

Hardy, Jeffrey (2010) 'Your Film's Thru-Line. From Concept to Audience' *Baseline Intelligence: Research Wrap*. On-line. Available HTTP: http://www. baselineintel.com/research-wrap?detail/C8/your_films_thru-line._from_ concept_to_audience_embrace (6 June 2011).

Hodgson, Geoffrey (1997) 'The Ubiquity of Habits and Rules', *Cambridge Journal of Economics*, 21, 6, 663-84. On-line. Available HTTP: http://cje. oxfordjournals.org/content/21/6/663.abstract (12 June 2011).

House of Lords (2010) 'The British Film and Television Industries: Decline Or Opportunity?' *Select Committee on Communications. Session 2009-10, 1.* London: House of Lords. On-line. Available HTTP: http://www.publications. parliament.uk/pa/ld200910/ldselect/ldcomuni/37/37i.pdf (6 June 2011).

Iron Sky (2011) 'How To Support', *Iron Sky Website*. On-line. Available HTTP: http://www.ironsky.net/site/support/how-to-support/ (20 June 2011).

Keegan, Victor (2007) 'The New Spielbergs Are in the Living Room', *The Guardian*, 27 September. On-line. Available HTTP: http://www.guardian. co.uk/technology/2007/sep/27/guardianweeklytechnologysection. comment2 (12 June 2011).

Kern, Phillipe (2009) 'The Impact of Digital Distribution: A Contribution'. *European Film Think Tank*. Seville: KEA European Affairs.

Keslassy, Elsa (2011) 'Bunch Takes a Wild Ride to B.O. Success', *Variety,* 30 April. On-line. Available HTTP: http://www.variety.com/article/VR1118036145 (6 June 2011).

Kohn, Eric (2011) 'Toolkit: 5 Lessons about Transmedia from the IFP/Power to the Pixel Cross-Media Forum', *Indiewire*, 20 April. On-line. Available HTTP: http://www.indiewire.com/article/2011/04/20/toolkit_5_lessons_about_ transmedia_from_the_ifp_power_to_the_pixel_cross-me (19 June 2011).

Launchlab (2008) 'Fabio Lima, Founder of MovieMobz. Starters for Ten', *Launchlab*. On-line. Available HTTP: http://www.launchlab.co.uk/article/ Starters-for-ten/Fabio-Lima,-founder-of-MovieMobz/526 (6 June 2011).

Miller, Danny and Jamal Shamsie (1999) 'Strategic Responses to Three Kinds of Uncertainty: Product Line Simplicity at the Hollywood Film Studios', *Journal of Management*, 25, 1, 97-116.

Milliken, Frances (1987) 'Three Types of Perceived Uncertainty about the Environment: State, Effect, and Response Uncertainty', *The Academy of Management Review*, 12, 1, 133-43.

NBCQ (2010) 'About NBCQ – New British Cinema Quarterly', *NBCQ – New British Cinema Quarterly Website*. On-line. Available HTTP: http://www.nbcq.co.uk/about/ (6 June 2011).

OECD (Organization for Economic Coordination and Development) (2011) *OECD Information Technology Outlook 2010*. Biggleswade: OECD Publishing.

PACT (Producers Alliance for Cinema and Television) (2010) *A New Business Model For UK Film Producers*. On-line. Available HTTP: http://www.northernmedia.org/tpl/uploads/PACT_producer_recoupment.pdf (6 June 2011).

Scottish Screen (2010) 'Investments 2010', *Scottish Screen*. On-line. Available HTTP: http://www.scottishscreen.com/content/sub_page.php?sub_id=213 (6 June 2011).

Skeletons The Movie Facebook Page. On-line. Available HTTP: http://www.facebook.com/pages/Skeletons-The-Movie/260736678117 (15 June 2011).

Skeletons The Movie Twitter Feed. On-line. Available HTTP: http://twitter.com/#!/SkeletonsMovie (15 June 2011).

Stirling, Andy (2003) 'Risk, Uncertainty and Precaution: Some Instrumental Implications from the Social Sciences', in Frans Berkhout, Melissa Leach and Ian Scoones (eds), *Negotiating Environmental Change: New Perspectives from Social Science*. Cheltenham: Edward Elgar, 33-76.

Tan, Tom and Serguei Netessine (2010) 'Is Tom Cruise Threatened? Using Netflix Prize Data to Examine the Long Tail of Electronic Commerce', *The Wharton School of the University of Pennsylvania*. On-line. Available: HTTP: opim.wharton.upenn.edu/~netessin/TanNetessine.pdf (15 June 2011).

Thompson, Anne (2011) 'Flicklaunch: Indie Distributor Builds on Facebook', *Thompson on Hollywood*. On-line. Available HTTP: http://blogs.indiewire.com/thompsononhollywood/2011/06/03/flicklaunch_indie_distributor_builds_on_facebook/? (15 June 2011).

UKFC (2010) *UK Film Council Statistical Yearbook 2010*. On-line. Available HTTP: http://www.ukfilmcouncil.org.uk/statsyearbook10 (6 June 2011).

UKFC/NorthernAlliance - Michael Franklin and Mike Kelly (2009) *Analysis of the Corporate Finance of SMEs in the UK Film Industry: A Report to the UK Film Council*. London: UK Film Council. On-line. Available HTTP: http://www.ukfilmcouncil.org.uk/media/pdf/8/a/Analysis_of_the_Corporate_Finance_of_SMEs_in_the_UK_Film_Industry.pdf (15 June 2011).

Ulin, Jeff (2009) *The Business of Media Distribution: Monetizing Film, TV, and Video Content*. Waltham: Focal Press.

Vogel, Harold (2010) *Entertainment Industry Economics: A Guide for Financial Analysis*, Cambridge: Cambridge University Press.

Vuorensola, Timo (2011) 'Crowdfunding – The New Way to Finance Movies', *Iron Sky* Website. On-line. Available HTTP: http://www.ironsky.net/site/support/finance/ (13 June 2011).

Welsh, Paul (2011) 'What is the State of Film Financing in the UK Today?' Public comments at the Edinburgh International Film Festival event, 18 June.

Notes

[1]   Contract theory is the study of how economic actors construct contractual arrangements, generally under conditions of asymmetrical information. There are further reading recommendations in Caves (2003).

[2]   Crowdfunding is the sourcing of money from large numbers of people via the Internet. Digital services that facilitate this operation include Kickstarter.

[3]   Twitter is an Internet microblogging platform where users can post text of 140 characters or less and images.

[4]   The 'like' button on Facebook allows users to share their appreciation of a particular piece of information with others. This function has now been made available to other websites so that Facebook users can 'like' things external to Facebook and share this with their network. The notion of 'like'-ing has become generic and need not refer specifically to the Facebook service.

[5]   The Pareto distribution, commonly known as the 80:20 rule, in this context refers to the notion that 20% of the films released generate 80% of the revenue. In reality the figures can be skewed more greatly. De Vany (2004) provides a detailed explanation of the fundamental dynamics of the film industry. A good summary of these characteristics is also featured in Vogel (2010).

[6]   The Long Tail refers to a concept popularised by Chris Anderson (2006), which posited a change to the economics of creative content sales generated by the Internet. This can be summarised as a shift from selling a lot of a few items to selling less of multiple items.

Convergence, Digitisation and the Future of Film Festivals[1]

Marijke de Valck

The democratisation brought about by the direct availability of, and better accessibility to digital media has had radical consequences for both institutions and individuals. The distribution landscape changes; key limitations of the physical world no longer hold in digital realms. Consumers no longer have to wait until a film is released theatrically in order to see it: they can download it directly. It is a radical shift that forces cultural organisations and media companies to reposition themselves in regard to new platforms, new rules and new players. They have to account for the new possibilities these things offer, as well as for the actual cultural practices that emerge. How people use media, how they react to the new opportunities for DIY content production and distribution, and what types of consumption patterns emerge in a landscape characterised by an infinite supply of niche content are just as relevant as the technological transformation itself.

I am particularly interested in the ways convergence and digitisation affect the functioning of the film festival network in a digital age. Will it be able to stay relevant when digital media ensure that art cinema is directly available and accessible? What is its added value in the context of convergence and digitisation?

The current focus on transformations in media technology and business models contributes to the popularity of the concept of convergence. It is not enough to study technological changes in delivery systems, argues Henry Jenkins (2006). We also need to scrutinise the shifts that are taking place in cultural systems and the protocols by which we are producing and consuming media, if we are to understand convergence's profound impact on contemporary media society. Jenkins explains:

> By convergence I mean the flow of content across multiple media platforms, the cooperation between multiple media

industries, and the migratory behavior of media audiences who will go almost anywhere in search of the kind of entertainment and experiences they want. (Jenkins 2006: 2)

Looking back, one can distinguish three phases in convergence development: the first wave of convergence hinged on the concentration of media ownership; the second on the digitisation of operating systems; while in the third wave, content emerged as 'a very liquid asset' that can be streamed across media platforms (Murray 2003: 9). Convergence's third wave, the post-dotcom crisis, is also a move beyond the phase of simple utopian visions; even though it is still impossible to predict the future, now is the time to draft probable scenarios. Digitisation and our understanding of it are no longer in their infancies; we have historic case studies and a wealth of theories at our disposal that may offer a solid foundation for developing a long view on the future of cinema and film festivals.

The International Film Festival Rotterdam, for example, launched a programme section dedicated to the future of cinema as early as 1996. As the title of the programme, Exploding Cinema, indicates, the festival envisioned a future in which the traditional cinema theatre would no longer be the only place where film would be exhibited. The very term Exploding Cinema is interesting in the light of recent debates on convergence. It reminds us that the actual assessment of digitisation is closely linked to the perspective chosen. Using the metaphor of an explosion, a strong divergent force, the festival chose to focus on (cinematic) aesthetics.

A decade later, in 2007, Cannes hosted a one-day conference on the Future of Cinema on the opening day of its sixtieth anniversary edition.[2] The panel discussions dealt with the fast evolving digital economy and tried to shed light on the question of how current transformations are shaping new roles for directors, producers and distributors. What's more, the topic of digitisation has been on the festival agenda for a considerable number of years.

Many other aspects of film festival operation – both artistic and commercial – have been influenced by digital developments and it will be impossible to list them all here. To name a few: festivals can assume the task of reporting on and framing the new aesthetic trends of hybridity (resulting in programmes such as Exploding Cinema); festivals are confronted with rapidly increasing numbers of films submitted for selection, which fundamentally alters the process of programming;

festival markets have to adjust to the demands of operating in an increasingly multimedia corporate environment.

In this chapter I address the challenges to film festivals' *raison d'être* by looking at the increased possibilities for digital distribution and exhibition and ask how these might affect the film festival network in the future. In so doing, I align myself with the business perspective of the contemporary convergence debates, while at the same time challenging some of its assumptions with insights derived from cultural studies.

The Long Tail: Abundant Choices, Diverse Tastes

> People are going deep into the catalogue, down the long, long list of available titles, far past what's available at Blockbuster Video, Tower Records and Barnes & Noble. And the more they find, the more they like. As they wander further from the beaten path, they discover their taste is not as mainstream as they thought (or as they had been led to believe by marketing, a lack of alternatives, and a hit-driven culture).
>
> Chris Anderson, *The Long Tail*, 2004

Digitisation poses a challenge to the established division between commercial distributors and film festivals. With the concentration of media ownership a major shift has taken place, from an industry based on cinema theatres to one revolving around copyright (Hediger 2005). In the copyright industry theatrical distribution is no longer the most profitable element in the commercial life cycle of a film. Video demonstrated the lucrative potential of ancillary markets as early as the 1980s, but its effect paled in the face of the changes brought about by digitisation. Nowadays, thanks to digital technologies, media products can easily and inexpensively be copied and distributed across various platforms. The result is a media economy in which niche products can be extremely profitable, and therefore are of interest to commercial parties as well. To describe this new economic model for media and entertainment businesses, in 2004 Chris Anderson coined the term the 'Long Tail' in a *Wired* article. For the first time in history cumulative sales of niche products would rival the profits realised from items with mass popularity, causing a major rupture in the way industrialised societies function. We can understand the challenge that digital distribution poses to film festivals better when we take a closer look at this new 'Long Tail' model.

Anderson formulated three rules for the 'Long Tail' economy: broad availability, low prices and assistance with search strategies. The third point is crucial for niche films. People are not very likely to go and look for 'difficult' products – which includes many films screened at film festivals – without prior knowledge or the advice of an intermediary. Appreciation and consumption of certain films will always be embedded in the larger cultural systems of education, criticism, programming and public debate. As Wesley Shrum observes: 'Taste in high art is mediated by experts, whereas taste in low art is not' (1996: 40). This is not to say that people could not develop a more sophisticated appreciation of film art, especially if they are inspired and encouraged by enthusiastic and knowledgeable peers. Without being explicitly alerted as to the existence of 'other' films, however, would they really go off the beaten track? And if they did, would they be able to find, say, a Hou Hsiao-hsien film amongst the abundance of films on offer? And even if they did, would they choose to devote enough time to this director's slow-paced films in order to begin grasping the subtlety of his style? Not very likely, especially if this is undertaken as a solitary exercise.

To Anderson, the old model was one marked by a poor match between demand and supply. He attributes the main problems to the limitations of the physical world: cinema theatres need to attract a minimum of visitors per film in order to break even; video and music stores must sell a minimum number of copies to be able to pay for the space required to store each item. For cinema, this meant that theatre owners would only programme films that were likely to generate the necessary demand. Hence the dominance of popular Hollywood films that feature stars, happy endings and spectacular settings, and can also count on lavish marketing budgets for mass promotion. Moreover, in the old cinema model, theatres were dependent on a limited demographic as only the local public, those living within a certain radius of the theatre, constituted potential customers; people from Hamburg don't tend to catch a film in Munich, nor do East-Londoners travel to Bristol for an evening of entertainment at the movies.

The question for film festivals is how the surge in new possibilities for digital distribution – a context where every possible genre and the smallest possible niches become easily accessible – influences the current festival model. In a media economy characterised by scarcity, film festivals were the appointed places towards which those people looking for special interest and hard-to-find films would gravitate. In a (future) media economy, characterised by abundance, media audiences can just as easily find and purchase their favourite niche products or discover new ones on the Internet or on their digital television (pay) channels. Why wait for a festival to screen the newest horror films from Japan when you can purchase them on-line? Why travel to Venice when you can watch a DVD at home? Would film festivals become superfluous in a market of abundance?

Finding Films and Acquired Tastes

For several decades film festivals have been helping people to find films and refine tastes in areas such as world cinema, experimental films or archival treasures. Festivals provide immersion in cinéphile peer communities and a variety of selections, discussions and opinions. Festivals, in other words, not only make a variety of films available, they also frame the films in a rich discursive context. Could digital distribution over the Internet or cable do a similar, or even better, job? We can learn valuable lessons from television here. With the multiplication of channels in the 1990s following the introduction of cable and satellite, television became the first mass medium (of moving images) characterised by abundance. As John Sinclair has argued, this meant the end of the golden age of broadcasting in which television was an instrument for creating imagined communities on the national level and interpersonal cohesion on the domestic level. It constituted the beginning of an era of fragmentation and individualised consumption: 'To the extent that the new services cultivate even more varied and specialised tastes and interests, they become a force for social differentiation rather than unification' (Sinclair 2004: 43). With digitisation these effects are intensified.

The main difference between broadcast television and digital television is that the first is a so-called 'push' whereas the second is a 'pull' medium (Jensen 1999). Whereas the television consumer of the past could sit on his couch passively exposed to the flow of programming, the television user today needs to be pro-active in choosing what to watch. The shift, in other words, is from a medium shaped by top-down programming to one dominated by user flows and expanded choices; however, early experiences with interactive and digital television challenged the old assumption that media consumers were eagerly awaiting the arrival of abundance and eager to choose among 500+ channels (Vittore 1997). Moreover, as John Caldwell argues:

> All of the predictions about digital's utopian promise as a responsive 'lean-in', 'pull' technology aside, programmers and the financial interests that deploy them will continue to attempt to 'push' content, to brand delivery systems, and to schedule media experience. (Caldwell 2003: 143)

In today's aggressive environment, where commercial producers and programmers turn to strategies of affective branding, spectacular aesthetics and populist content, it is, I argue, not enough to make festival films available on-line. The on-line dimension of film festivals is mostly a supplement to the 'live' festivals as localised, scheduled occasions. Festivals need to draw attention to alternative titles and provide a socio-cultural environment where viewers are stimulated to watch and contemplate these films. As Caroline Pauwels and Joy Bauwens have convincingly argued with regard to television viewers, the idea that people are autonomous in their viewing choices is a myth. They state that 'what we consume is always a reflection of the socio-cultural conditions in which we exist [...] It is precisely the social determination of choices that the optimistic perspectives [on television consumer sovereignty] scarcely pauses to consider' (2007: 155). When we apply a Bourdieusian perspective on our cultural viewing habits and taste distinctions, the idea of socially-nurtured consumption patterns applies to cinema even more strongly than to television.

November 2005 marked the official launch of YouTube, a website where users can watch and upload videos; content varies from existing material such as video clips, movie trailers or television excerpts to user-generated content like video blogs, mash-ups and short amateur videos. In the space of a year, YouTube turned the established media world completely upside down by democratising the means of distribution. Previously, distribution and exhibition of film, television and video were activities reserved to big, wealthy media corporations who could afford the labour and the technology-intensive structures these required. YouTube breached the hegemony with smart use of digital technology: all of a sudden, everybody with an Internet connection could make material directly available on-line.

Time Magazine underlined YouTube's impact in November 2006 by naming 'you' – the average user – as Person of the Year. For some, push media are outdated in the digital age (Gobé 2001). We no longer want to be told what to watch, let alone think, by others. Instead, today we're all 'prosumers' (an amalgam of producer and consumer, see Toffler

1980) who want to take control and who will arrive at superior solutions and achievements thanks to our collective intelligence, the so-called wisdom of crowds (Tapscott and Williams 2006). Others argue that in an age of unlimited choice people will rely more heavily on guides, filters and other tools to navigate through the immense supply.

Psychologist Barry Schwartz, for instance, has claimed that the combination of freedom of choice and a large supply of products and services from which to choose will produce a paradox: we are less satisfied with our choice than when there were fewer options (Schwartz 2004). A similar line of reasoning has been put forward with respect to media. John Ellis, for example, observes a certain 'choice fatigue' among television viewers confronted with an array of 100+ channels. There is only limited time to browse through the options and watch selected items. This causes stress and displeasure and might lead viewers to restrict themselves to familiar channels or forums populated by like-minded individuals (Ellis 2000).

Both the utopian vision of democratising the public sphere through the increased participation of 'ordinary' people and the critical concerns about elements that cause the public sphere to deteriorate are relevant here. They will help chart what forces are at work in the repositioning of film festivals in the age of YouTube.

Festival Space That Matters

Theoretically, we could replace actual festival visits with viewing films via the Internet and participating in voting systems on-line. Moreover, as Jenkins observed, fundamental shifts are occurring in the ways in which we consume media content. It is not unthinkable, then, that established patterns of cultural consumption might also shift and adapt. But will they? In order to formulate a likely scenario and long-term vision for the future of film festivals, I believe we should begin by investigating some pioneering examples of film festivals staged on the Internet. One would suspect that they have the best of both worlds: unlimited availability of (niche) titles and an 'expert' frame that can function as both portal and guide to the films on offer.

Let's take a brief look at two on-line film festivals – the American Media That Matters Film Festival and the Japanese CON-CAN Movie Festival.

Media That Matters is currently in its eleventh edition (May 2011-May 2012). The festival showcases 'short films on the most important topics of the day…[and] engages diverse audiences and inspires them to take action' (Media That Matters undated). Issues raised include criminal and economic justice, gender, gay/lesbian, human rights, media, politics and health. The CON-CAN Movie Festival (2011, in its eighth year) also streams short films on-line: 'We at CON-CAN Media Plaza' – the organisers state – 'believe that what the world needs most is a communications plaza where like minded neighbours with caring and rich hearts can connect' (Yoshino 2010).[3]

The festival programmers select a wide variety of films and aim to bring together viewers and filmmakers from around the world. Like all on-line film festivals these initiatives have only played a peripheral role in the festival network so far. The reason for this peripheral status should, however, not be attributed to the focus on short films. Shorts are widely recognised as an important genre and receive attention at most prestigious international film festivals as well.[4] They have always attracted the attention of the international film festival community because the format is less susceptible to commercially-imposed constraints and thus allows for aesthetic experimentation and bolder choice of topics. Short films are, furthermore, a sensible choice for these first generation digital festivals because of bandwidth limitations and the shorter average attention span that is commonly believed to characterise activity on the Internet.

It is telling that many of these festivals combine their on-line presence with events that take place in the real world. Every year in June, Media That Matters presents a new selection of 16 films, chosen by a jury consisting of filmmakers, educators, writers, non-profit leaders, film programmers, activists and youth. They host a festive event in New York, the city where the festival organisation is located, and invite a celebrity to present the selection (past guests include Tim Robbins and Woody Harrelson). This event, in other words, closely resembles the format of real-time festivals and the event organised in New York functions as launching pad for Media That Matters activities such as community screenings and special events which take place throughout the year, both on-line and off-line. CON-CAN, in turn, offers a quite elaborate on-line schedule that involves rounds of audience review as well as expert and jury selection. Instead of opening with an off-line event, the festival culminates in one – the award ceremony in Tokyo. These examples raise the question of whether on-line festivals depend on real-time events?

Clearly, physical events have major advantages over their on-line offspring. For one, events taking place in actual space and time are more capable of creating a festive atmosphere, which not only alerts and attracts visitors to the screenings, but also puts them in the mood for 'discoveries'. Festival visitors are thus more open and willing to try and make sense of unfamiliar content (Nichols 1994). Year-round availability of films through digital distribution is less likely to create the right setting for this type of highly attentive media consumption. Many cinéphiles simply crave the theatrical immersion (Klinger 2006). The big screen is still considered the premier choice and the most authentic experience for film screenings, which means that in a network revolving around cultural value addition, the most prestigious events will use cinema theatres and give film lovers the opportunity to watch the complete programme on the superior silver screen. What's more, cinema theatres and festival locations can add prestige when drawing on a rich history (De Valck 2007: 138-9).

Another set of reasons why spatial characteristics are central to the way festivals function is linked to actual presence. Festivals need rituals and ceremonies to add value and attract media attention and these are much harder to conceive of in virtual space. Major international film festivals cannot be media events without celebrities posing for photographers on the red carpet. Neither are competition programmes likely to generate sufficient prestige if they don't conclude with an official award ceremony in which the prize-winner mounts a stage to receive his/her prize in person (English 2005: 31-5). Indeed the on-line festivals from this example, Media That Matters and CON-CAN, both arrange ceremonies in actual locations. Furthermore, it is important that people at festivals have the ability to meet and talk in person. Face-to-face interactions stimulate regular visitors to discuss and develop their appreciation of cinema. The possibility of meeting directors, stars, industry professionals or other experts in person adds a spectacular dimension to the festival event and makes it more competitive than Internet forums and communities in the contemporary experience economy. In a media economy characterised by abundant consumer choice, it is the embedding in a supportive and spectacular socio-cultural context – i.e. immersing oneself into the festival ('in') crowd – that is crucial in stimulating people to watch festival films. It is the actual festival space that matters. Contrary to what the Long Tail model would have us believe, the fact that festival space is only accessible for a limited amount of time strengthens its appeal even more. It generates exclusivity and thus raises the prestige and news value of programmed films.

The Future of Festivals: The Audience as Stakeholder

It is my expectation that current digital developments will have their biggest impact on the way festivals engage with their audiences. Festivals are gatekeepers in two ways: as judge and as guide (De Valck 2010). These functions will be kept by those festivals that normatively involve competitive awards. More room, however, will have to be made for the amateur cinéphile. Digitisation, and Web 2.0 technologies in particular, allows a media landscape in which lay users are more directly involved and have greater means to express their opinion or share experiences. The new generation of cinéphiles will claim this space. In other words, the audience as stakeholder will be more important in the digital age. The time when programmers' choices and tastes were sacred is no more, but I believe that if cultural institutions like festivals are transparent about their (subjective) choices, there will in fact always be a need for their expert opinions and valuations.

Despite my fear over whether or not niche products will be indeed found in the 'Long Tail' and my reservations about the extent to which audiences will develop a liking for 'difficult films' through self-learning, I do believe that film festivals could lose ground to digital distribution platforms on other fronts. In terms of economics, digital distribution and the Long Tail model offer commercial opportunities that festivals simply cannot match. Festivals are bound by the limitations of the physical world and will therefore remain non-profit organisations that depend on funding, sponsorships and/or ticket sales. Film festivals are unable to turn a profit on individual titles because of their format: many films are programmed alongside each other, each film only screening an average of two or three times. This has severe implications for the viability of the festival network as an alternative business model. Although festivals find audiences and media exposure for films, they also tend to place filmmakers in a dependent position, restricting their chance of generating an income from the fruits of their labour. Digital distribution, on the other hand, can result in commercial success. In the Long Tail even the smallest niche can generate revenues. Why would filmmakers lend their creations to festivals for free when they can reach audiences *and* make money with distribution through digital platforms?

We are faced with the contradictory situation that the physical characteristics of the film festival network are at the same time its weakest link – keeping filmmakers captured in a subsidised ghetto – and indispensable to its success as an alternative distribution and exhibition circuit for films that have (niche) artistic value and/or socio-political relevance. Many festival films are atypical niche products that depend to a large extent on discursive framing, embedding in a socio-cultural context, and persistence in acquiring tastes. As is shown in this chapter, festival space matters because it supports the visibility and prestige of festival films in ways that digital distribution cannot. In order to draw scenarios for future changes in the festival network we will have to complement insights derived from new business models with knowledge of cultural systems and cultural consumption. Learning from Jenkins' assessment of the black box fallacy (2006: 13-6), we are warned not to fall into the trap of thinking one medium (one mode of distribution) will be the end result of this period of convergence. It is, in other words, not a question of either one of the two emerging as the survivor of a 'convergence shake-out'. The CON-CAN Movie Festival might be a forerunner of things to come. So the future of festival screenings appears bright. The future of cinema seems even brighter when we consider the advantages of the Long Tail model. Digital distribution might prove to be the perfect companion to actual festival events, creating opportunities for further expansion and consolidation of the circulation of niche films among worldwide audiences.

That festivals have important advantages over the new digital exhibition opportunities should therefore not imply that they will remain unaffected by the transformations. Beside the off-line event, festivals could open on-line portals and continue to function as meeting places for lovers of world, art and independent cinema in the digital realm. Web 2.0 technologies and social media offer plenty of new ways to exchange information and knowledge, and to consolidate cinéphile passion in communities, not only during the festival, but also throughout the whole year.

Works Cited

'1962 – Oberhausen Manifesto' (1962) *Kultur Kenner*. On-line. Available HTTP: http://www.kulturkenner.com/static_pages/1962-%E2%80%93-oberhausener-manifest (15 August 2011).

Anderson, Chris (2004) 'The Long Tail', *Wired*, 12, 10, October. On-line. Available HTTP: http://www.wired.com/wired/archive/12.10/tail.html (20 June 2011).

_____ (2006) *The Long Tail: Why the Future of Business Is Selling Less of More.* New York: Hyperion.

Caldwell, John (2003) 'Second-shift Media Aesthetics: Programming, Interactivity, and User Flows' in John Caldwell and Anna Everett (eds) *New Media: Theories and Practices of Digitexuality*. New York and London: Routledge,127-44.

De Valck, Marijke (2007) *Film Festivals. From European Geopolitics to Global Cinephilia*. Amsterdam: Amsterdam University Press.

De Valck, Marijke (2010) 'De Rol van Festivals in het You-Tube Tijdperk', *Boekman*, 83, 54-60.

Ellis, John (2000) *Seeing Things: Television in the Age of Uncertainty*. London/ New York: I.B. Taurus.

English, James F. (2005) *The Economy of Prestige: Prizes, Awards and the Circulation of Cultural Value*. Cambridge, Massachusetts: Harvard University Press.

Gobé, Marc (2001) *Emotional Branding*. New York: Allworth Press.

Hediger, Vinzenz (2005) 'The Original Is Always Lost' in Marijke De Valck and Malte Hagner (eds) *Cinephilia: Movies, Love and Memory*. Amsterdam: Amsterdam University Press, 135-49.

Jenkins, Henry (2006) *Convergence Culture: Where Old and New Media Collide*. New York and London: New York University Press.

Jensen, Jens F. (1999) 'The Concept of Interactivity in Interactive Television and Interactive Media' in Jens F. Jensen and C. Toscan (eds) *Interactive Television: The TV of the Future or the Future of TV?* Aalborg: Aalborg University Press.

Klinger, Barbara (2006) *Beyond the Multiplex: Cinema, New Technologies, and the Home*. Berkeley, Los Angeles and London: University of California Press.

Media That Matters (undated) 'About', *Media That Matters Website*. On-line. Available HTTP: http://www.mediathatmattersfest.org/about (20 June 2011).

Murray, Simone (2003) 'Media's Convergence's Third Wave: Content Streaming', Convergence, 9, 1, March, 8-18.

Nichols, Bill (1994) 'Discovering Form, Inferring Meaning: New Cinemas and the Film Festival Circuit', *Film Quarterly*, 47, 31, Spring, 16-30.

Pauwels, Caroline and Jo Bauwens (2007) '<Power to the People>? The Myth of Television Consumer Sovereignty Revisited', *International Journal of Media and Cultural Politics*, 3, 2 149-65.

Schwartz, Barry (2004) *The Paradox of Choice: Why More Is Less*. New York: HarperCollins.

Shrum, Wesley Monroe Jr. (1996) Fringe and Fortune: *The Role of Critics in High and Popular Art*. Princeton, New Jersey: Princeton University Press.

Sinclair, John (2004) 'Into the Post-broadcast Era' in John Sinclair and Graeme Turner (eds) *Contemporary World Television*. London: BFI, 42-60.

Tapscott, Don and Anthony D. Williams (2006) *Wikinomics: How Mass Collaboration Changes Everything*. New York: Portfolio.

Toffler, Alvin (1980) *The Third Wave*. New York: Bantam Books.

Vittore, Vince (1997) 'The New Video Mix: Couch Potatoes May Not Need 500 Channels, but They'll Pay for Better Options', *Telephony Online*, 8 December. On-line. Available HTTP:http://telephonyonline.com/mag/telecom_new_video_mix/ (20 June 2011).

Yoshino, Masahiro (2010) 'Welcome to the Con-Can Media Plaza', CON-CAN Website. On-line. Available HTTP: http://en.con-can.com/aboutus/message.php (15 August 2011).

Notes

1   This chapter is an updated and reworked version of an earlier essay by the author, '"Screening" the Future of Film Festivals? A Long Tale of Convergence and Digitization', *Film International*, 6, 4, October 2008, 15-23. For its update it draws partially on the cited Dutch piece (De Valck 2010).

2   The Future of Cinema conference, 22 May 2007, hosted by the Cannes Market, Filmfestivals, MM2 Editions and Moving Pictures.

3   '"The world is one big family" is our key principle here at the CON-CAN Movie Festival' (Yoshino 2010).

4   The oldest short film festival is the International Short Film Festival Oberhausen, which was established in 1954, received FIAFP accreditation as early as 1960, and presented an influential Manifesto in 1962. In the Manifesto, 28 young German filmmakers declared their dedication to contribute to the new German film. They observed that in the previous couple of years short films had won many prizes at festivals and received favourable critiques. This was a sign to them that the future of the German film was in the hands of those who understood the new film language. 'The old film is dead. We believe in the new film' [author's translation] (1962 Oberhausen Manifesto).

CINEMA MOVES
ON-LINE

Mission Unreachable:

How Jaman Is Shaping the Future of On-line Distribution

Jon Silver, Stuart Cunningham

and Mark David Ryan

Perhaps the most innovative of all independent on-line distribution ventures specialising in rest of the world content is Jaman. Founded in 2007 by IT entrepreneur Gaurav Dhillon and based in San Mateo, California, Jaman is a quality specialist distributor of non-Hollywood films. The company was set-up for a total of U.S.$23 million (from private and venture capital), far less than the U.S.$50 million spent by the Hollywood majors on Movielink. Seventy-five per cent of Jaman's start-up capital was invested in technology (of which 55-60% went to engineering the site and 15-20% to ingest costs), and another 25% into content acquisition and marketing expenses.

Jaman enables viewing via a peer-to-peer (P2P) network that provides 720p DVD quality to a downloadable media player that gives movies a cinematic look and feel. The company's mission was to create an on-line destination for world cinema. Dhillon, a film buff, was surprised to learn that only 1% of movies produced each year actually gain a theatrical release (Dhillon and Galaria 2007). After years of attending international film festivals and viewing quality cinema from diverse countries around the globe, Dhillon began to ask 'why couldn't a really good film made in Europe be enjoyed by somebody in India?' (Dhillon 2010). Jaman arose from Dhillon's realisation that the Internet presented 'the best way to bridge that gap'. 'Like a Sundance on the Web', Jaman allows the user to watch a film, review it, recommend it and see what the favourites were in Jaman's on-line community (Dhillon and Galaria 2007). The site is designed to facilitate viewing and discovery through trusted networks – seek, share and discuss with like-minded people. 'We emphasised the international, independent nature of it

133

because that is the least served. I figured I could do well by doing good', said Dhillon (Agence France Press 2007).

Since inception, Jaman has developed strong strategic alliances with prominent film festivals, effectively 'converging with the festival distribution circuit and extending the festival exposure' (Iordanova 2010: 37). In the words of Dhillon, 'in many ways we have created a film festival that never ends' (Keating 2007). The site enables audiences to search for films in Jaman's catalogue that have screened at major international festivals, including Cannes, Venice and Sundance. Jaman also has a history of partnering with film festivals to showcase their films on-line. In April 2007, Jaman partnered with the Tribeca Film Festival in New York, and one week later partnered with the 50th San Francisco International Film Festival (SFIFF). The film industry trade magazine Variety heralded the significance of the Jaman-Tribeca partnership:

> Under the pact with Tribeca, six films screening at this year's fest [...] will be offered simultaneously for free download by users anywhere in the world for a period of seven days. The deal is [...] the first time a major festival will have given online exposure to part of its full-length feature programme at the same time the movies unspool at the fest. (Dawtrey 2007)

For Graham Leggat, Executive Director of SFIFF,

> The groundbreaking partnership with Jaman enables us to give SFIFF a truly radiant worldwide reach. For the past fifty years, the International has been bringing the world to San Francisco. Now the International Online will bring our films and filmmakers to the world. (Jaman 2007)

SFIFF films selected for the International Online programme were made available worldwide to a select number of viewers during an exclusive time window following the festival's final theatrical screening.

Jaman continued with fresh innovation in 2008, running a six-month Hong Kong Online Film Festival. It partnered with Fortune Star, a premier Asian film distributor, to showcase an 'epic retrospective' on Hong Kong cinema, featuring comedies, dramas, thrillers and martial arts films (Jaman 2008b). In 2011, Jaman featured numerous films from different festivals around the world, including four Palm Springs International Film Festival selections: *Yureru* (*Sway*, Miwa Nishikawa,

Japan, 2006), *Agua* (*Water*, Verónica Chen, Argentina/France, 2006), *Ma femme... s'appelle Maurice* (*My Wife Maurice*, Jean-Marie Poiré, France/Germany, 2002) and *Is It Just Me?* (J.C. Calciano, U.S., 2010).

Jaman launched with an available catalogue of 1,000 films from various parts of the world. This equated to a larger film library than Apple's iTunes at the time of its commencement a year earlier. Jaman negotiated supply deals for its catalogue with a range of content creators and distributors, including: short films from 60 Frames (Businesswire 2008) and feature films from the BFI, Pathé, Content Media and Axiom Films (Business of Cinema 2009); Eros Entertainment, Lionsgate, First Look, Magnolia (Jafaar 2009); NDTV Lumiere (Frater 2008); Arts Alliance (Woodson 2008); Fortissimo Films, Trust Film Library (Scandinavia), Fortune Star (Hong Kong) and Dreamachine (Goldstein 2007). Though specialising in rest of the world and independent cinema, Jaman signed a licensing agreement deal with Paramount Digital Entertainment in 2008. Jaman's catalogue includes renowned English-language titles such as *Into the Wild* (Sean Penn, U.S., 2007), *The Kite Runner* (Marc Forster, U.S./China, 2007), *Super Size Me* (Morgan Spurlock, U.S., 2004), *Dogville* (Lars Von Trier, Denmark/Sweden/UK/France/Germany/Netherlands/Norway/Finland, 2003) and Bollywood blockbusters including *Sholay* (Ramesh Sippy, India, 1975), *Chalte Chalte* (Aziz Mirza, India, 2003), *Devdas* (Sanjay Leela Bhansali, India, 2002) and *Eklavya* (Vidhu Vinod Chopra, India, 2007) among many others.

While Jaman had acquired 7,000 film titles by 2010 – one of the largest on-line libraries anywhere – only 3,400 were available to U.S. Jaman members on a rental or download-to-own basis. In some countries, for example Australia, as few as 500 films may be available, the reason being that Jaman has been unable to secure worldwide Internet rights to distribute the great majority of its films. Independent distributors and filmmakers typically sell individual international territory rights to maximise pre-sales or license fees, rather than sell universal rights to one distributor, a point we return to below. Genres available range from action-adventure, kung-fu, science-fiction/fantasy and horror, to special interest films such as Bollywood movies, documentaries and Japanese anime, to niche products including shorts, gay and lesbian films and cult movies. The majority of Jaman's business is rental-on-demand. Users can rent a film at a low U.S.$2.49, or download-to-own for prices of U.S.$4.99 and U.S.$9.99. The site offers a selection of free movies for streaming in high definition supported by advertising.

Table 1: The Jaman Platform

Upload and Ingest	Transcoding, Metadata, Rights Management
Delivery	DRM, Flash Player, Ad Network Integration, Downloadable Player (PC, Mac OS X), TiVo, Set-Top Boxes, iPhone Application, Mobile Devices
Audience Participation	Ratings & Reviews, Facebook Connect, Fanning, Embeddable Widgets, Fora, Live Events
Discovery	Movie Mood Finder, Recommendation Engine, Editorial Merchandising, Categories, Genres and Collections, Gifting Friends
Add-ons	Connected BluRay DVD, IP Video, Smart HDTVs, Yahoo Widgets, Roku, VuNow

Source: Jaman (2011) 'Jaman Networks Platform Overview', *Jaman*. On-line. Available HTTP: http://www.jaman.net/technology/ (7 June 2011).

The Jaman platform comprises a hosted server infrastructure, a distributed transcoding farm and user-facing client applications on a variety of platforms. These client applications communicate with the service infrastructure using industry-standard web services' (Jaman 2011). The platform design, as shown in Table 1 above, displays sub-menus of software modules that provide Jaman's unique user experience, namely: upload and ingesting movies, delivery, audience participation, discovery and add-ons. The website's design is a good example of how films can be made available on a variety of viewing devices ranging from smart HDTVs to set top boxes like Roku and TiVo, and also to mobile devices. Jaman uses a sophisticated proprietary process for ingesting premium quality film content into its system for delivery and 'encodes each film into 7+ formats that support auto-selecting, multi-rate streaming in H.264 and DRM protected files for download to Jaman's installable player; TiVo; iPhone and other playback devices' (Jaman 2011).

As of late 2010, Jaman had 1.8 million registered users and was attracting viewers from most countries in the world. Seventy-five per cent of all use is generated from outside the U.S.; Jaman does very well in English speaking parts of the world, particularly current and former Commonwealth countries. The UK accounts for 29% of users,

North America (U.S. and Canada) 26% and India represents 23%. The consumption of Bollywood titles occurs mostly outside India, in the Middle East and the U.S. There is a strong diasporic audience for Indian movies: the United Arab Emirates and Saudi Arabia account for 30% of all users and the UK (with its own large south Asian population) comprises 29% (Dhillon 2010). BizShark's (Web) Traffic Heat Map showed that other countries with a small but growing Jaman user base include: South Korea, Japan, China, Malaysia, Egypt, Iran, Dubai, Pakistan, Finland, Sweden and Germany (BizShark 2011). An Alexa Web traffic search of Jaman revealed that the largest segment of Jaman users were male, aged 18-24 years, who typically browse the website from home. The next largest user group were females, aged between 35-54 years; there was also considerable use by females of over 65 years and also a high usage by people who browse from work (Alexa 2011). The vast majority of Jaman's user base are long-term users – once registered, viewers typically remain an active part of Jaman's on-line community. As Jaman has a diverse range of viewers from both developed and developing countries with varying broadband penetration and information communication infrastructure, a key challenge confronting the site's development was the creation of a content delivery system which delivered the same speed (for downloads and streaming), quality and functionality anywhere in the world (Kho 2008).

Until recently, a key aspect, which made Jaman unique in the marketplace, was the social experience it offered users. Jaman is sometimes referred to as 'social cinema': a website which brings together the critique and review of a cinéphile website (the forums of Rue-morgue for fantasy film fans for example) with the social interaction, community and functionality of a social media site (for example Facebook). Jaman could be considered a pioneer in this space; a leader in the packaging of commercial movie downloading in an interactive social experience. Such an approach is, however, becoming increasingly commonplace for movie download sites, including Jaman's competitors, such as Hulu.

Jaman provides viewers with 'staff favourites', 'most watched' and 'most discussed' lists and also a 'people finder' to help users/members discuss films with others in the Jaman community who share similar tastes. There are user-reviews using a star rating system, blogs and a sub-titler that permits members to re-write captions on foreign film clips (Block 2009). Jaman is a cleverly designed site that facilitates the discovery of new films through its sliding 'movie finder' which can be set on choice scales such as serious vs. funny, deep vs. shallow, mellow vs. charged or tears vs. bullets. Once a viewer's preferences are locked in, Jaman generates a series of recommended films to match their mood, and begins to make personalised recommendations. Jaman was one of first on-line distribution companies to include Facebook Connect functionality, an application which allows users to sign into Jaman using an established Facebook account without having to register separately for Jaman. The website also integrates Twitter and Skype, user discussion boards and blogs for reviews and news of the latest acquisitions. It leverages various platforms and devices to deliver content, including TiVo, Apple TV, Roku, PCs and Macs, and mobile devices including iPhone.

Dhillon has identified three major barriers facing Jaman. Piracy is unavoidable and, he argues, exists because quality films from around the rest of the world are not available at local destinations and prices. For Dhillon, if Jaman's catalogue could be offered at low enough prices in countries like India – in a similar vein to the *iTunes* model – there may be greater incentive for consumers to purchase titles legitimately, rather than downloading them illegally via BitTorrent sites. A second barrier is territorial restrictions on rights availability: 'Our single greatest impediment is rights – you can't get non-exclusive rights to films. If you could assemble the rights, you could assemble a world cinema channel' (Dhillon 2010). Jaman has been unable to secure worldwide Internet rights to distribute a number of its films. So while Jaman's audience is global and the company's catalogue of licensed movies is impressive, many are geo-blocked and only accessible to viewers within the U.S. Moreover, legitimate on-line distribution ventures such as Jaman currently compete against illegal BitTorrent websites and P2P downloading that do not have universal rights restrictions and don't incur the costs of rights acquisition. According to Dhillon: 'If we could assemble the rights, without limits, for a substantial body of film, with a substantial international presence [then this] would make us successful [...] You need the rights available on a subscription model, with a worldwide emphasis to be successful' (Dhillon 2010). He elaborates:

> We have shown at Jaman [...] that the viewing and the social wrapping around the viewing can provide an alternative enjoyment [to traditional movie viewing] [...] We've shown that, but we've faced challenges. Ultimately what happens to Jaman long term [...] is going to be determined more by the

lack of rights, more than the lack of technology, and I would argue even more than the potential lack of consumption. (Dhillon 2010)

Jaman experienced great turmoil during the global downturn in 2008-10, the impact of which was that the traditional venture capital needed for this type of operation and the next stage of growth disappeared overnight (Dhillon 2010). In response to these challenges, Jaman has diversified into new areas of economic activity, particularly IT services, in an attempt to generate other revenue streams and to diversify risk. Founded in 2009, Jaman Networks is a 'white-label' technology provider licensing Jaman's underlying technology platforms to companies looking to enter the on-line marketplace. Their service offers 'content owners, retailers, ISPs and consumer electronics companies an end-to-end solution for worldwide Internet distribution of Hollywood movies, independent film and television content' (Jaman Networks 2011). While Jaman has experienced corporate restructuring and downsizing recently, the company remains one of the most successful and innovative companies operating in the on-line distribution marketplace offering speciality cinema.

In December 2011, Jaman temporarily suspended its on-line services in order to move its content to the cloud. This is an important development because major competitors in on-line distribution such as Amazon, Apple, Disney Studio All Access and UltraViolet (a consortium of Major Hollywood studios and other key stakeholders in the digital value chain) were also moving rapidly to make their content available in the cloud. The move is important strategically because it keeps Jaman at the cutting edge in terms of the technology and positions it favourably to its on-line audience.

Works Cited

Agence France Press (2007) 'Independent Film Makers Win Online Stage', *The Age*, 29 October. On-line. Available HTTP: http://news.theage.com.au/technology/independent-film-makers-win-online-stage-20071029-16rz.html (7 June 2011).

Alexa (2011) 'Audience Demographics for Jaman.com', *Alexa*. On-line. Available HTTP: http://www.alexa.com/siteinfo/jaman.com (4 April 2011, 10am).

BizShark (2011) 'Jaman.com/traffic', *BizShark*. On-line. Available HTTP: http://www.bizshark.com/company/jaman.com/traffic (4 April 2011).

Block, Dana (2009) 'Jaman Launches Facebook Connect to Unite Film Lovers around the World', *Social Media Portal*, 9 February. On-line. Available HTTP: http://www.socialmediaportal.com/PressReleases/2009/02/Jaman-Launches-Facebook-Connect-to-Unite-Film-Lovers-Around-the-World.as px?ReturnUrl=%2FSearch%2FDefault.aspx%3FTag%3DOn-line%2Bcom munity%26Pg%3D1%26Sz%3D50 (14 June 2011).

Business of Cinema (2009) 'Jaman Rolls Out International Operations', *Business of Cinema*, 14 January. On-line. Available HTTP: http://www. businessofcinema.com/news.php?newsid=11523&page=44 (7 June 2011).

BusinessWire (2008) 'Jaman Expands Library To Include Original Internet Series from 60 Frames'. *Businesswire*, 8 December. On-line. Available HTTP: http://www.businesswire.com/news/home/20081208005364/en/Jaman-Expands-Library-Include-Original-Internet-Series (8 September 2011).

Dawtrey, Adam (2007) 'Tribeca Downloads Jaman: Movie Download Service Strikes Deals', *Variety*, 23 April. On-line. Available HTTP: http://www. variety.com/article/VR1117963642?refCatId=20 (7 June 2011).

Dhillon, Gaurav (2010) Skype interview conducted by Stuart Cunningham and Jon Silver, 1 April.

Dhillon, Gaurav and Faisal Galaria (2007) 'Hi-def Independent Films Online with Jaman', Podtech interview conducted by Robert Scoble, *Classic ScobleShow*, 27 June. On-line. Available HTTP: http:// connectedsocialmedia.com/2931/hi-def-independent-films-online-with-jaman/ (12 August, 2011).

Goldstein, Gregg (2007) 'Jammin with Jaman.com', *Hollywood Reporter*, October 1. On-line. Available HTTP: http://www.hollywoodreporter.com/news/jammin-jamancom-151369 (12 August, 2011).

Frater, Patrick (2008) 'NDTV Lumiere Pacts with Jaman; Deal Covers Streaming, Downloading of 30 Films', *Daily Variety*, August 13. On-line. Available HTTP: http://www.variety.com/article/VR1117990535.html?categoryid=19&cs=1 (7 June 2011).

Iordanova, Dina (2010) 'Rise of the Fringe: Global Cinema's Long Tail', in Dina Iordanova, David Martin-Jones and Belen Vidal (eds) *Cinema at the Periphery*. Detroit: Wayne State University Press, 23-46.

Jaafar, Ali (2009) 'Jaman logs site in U.K.', *Daily Variety*, January 14. On-line. Available HTTP: http://www.variety.com/article/VR1117998549. html?categoryid=20&ref=ra&cs=1 (7 June 2011).

Jaman (2007) 'San Francisco Film Society and Jaman Announce the Launch of the International Online at the 50th San Francisco International Film Festival', *Jaman, 22* January. On-line. Available HTTP: http://www.jaman.com/m/news/releases/1_22_07.html (7 June 2011).

_____ (2008a) 'Jaman Delivers Award Winning Film "Punching at the Sun" to Movie Lovers around the Globe', Press release at Sundance Film Festival, Jaman, 22 January. On-line. Available HTTP: http://www.jaman.com/m/news/releases/01_22_08.html (10 August 2011).

_____ (2008b) 'Jaman Celebrates Hong Kong Movies with Its First Online Film Festival', *Jaman.com*, 29 January. On-line. Available HTTP: http://www.jaman.com/m/news/releases/01_29_08.html (7 June 2011).

_____ (2011) 'Jaman Networks Platform Overview', *Jaman*. On-line. Available HTTP: http://www.jaman.net/technology/ (7 June 2011).

Jaman Networks (2011) 'Who We Are', *Jaman*. On-line. Accessed HTTP: http://www.jaman.net/company/ (7 June 2011).

Keating, Gina (2007) 'Jaman Aims for Video Niche Markets', *Reuters*, 23 February. On-line. Available HTTP: www.reuters.com/assets/print?aid=USN2345521720070223 (7 June 2011).

Kho, Nacy (2008) 'Making a Sticker Cinema Site: Edgecast's CDN Keeps Jaman's Vistors On-site Longer', *Streaming Media Magazine*, February/March, 193.

Woodson, Alex (2008) 'Jaman Plucks Spurlock Pics', *Hollywood Reporter*, 24 April. On-line. Available HTTP: http://www.hollywoodreporter.com/news/jaman-plucks-spurlock-pics-110146 (12 August, 2011).

'IMDb Helps Me Sleep at Night': How a Simple Database Changed the World of Film

Alex Fischer

The Internet Movie Database (IMDb) is the preeminent source for movie facts, news and promotional material. Averaging 57 million visits a month, the website has become, since its inception in 1990, a major force in raising public awareness of film titles and connecting filmmakers and other industry professionals to audience members around the globe. Committed to being trustworthy, factual and up-to-date (Needham and Gains 2011) the site has become an indispensable part of the new digital film ecology, developing on-line communities and professional networks that extend to the farthest reaches of modern day filmmaking. In fact, IMDb is so ingrained into the contemporary cinematic culture, that it's almost fair to say that if a film isn't listed on the database it simply does not exist.

This case study chronicles the operational history of IMDb. The information is presented in three sections followed by a timeline highlighting the events that function as milestones in the company's impressive trajectory. The first section examines how an on-line collective of 20 individuals amassed one of the largest continually growing databases in world. The second section discusses the acquisition of the database by the Internet juggernaut Amazon and the catalyst-like effect this acquisition had in expanding the technological reach of the company. The third section ponders the possible future role of IMDb as a video-on-demand content provider.

Goodwill Hunting

This is very much a labor of love. When we started the company, there was no commercial use of the Internet.

Col Needham, founder and CEO of IMDb (in Siklos 2006)

The Internet Movie Database began in 1990 when Col Needham, a computer engineer working for Hewlett-Packard in the English city of Bristol, decided to post a bulletin board database called rec.arts. movies.movie. This database was devoted to movie credits and, as Needham explains, was the result of seeing too many films and losing track of information such as which actors starred in particular movies (Needham 2011). The desire to make the database virtual stemmed from his childhood familiarity with programming and from an understood need to avoid a paper-based catalogue due to its physical limitations.[1] Among the limitations of a physical catalogue was the single-sidedness of the information collected. That is, the World Wide Web offered an advanced means of gathering information via an open editable model, a model which sees metadata continually created and updated by users and which is the foundation of the crowdsourcing principal on which e-information banks such as Wikipedia are modelled.

From the very beginning, rec.arts.movies.movie was based upon the principal of collaboration and specialisation. Jean-Michel Frodon calls this collaborative growth 'one of the most spectacular adventures of the young history of the Internet' (2008) and it is hard to disagree. In fact, the creation and development of film credit categories such as scriptwriter, foley artist, composer, etc., was undertaken by individuals specifically interested in those particular aspects of film production (Needham 2011). What made this collaboration so unique was the snowballing effect manifested by altruistic individuals willing to donate time and knowledge to explore the interactive capabilities of the Internet. When users logged onto rec.arts.movies.movie, they could discuss topics, answer questions and post information thus effectively growing the database in a way traditional publishing could not. From the original 20 members who routinely spent spare time and weekends contributing information, one of the world's most extensive film resources, utilised by millions of users, would ultimately take root.

Another advantage of the virtual database is its unique way of conquering time and space. In October 2011, IMDb turned 20 years old. This means the database has been accumulating information non-stop for over two decades. This prolific collection of data is largely due to the fact the Internet has no physical boundaries and never closes.[2] So, even though Needham may be off-line at his home in Britain, his counterparts in America would continue working, thus effectively creating a 24-hour work schedule. Additionally, the advantage of working on-line has enabled contributors to keep correcting inaccurate information over time. There are several stories of individuals trying to advance their film careers by attaching their name to film credits. Needham explains that such false claims are generally corrected within minutes, something printed disclaimers can never achieve (Needham 2011).

Through the early 1990s, rec.arts.movies.movie continued to expand, taking advantage of recently installed servers in countries such as the U.S., Australia, Germany, Italy, South Korea, Japan, South Africa and Iceland (Frodon 2008). These servers enabled rec.arts.movies. movie to have a greater worldwide presence, increased the speed at which users received requested information and kept the database from being overrun by individuals eager to use the site.

The popularity of the database prompted Needham and other content providers to rethink the legal standing of rec.arts.movies.movie, and in 1996 IMDb became officially incorporated. The official branding of the database meant IMDb would receive an aesthetic facelift to improve and encourage user participation. Improvements included a revamped centralised e-mail interface that enabled individuals to contact and submit information to the database. The shares were divided among the 20 individuals 'who had contributed most to fuel the database' (Frodon 2008). It was from this moment on that the motivation pushing IMDb became intertwined with commercial interests. Challenges they faced were creating a free website and making and keeping the database sustainable. The creation of the database was entirely based upon good will; it was, as Needham says, a labour of love. So, making the site profitable required adding new dimensions. One of these dimensions was advertising. Given the amount of film-related user traffic, the site seemed destined to become an integral part of the Hollywood film release strategy. In fact, the company almost seemed to tempt Hollywood by officially launching just before the 1996 Academy Awards®. By the summer of 1996, IMDb had sold its first advertising slot for the film *Independence Day* (Roland Emmerich, U.S., 1996) (Needham 2011).

This sale marked an important step forward as it enabled Needham, who had devoted the majority of his adult life to building the database, to become the first IMDb employee (Frodon 2008). From this point on, IMDb had established a firm foothold within the film industry and the profitable nature of the database was not lost on potential investors. In fact, numerous companies tried to acquire the company prior to late 1997 when Jeff Bezos, the creator of Amazon, contacted Needham to discuss the takeover that was eventually to be finalised three months later. The next section discusses how the incorporation of IMDb into the Amazon universe enabled the company to continue its exponential growth and establish itself as a dominant fixture in film culture.

The Amazin' Growth of IMDb

In January 1998 the Internet Movie Database officially became an Amazon holding company. The motivation to acquire IMDb was based upon the notion that the database could help Amazon sell movies (Siklos 2006). And indeed, for a while, links to DVDs of films available via Amazon did feature on the site; however, life as part of the Amazon empire did not radically change the way in which the IMDb operated. The on-line retailer was not intent on changing the look or feel of the database. Rather it seems as though Amazon just wanted to be a part of the action and, by purchasing IMDb, it gained not only the single largest film database in the world, but also access to its users.

The benefits of the Amazon buyout for IMDb were numerous. Paramount was access to Amazon's capital which could be used for research and development to improve the service provided to the database's millions of visitors. With regard to Col Needham and the other stakeholders, the Amazon buyout translated into a mixture of actual payment and Amazon stock estimated to be worth U.S.$55 million (Siklos 2006). [3]

It is logical to assume that being purchased by the largest on-line retailer would send the hobbyists into retirement, but the acquisition seemed to inspire IMDb's enthusiasts to modify the database so as to allow greater connectivity between people and film. The first major change occurred in 2002 with the introduction of IMDb Pro. Besides creating a discernable revenue stream, this subscription-based, enhanced version of the database allowed members greater access to information such as movie budgets and provided listings for directors, actors and producers, as well as the contact details of motion picture businesses. The service was primarily aimed at film industry professionals and marked a considered move by IMDb to diversify its user base. No longer was the site solely a source of factual information; rather, it could be used to seek out employment, raise awareness of projects or contact individuals and businesses via a common affiliate.

As for the non-professionals, IMDb became the one-stop-shop for up-to-date entertainment news, promotional material, blogs and articles about specific productions. It also served as a space for expressing opinions through the 'Starmeter' and various questionnaires posted by users and IMDb employees. Evidence of the contagious nature of the site can be observed in the 67% increase in traffic it experienced between 2005 and 2006. This jump in activity made the IMDb the tenth most-popular entertainment site on the Internet according to ComScore Media Metrix (Siklos 2006). One of the reasons for the site's popularity can be attributed to the interconnectivity of its information. That is, utilising the database's search function exposes the user to an extensive hyperlink-based listing of related topics and this interconnectivity ultimately enriches the IMDb experience by providing users with a 'rabbit hole' of information whose topical boundaries have no ends. Additionally, the site also provides movie fans with the chance to interact. Discussion forums related to individual films enable viewers around the globe to enter into dialogue and form virtual networks that simply could not exist in the physical world.

Whether the popularisation of IMDb can be directly attributed to Amazon's influence is not known, however the on-line retailer did give IMDb additional legitimacy that could have raised the perceived social worth of the database simply through affiliation. It would not be surprising if Amazon provided advice on how to engineer on-line transactions – such as allowing users to purchase movie tickets from the IMDb site, which ultimately increased the overall service worth of the database. There is also synergy between IMDb and the other Amazon-owned subsidiaries such as Withoutabox and CreateSpace. Through these companies, IMDb can position itself as the marketing and promotional centre for independent film production. It has long been speculated that another, more covert reason why Amazon bought IMDb was in preparation for the retailer to enter the video-on-demand (VOD) marketplace. According to Siklos (2006), the 1998 buyout was connected to the development of a downloadable service that would enable Amazon customers to burn their own DVD copies of Hollywood films from their desktop. Although IMDb provides the ideal platform to perform this service since it already contains factual information about films it is a service that has yet to materialise; however, it is still not out of the question.

The next section discusses what future role the IMDb envisages for itself as a content provider and how Needham's vision of this future could mark a new era in film distribution.

IMDme

Early on in this chapter it was suggested (and not for the first time) that if a film isn't listed on IMDb it simply does not exist. While this is an obvious overstatement there are signs that all cinematic roads might indeed eventually lead to IMDb.[4] In recent years, the database has become extremely important in promoting independent and niche cinema. For example, those filmmakers submitting work to film festivals through the film festival intermediary Withoutabox are given the option to register an IMDb account for their film. This is a free service that allows rights holders to upload videos, posters, trailers and other promotional material in a bid to raise awareness of their production. Similarly, the studio system has realised the marketing potential of the site, and teaser and trailer campaigns are used to build hype that can lead to millions of box office dollars.

The digital distribution of Hollywood films in the near future seems unlikely. Tried and true distribution methods which see films moved through a theatrical pipeline continue to function. For independent productions, though, IMDb offers a wealth of benefits, with one of the greatest being audience connectivity (Needham 2011). This audience connectivity sees the physical limitations associated with geographic isolation become irrelevant as both films and audiences become part of an elaborate virtual cinema space. The only sticking point is payment to rights holders. Several models are being tested at the moment, such as the self-distribution method available through the Amazon affiliate network.[5] For the most part, however, digital distribution remains unformalised, though much has been learned from the trials and tribulations encountered by the music industry during its early days (Needham 2011).

If IMDb has a weakness, it is its focus on Western cinema. That is, although IMDb does list Chinese, Indian and African titles, they represent only a disproportionate fraction of the number of films produced. This situation is acknowledged by Needham who believes the same user content contribution method that built IMDb over 20 years ago will be applied again by filmmakers, critics and fans from under-represented film traditions (Needham 2011).

Conclusion

Col Needham knows that there are always more films to see than there is time in the human lifespan to watch them (Needham 2011). It seems an appropriate observation for a film buff, who has dedicated his life to cataloguing movies. At last count, Needham owned 8,000 DVDs. He attributes much of the success of IMDb to a serendipitous timing that saw the database coincide with the rise of VHS and a new form of cine-fandom that allowed people to physically own movies.

Over the course of the last 20 years, the Internet Movie Database has grown to become *the* trusted source of film facts. What began as a rudimentary discussion board has become a multi-million dollar business. Needham is not shy in positing IMDb as possibly 'the world's first profitable Internet company' (Needham 2011). Utilising the strengths of the virtual space he was been able to successfully harness the collaborative experience that powers on-line interaction.

There is no sign that IMDb will stop collecting film data and, as more rights holders use the database as a screening platform, the content will become more varied and layered. It has already become a fundamental part of contemporary cinema and is used by a range of individuals, from the casual weekend movie-goer to the serious academic. A single glance at the webpage displays a vibrant cultural tool used to promote, inform and ultimately form part of a collective viewing experience.

The database has even been known to cure sleepless nights. According to Needham, IMDb often receives notes of praise from individuals unable nod off at night because they are haunted by some specific lines or an actor, but cannot recall the film (Needham 2011). Such a triumph of community in the face of adversity is certainly worth critical praise and offers a much more interesting alternative to counting sheep.

Table 1: Timeline of IMDb Organisational Growth

Year	Event
1990	Col Needham uploads rec.arts.movies.movie – individuals begin contributing information specific to their field of interest.
1990	1,100 titles are listed on the database.
1993	The rec.arts.movies.movie database is mirrored onto servers in the U.S., Australia, Germany, Italy, South Korea, Japan, South Africa and Iceland.
1996	The rec.arts.movies.movie database officially becomes the Independent Movie Database (IMDb).
1996	First advertising spot is sold to Fox Studios to promote the film Independence Day.
1996	Col Needham becomes the first employee of IMDb.
1997	IMDb reaches 18 million registered users.
1997	IMDb is offered buyout deals by several companies, including Amazon.
1998	IMDb officially becomes a subsidiary of Amazon.
2002	IMDb Pro is launched. The service specialises in content for film industry users.
2006	IMDb is ranked as the tenth most popular entertainment-based website, according to the ComScore Media Metrix.
2007	210,00 titles are listed on the database.
2010	220,000 titles are listed on the database.

Source: Compiled by the author.

Works Cited

Frodon, Jean-Michel (2008) 'Evénement. Le Cinéma supersite', *Cahiers du Cinéma*, 634, May, 634. On-line. Available HTTP: http://www. cahiersducinema.com/Evenement-Le-cinema-supersite.html (24 June 2011).

Needham, Col (2011) 'Spotlight on IMDb Founder Col Needham', Edinburgh International Film Festival event, 19 June.

Needham, Col and Christian Gains (2011) Unpublished interview conducted by Alex Fischer, 19 June.

Siklos, Richard (2006) 'From a Small Stream, a Gusher of Movie Facts', *New York Times*. On-line. Available HTTP: http://www.nytimes.com/2006/05/28/ business/yourmoney/28frenzy.html (24/7/11).

Withoutabox (2011) 'Homepage', *Withoutabox*. On-line. Available HTTP: https:// www.withoutabox.com (23 February, 2011).

Notes

1   At the age of 14 Needham established a software company in order to sell simple video game programs (Frodon 2008).

2   Of course, there are limitations related to black outs or instances where lines of communication are cut off.

3   Included in this buy-out were two other European companies. The exact figures or division of money/stock options has not been disclosed.

4   As of 2010 more than 220,000 titles were listed on IMDb (Needham 2011).

5   Key players in this network include CreateSpace, Withoutabox and IMDb.

'The Fully Clickable Submission': How Withoutabox Captured the Hearts and Minds of Film Festivals Everywhere

Alex Fischer

What is the film festival of the future? This simple, forward-looking question carries the implication that the functional structure of film festivals will somehow be different from their predecessors. Indeed, even a basic investigation into the individual histories of iconic events such as Cannes provides evidence that successful film festival operation is underpinned by the ability to adapt to a continuously changing environment.[1]

The forces that drive the change include, but are not limited to, technological advances, the rise of particular cinematic movements or styles and the availability of key resources such as films, venues, funding and audiences. While all these agents of change influence how a film festival functions, it is the ability to secure key resources that ultimately dictates if a film festival is able to operate or not.

The film festival of the future will have its architectural plans sketched with accessibility in mind; it will no longer rely so much on its presumed role as a critical node. In the future, the film festival's capacity for self-preservation may diminish due to the appearance of film festival intermediaries, private companies that are fast becoming a resource 'middle man', thus effectively eroding the film festivals' one-time monopoly as sites of passage (de Valck 2007) for filmmakers in pursuit of distribution deals.

The most prominent among the new film festival intermediaries is Withoutabox. Launched at the Toronto International Film Festival in 2000 by two American independent filmmakers, this Internet-based business was the first company to offer a streamlined, one-size-fits-all, application service designed to expedite the submission process for both filmmakers and film festivals. It has since grown, expanding its role and competing against other intermediaries such as B-Side, Dataflow, Eye on Films, Eventival and Festival Scope, to provide an effective, virtual means of connecting filmmakers and film festivals. The following chart provides more information as to the role and impact of these six intermediaries.

Table 1: Film Festival Intermediary Sites

Intermediary	Service Offered	Number of participating film festivals
B-Side (now Slated)	Social media platform specialising in enhancing audience experience at film festivals.	643
Dataflow	Internet-based festival management software soon to offer downloadable screener technology to film festivals.	Unknown.
Eye on Films	Distribution of first-time feature films via a global network of film professionals.	14
Eventival	Festival management software soon to offer downloadable screener technology to film festivals.	20
Festival Scope	On-line screening platform.	42
Withoutabox	On-line film festival application form, self-distribution opportunities, direct marketing to filmmakers, On-line screener submission.	5,000+[2]

Source: Compiled by the author.

Presently, nearly all film festival intermediaries enable filmmakers to submit their films to festivals electronically. This process involves a digital copy of the film being transferred to the nominated intermediary's digital storage space. For all intents and purposes the uploaded copy is secure from potential piracy (as indicated by the presence of numerous disclaimers intended to ease the fears rights holders). This development has revolutionised the submission process as it allows filmmakers to create their own personal film festival circuit. Additional advantages of submitting a film to a film festival via the Internet include:

- Eliminating the physical medium, thus enabling film festival organisers access to a film without having to wait for a VHS, a DVD or a film print to arrive. This has a far-reaching effect in expediting the programming process by allowing faster decision-making regarding a film's inclusion.
- Lowering costs attributed to the physical shipment of a film. Most intermediaries will allow filmmakers to upload their films for free, while film festivals are expected to purchase subscriptions.[3] (In the past filmmakers could make only a limited number of submissions as it was a common practice for festivals not to return submitted film dubs; filmmakers who wanted to submit to more festivals were incurring additional expenses for extra prints.)
- Improved communication between filmmakers and film festivals. Filmmakers can now monitor the progress of their submission and ensure technical glitches are rectified. Similarly, film festival organisers are able to contact selected filmmakers for promotional materials, such as a trailer, to enhance websites and increase the likely patronage to a particular film.
- Filmmakers can create and manage a customised personal film festival circuit and react more efficiently in instances where the film is rejected by a festival.

This chapter explores the impact film festival intermediaries have on current film festival operation and the role of technology in changing the culture of independent film distribution. The first section provides background as to how Withoutabox came into existence, examining the evolution of the business from a basic connection point between filmmakers and festivals to a highly complex service provider capable of instituting a new means of global distribution. The second section discusses how film festival intermediaries in general are likely to influence future film festival operation. The focal point of this section is those possible structural changes that may result as the potential for a digital distribution network is fully realised.

The Arrival and Evolution of Withoutabox

Withoutabox occupies a unique niche that is largely a response to the problems associated with film programming as, historically, film festival operation has always been adversely influenced by the physical nature of film prints. This was especially true for festivals located geographically outside of the main European film festival network. David Donaldson, director of the Sydney Film Festival (1954-7), explains that the 'primary criterion' of programming an event in the 1950s was whether the films were already located in Australia or whether it looked like they would arrive in time for the event (Webber 2005).

With the modernisation of air transportation, the operational constraints faced by Donaldson and other film festival organisers of that era diminished. It wasn't until the establishment of the Internet, however, that new options for programming on a global scale could be seriously explored. Not only did e-mail enable greater and quicker communication, but the connectivity between film festivals and filmmakers, distributors, sales agents and the like became more developed. Similarly, technological advances and the availability of inexpensive filmmaking hardware such as digital camcorders and non-linear editing equipment meant that more films produced without distribution already in place were likely to seek to play at film festivals as an alternate exhibition platform.

The founders of Withoutabox capitalised on this situation. Their business was to become an official conduit between film suppliers and film festivals, a service which 'allows filmmakers to access and apply to film festivals worldwide with one online entry form' (Business Wire 2001). The business idea grew out of the challenges the company's American founders, David Straus and Joe Neulight, had experienced while making and trying to self-distribute their own films while enrolled in a Masters of Fine Arts at UCLA. According to Straus: 'We were frustrated filmmakers trying to break into the market and we thought transforming the entire distribution paradigm would actually be an easier thing to do' (Straus and Neulight 2007).[4]

Straus and Neulight considered entering a film into the film festival circuit to be both 'costly' and 'cumbersome' (Q 2007). Straus explains that the idea to offer an International Film Festival Submission Service (IFFSS) was not so much driven by desire to provide 'exposure' for independent filmmakers but was rather meant to enable them to access 'useful information systems' that allowed them to run their own 'cottage businesses' (Straus and Neulight 2007). Initially, the IFFSS rolled out at several prominent, North American-based film festivals – the Toronto International Film Festival, the Cleveland International Film Festival, the Ann Arbor Film Festival, the San Francisco International Film Festival, the AFI Fest and the Sundance Film Festival – which were selected as 'Test and Development Partners' (Business Wire 2001).

Enlisting such an impressive array of film festivals was no doubt strategically important; within a year of its official launch on the Withoutabox website, the IFFSS was in use by more than 100 film festivals. As Straus explains, 'When you consider the size, diversity and geographic scope of our partner festivals, we will be reaching approximately 80-percent of the filmmaking community in North America by Spring 2002' (Business Wire 2001). Current figures of Withoutabox's client base list more than 5,000 film festivals world-wide and 300,000 filmmakers and writers as registered participants (Withoutabox 2011). Such tremendous growth indicates the universal value of the services offered by Withoutabox and has no doubt solidified the company's position as the premier intermediary for filmmakers and film festivals.

Such popularity has also translated into sizable profits for the company. While budgetary figures are not publicly available it is known that Withoutabox charges only the film festivals for its service. Filmmakers are able to use Withoutabox for free, but must pay individual film festival submission fees from which Withoutabox takes a percentage.[5] Over the years the cost of using Withoutabox has risen, causing some film festival organisers to re-think their use of the intermediary. According to Adam Roffman from the Independent Film Festival of Boston, 'there are some services that we just don't find worth the money' (Swanson 2008).

The growing popularity of the IFFSS among film festivals can be attributed to the ease with which organisers can now overcome the challenges commonly faced when dealing with unsolicited film entries. Unlike invited films or those contracted and programmed through a distributor or sales agent, unsolicited entries pose a major time constraint, both in terms of paperwork and viewing. Doug Guthrie of the Northampton International Film Festival explains that Withoutabox saves 'two weeks or 80 hours' worth' of work by streamlining the entry process (Swanson 2008).

When Withoutabox first began operating, film producer Jonathan Dana noted that the IFFSS was a 'well thought-out and researched system that will move information through the movie pipeline in an entirely new way' (Business Wire 2001). Ten years later this 'movie pipeline' has grown to include distribution services to independent filmmakers through a partnership with CreateSpace (previously CustomFlix).[6] This partnership ultimately sees Withoutabox operating as an alternative distribution platform and therefore fulfilling a similar role to the film festivals it once served. No doubt there are major differences between film festivals and the Withoutabox/CreateSpace model; however, because Withoutabox offers a distribution-based service it has the potential to diminish the monopolistic role film festivals once occupied as sites of discovery for many rights holders. Moreover, given its pre-existing connection to filmmakers and its reputation it has the potential to overshadow many smaller film festivals that lack the same name recognition.

The evolution of Withoutabox seems to be financially motivated. This is in contrast to most film festivals, whose organisers have a tendency to focus on cultural rather than financial gains.[7] It therefore should come as no surprise that as soon as IFFSS was publicly released, Withoutabox began modifying its service so as to remain competitive and in-demand. While many of these modifications were related to interfaces (e.g. film festival information, more specific entry forms, etc.), it was the creation of an exhibition-based project called 'The Distribution Lab' that signalled the future of the company.

First announced in 2006, this initiative was described as a 'program that will offer a suite of services to support filmmakers who plan to release their films themselves' (Hernandez 2006).

The publicly available information on the early operation of The Distribution Lab and its overall effectiveness is scarce. What is known is that Withoutabox aimed to develop a system that allowed filmmakers to self-distribute using the same streamlined and efficient methods that had made its International Film Festival Submission Service so successful. These methods included offering hands-free manufacturing and transportation of DVD screeners to film festivals and customers.[8] So, Withoutabox would effectively create, author and post all DVDs for filmmakers and would provide, according to Joe Neulight, 'the long-awaited fully clickable submission. No need to touch or put anything in the mail. This service will enable it to be done for them [filmmakers] anywhere in the world' (CreateSpace 2006)[9].

In order to facilitate this 'fully clickable submission' service, Withoutabox partnered with CustomFlix, an Amazon-owned company specialising in on-demand video publishing. Dana LoPiccolo-Giles, Managing Director of CustomFlix, describes the company's role as offering 'Withoutabox's filmmakers fully-tracked and delivered film festival submission DVDs at prices that will be hard to beat, even for filmmakers doing it themselves' (CreateSpace 2006). The option to use CustomFlix was offered to filmmakers in their application to film festivals via the Withoutabox festival submission form.

To further enhance the attractiveness of the new distribution-based service, Withoutabox formed a strategic alliance with Filmfinder, a film title search engine, and Rightsline, a company specialising in asset tracking software. According to Neulight, these additional partnerships 'allow [Withoutabox] to offer the most comprehensive open marketplace to our 90,000-plus rights owners along with thousands of buyers, sales agents and distributors throughout the world' (Brooks 2006).

The self-distribution project seemed to have all the correct pieces in place; however, it failed to make any ground-breaking announcements or newsworthy headlines that could demonstrate how profoundly it had transformed the independent distribution scene. It wasn't until 2008, when Withoutabox was purchased by the Internet Movie Database (IMDb), that an improved self-distribution model was created. In fact, news of this acquisition was seen as so important that it dominated the pre-festival headlines prior to the 2008 edition of Sundance (Graser and Thompson 2008).[10] The new alliance saw filmmakers distributing their films over the Internet as opposed to mailing physical copies. Additionally, with a monthly average of over 50 million unique visitors (Puget Sound Business Journal 2008), IMDb gave Withoutabox unprecedented connectivity through which it could offer its services.

Since IMDb is a subsidiary of Amazon, the previous alliance between Withoutabox and CustomFlix grew into a more collaborative relationship.[11] That is, both Withoutabox and CustomFlix were now owned by the same parent company so a symbiotic partnership had the potential to flourish. Evidence of the collaborative nature between the two companies can be found in public statements in which CreateSpace (previously CustomFlix), explains that it 'shares Withoutabox's mission of connecting filmmakers profitably to their worldwide audience' (Withoutabox 2011). This like-mindedness led to the creation of an enhanced distribution service that enabled filmmakers to retain exhibition rights and control all aspects of their film's distribution, from the cover artwork to the retail price of the film so that filmmakers 'start making money with their first sale, and on each subsequent sale' (Withoutabox 2011).[12]

The competition Withoutabox faces from other intermediaries is not significant. The only potential challenger is the Texas-based B-Side, a 'full service distribution company' which delivers feature films via 'retail and rental outlets, digital streaming and download services, VOD, and television' and which has been operating since 2005 (B-Side 2011). Initially, B-Side competed directly with Withoutabox by offering a 'Submission 2.0' service that automatically matched submitted films with film festivals having 'a history of screening similar work'. The company also planned to provide a similar service to film festival organisers as Withoutabox but at half the rate (Jones 2008).

Interestingly, in 2010 B-Side's technology was bought by the New York-based company Slated. Slated calls itself a 'data and investment marketplace for the film industry' (Slated 2011) and has shifted its focus from facilitating film festival submission to enhancing the connection audience members have with a film festival. Slated offers a 'Festival Genius' service consisting of 'an interactive festival schedule that engages audience members and filmmakers with social features such as ratings, reviews, recommendations, and blogs' (B-Side 2011). According to Slated, the Festival Genius programme 'has helped 643 festivals get 6,459,944 people to watch 69,566 films' (Slated 2011).

Other existing intermediaries offer a more individualised, boutique-style service, such as access to specialist film festival data management software akin to Filemaker Pro, rather than by acting as an intermediary between the events and the filmmakers. Eventival is one such company which offers a complete film festival management package. Similarly to Withoutabox, the company's founders identified a distinct niche to service film festivals as early as 1999 (Eventival 2011); they currently have 20 film festival clients including the Hong Kong International Film Festival, the Estonian-based Tallinn Black Nights Film Festival, and the Argentinian-based Ventana Sur.[13]

If anything, the competition between Slated, Eventival and Withoutabox is more opportunity-driven than direct. By targeting different niches of the film festival service industry the smaller companies avoid confrontation with Withoutabox. This is not to say that they don't compete, but rather that the field is large enough for each company to focus on putting forward the best product and leaving the festivals to decide which intermediary to use.

Filmmakers also benefit from the service offered by Withoutabox. The single application accelerates the submission process and provides users with a list of participating Withoutabox film festivals. So, filmmakers can effectively enter their work into global circulation via a film festival track of their own design. Filmmaker Ryan Gielen explains that, 'Once I've created a [Withoutabox] profile, I scroll through the festivals to add them to my shopping cart' (Puget Sound Business Journal 2008).

Such an effective use of virtual space presents tremendous opportunities when contrasted with the tyranny of distance experienced by film festivals in the past, and the filmmakers' burden of shipping screeners and prints to festivals. The appearance of Withoutabox in 2000 supplied the new and effective means by which film festivals and filmmakers now connect. Over the next decade advances in digital technology are likely to see the services offered by Withoutabox further evolve and the global circulation of films by independent filmmakers increase.

The Future of Film Festivals

One method by which film festival organisers overcome the challenges and demands of their environment is through the formation of a network. As Marijke de Valck explains, 'the film festival network is successful and capable of self-preservation precisely because it knows how to adapt to changing circumstances' (2007: 35-6). This self-preservation is largely due to the role of film festivals as 'sites of passage' and their intrinsic position as gatekeepers and distributors of obscure and/or non-mainstream cinema. Film festivals act as the primary node within the network and are therefore critical to its ability to function; 'without them, an entire network of practices, places, people, etc. would fall apart' (2007: 35-6).

Placing film festivals at the centre of a network reveals how film festival organisers are able to successfully gain and retain access to key resources required for operation. Yet it is becoming increasingly clear that the networked nature of film festivals may be more imaginary than real (Iordanova, 2009: 26; Fischer, 2009). The mutual dependency of film festivals, which allows them to move sharable commodities like film through this network, may be purely circumstantial and, as new forms of technology arise enabling filmmakers to have unfettered access to film festivals on a global scale, a more realistic, coordinated circulation of film materials may be observed.

The evolution of Withoutabox from a connection point to a distribution centre has ramifications for how future film festivals will operate. This is especially true of film festivals that rely upon unsolicited, independent film entries for programming. If film festivals' established position as sites of passage that filmmakers seeking exhibition must enter in order to improve the circulation potential of their work, the CreateSpace distribution service offered through Withoutabox constitutes an alternative and radically disruptive networking site.[14] In the context of changing submission models, film festivals focusing on independent work – such as the American-based Dances with Films, the French-based European Independent Film Festival, and even the renowned Sundance – may experience decline in the number of entries they receive as more filmmakers choose the self-distribution route.

Other festivals, which do not source significant numbers of independent films, will most likely continue to work with intermediaries and benefit from the technology these private companies are able to offer as part of their service. For example, as Internet bandwidth has increased, so too has the potential for film festivals to procure and exhibit films digitally. In fact, the Berlin International Film Festival recently announced that it would add a number of its titles onto the on-demand viewing platform Festival Scope (Mitchell 2011).

In closing, it is important to note that some film festivals no longer use the services offered by Withoutabox. It is unlikely that festival organisers feel directly threatened by the company; rather they have expressed concern regarding the impersonal interaction the intermediary facilitates. For example, organisers of the American-based Dark Carnival Film Festival insist that Withoutabox 'puts the filmmaker at the bottom of the foodchain' by propagating the idea that unsolicited film entries are a lucrative money making enterprise (Scared Movie Blog 2010). While it is true that the use of a streamlined application and submission process eliminates the human touch in handling unsolicited entries, the number of film festivals that are likely to stop using Withoutabox is extremely low. It is a novel intermediary that has enabled film festivals to finally operate in more efficient manner; returning to previous methods of operation would be counterproductive.

Works Cited

B-Side (2011) 'B-Side Uses the Power of Audience to Discover and Market Films', *B-Side* Website. On-line. Available HTTP: http://bside.com/about/ (8 May, 2011).

Blažević, Igor (2009) 'Raising Funds to Support a Human Rights Film Festival', in Tereza Porybná (ed.), *Setting up a Human Rights Film Festival: A Handbook for Festival Organizers Including Case Studies of Prominent Human Rights Events*. Prague: People in Need, 45-67.

Brooks, Brian (2006) 'Withoutabox Acquires Film Finders; Embarks on Relationship with Rightsline', *IndieWIRE*. On-line. Available HTTP: http://www.indiewire.com/article/withoutabox_acquires_film_finders_embarks_on_relationship_with_rightsline/ (4 April, 2011).

Business Wire (2001) 'Sundance Submission Go Paperless Via Without A Box, Inc.; Top Film Festival Among First to Use...', *Business Wire*. On-line. Available HTTP: http://www.allbusiness.com/media-telecommunications/movies-sound-recording/6171468-1.html (23 February, 2011).

Carter, Annie (2010) 'How Did Netflix Start', *eHow*. On-line. Available HTTP: http://www.ehow.com/facts_6757161_did-netflix-start_.html (8 May, 2011).

CreateSpace (2006) 'Withoutabox & CustomFlix Team Up to Offer Complete On-Demand DVD Fulfillment', *CreateSpace*. On-line. Available HTTP:https://www.createspace.com/Special/AboutUs/PR/20060320_WithoutABox.jsp (8 April 2011).

Davies, Laura (2006) 'Hitting Send', *Filmmaker*. On-line. Available HTTP: http://www.filmmakermagazine.com/issues/fall2006/line_items/hitting_send.php (10 May 2011).

de Valck, Marijke (2007) *Film Festivals: From European Geopolitics to Global Cinephilia*. Amsterdam: Amsterdam University Press.

Eventival (2011) 'History of Eventival', *Eventival Website*. On-line. Available HTTP: http://www.eventival.com/about-us/history/ (4 April 2011).

Fischer, Alex (2009) 'Conceptualising Basic Film Festival Operation: An Open System Paradigm', PhD Thesis. Gold Coast, QLD: Bond University, School of Humanities. On-line. Available HTTP: http://epublications.bond.edu.au/cgi/viewcontent.cgi?article=1076&context=theses> (23 June 2011).

Four Eyed Monsters (2006) 'Four Eyed Monsters Announce Self Distribution Through New Withoutabox, INC. Initiative', *Four Eyed Monsters Blog*. On-line. Available HTTP: http://foureyedmonsters.com/four-eyed-monsters-announce-self-distribution-through-new-withoutabox-inc-initiative/ (7 April 2011).

Graser, Marc and Anne Thompson (2008) 'IMDB, TiVo Move Closer to Distribution', *Variety*, 16 January. On-line. Available HTTP: http://www.variety.com/index.asp?layout=festivals&jump=story&id=2470&articleid=VR1117979206 (10 May 2011).

Hernandez, Eugene (2006) 'PARK CITY '06 BIZ DAILY: New Self-Distribution Initiative Unveiled; Park City Filmmakers Sign On for Pilot Program', *IndieWIRE*. On-line. Available HTTP: http://www.indiewire.com/article/park_city_06_biz_daily_new_self-distribution_initiative_unveiled_park_city_/ (23 February 2011).

Iordanova, Dina (2009) 'The Film Festival Circuit', in Dina Iordanova with Ragan Rhyne (eds) *Film Festival Yearbook 1: The Festival Circuit*. St Andrews: St Andrews Film Studies, 23-40.

Jones, Michael (2008) 'B-Side Opens Film Fest Submission Site', *Variety*. On-line. Available HTTP: http://www.variety.com/index.asp?layout=festivals&jump=story&id=2500&articleid=VR1117982230 (9 May 2011).

Mitchell, Wendy (2011) 'Festival Scope Adds Dozens of Berlinale Titles', *Screen Daily*. On-line. Available HTTP: http://www.screendaily.com/festivals/berlin/festival-scope-adds-dozens-of-berlinale-titles/5024318.article (4 April 2011).

Puget Sound Business Journal (2008) 'IMDB Acquiring Without A Box', *Puget Sound Business Journal*. On-line. Available HTTP: http://www.bizjournals.com/losangeles/stories/2008/01/14/daily40.html (4 April 2011).

Q (2007) 'David Straus, CEO-CoFounder, WITHOUT A BOX', *Future Q*. On-line. Available HTTP:http://www.futureq.net/bios/nov07_strauss.html (6 May 2011).

Scared Movie Blog (2010) 'Without a Box, Helpful or Harmful?' *Filmmakers Blog*. On-line. Available HTTP: http://sacredmovie.blogspot.com/2010/06/without-box-helpful-or-harmful.html (4 April 2011).

Slated (2011) 'Welcome', *Slated* Website. On-line. Available HTTP: http://slated.com/ (8 May 2011).

Straus, David and Joe Neulight (2007) 'Power to the Pixel 2007 Conference'. On-line. Available HTTP: http://www.youtube.com/watch?v=ZET_vEGDF2K (9 May 2011).

Swanson, Jen (2008) 'With or Withoutabox', *The Independent*. On-line. Available HTTP: http://www.aivf.org/08/11/or-withoutabox (6 May 2011).

Webber, Pauline (2005) 'Opening Quote: Ch 1, "Is it Here? Does it Look like Arriving?"', *History of the Sydney Film Festival*. Unpublished Master's Thesis, University of Technology Sydney.

Withoutabox (2011) 'Homepage', *Withoutabox*. On-line. Available HTTP: https://www.withoutabox.com (23 February 2011).

_____ 'Frequently Asked Questions: Which Festivals Use Withoutabox?' *Withoutabox*. On-line. Available HTTP: https://www.withoutabox.com/index.php?cmd=faq.filmmaker (23 February 2011).

Notes

1. Following the1968 shutdown of the Cannes Film Festival, organisers were required to restructure the event's programming streams so as to reflect changing social conditions.

2. This figure is taken from the Withoutabox homepage. Interestingly, this figure is well above the 1,200 to 1,900 film festival mark identified by Marijke de Valck (2007). It is possible that Withoutabox's number is more accurate given its direct access to film festivals; however, more research must still be conducted as to what actually constitutes a film festival as opposed to a film market or film series.

3. It is important to note that most film festivals charge an entry free for film submissions so the concept of a free upload via an intermediary only reduces the costs associated with physically mailing screeners to a film festival. There are, however, VOD suppliers such as IMDb that will allow rights holders to upload films for free and without an entry fee as part of a basic service package. This is commonly viewed as a strategy to build content and popularise a site.

4. It is interesting to note that frustration prompted the creation of Netflix, a no-late fee, postal DVD rental service. When the company's founder felt he had been unfairly charged a U.S.$40 fee from a video shop for an overdue rental he decided to change the movie rental scene..

5. The actual percentage paid to Withoutabox by film festivals varies according to the type of service an individual event desires. It is speculated that well-known film festivals such as Sundance do not pay a fee but instead contribute to Withoutabox's company profile though publicity at the event and name recognition.

6. CreateSpace is an on-line business specialising in providing authors and filmmakers with a means to self-publish and distribute their work via the Internet.

7. Further discussion about the loss-making nature of film festivals can be found in Igor Blažević's chapter discussing fund raising for human rights film festivals. (Blažević 2009).

8   Films such as *Four Eyed Monsters* (Arin Crumley and Susan Buice, U.S., 2006) were said to have received guidance from Withoutabox towards a successful distribution model for their independent film, including reliance on social networking sites such as Audience and on-demand software such as Demand Ticketing and Pay-to-Play Accounting (Four Eyed Monsters 2006).

9   The inception of this service occurred when DVD was the preferred format for exhibition and before streaming on-line became a practical means of distributing films.

10   Also announced pre-Sundance in 2008 was an acquisition deal between TiVo and Jaman (see Graser and Thompson 2008).

11   See the chapter by Silver, Cunningham and Ryan in this book for more information regarding the interconnectivity of these affiliated Amazon-owned companies.

12   Withoutabox does not pay filmmakers so the only means of developing an income stream using the intermediary is through cash prizes won at festivals or by utilising the distribution services it offers in collaboration with other Amazon-owned affiliate businesses.

13   It is interesting to note that the Hong Kong International Film Festival is a member of Withoutabox, while Tallinn Black Nights Film Festival and Ventana Sur are not.

14   A good example of a company that has major disruptive potential is Distrify, an on-line distribution service that presents what is considered a low cost model for independent filmmakers.

Spotlight on MUBI:
Two Interviews with Efe Cakarel,
Founder and CEO of MUBI

Paul Fileri and Ruby Cheung

In 2008, an entrepreneurial movie-lover named Efe Cakarel had an epiphany: he would create an on-line service powerful enough to provide a comprehensive catalogue of films that could be viewed anywhere in the world via the Internet. Within two years this idea had become reality and The Auteurs had established itself as one of the world's premier video-on-demand (VOD) services, with '260,000 registered global members in 177 countries' (Thompson 2010).

Sporting the motto 'Your on-line cinema. Anytime, anywhere', Cakarel's vision remains as dynamic and fluid as the virtual environment it inhabits. Evolutionary milestones include a re-branding of the company (The Auteurs is now MUBI)[55] and a partnership with Sony Computer Entertainment Europe that allows viewers to access films via the PlayStation 3 console.

To date, MUBI offers a film library totaling more than 20,000 titles (MUBI 2011) which are screened as Flash files. This technology requires viewers to have up-to-date software that can be downloaded from the MUBI website for free. Interestingly, iOS devices such the iPad and iPhone cannot support Flash files, so the company plans to switch to HTML5, the fifth revision of the hypertext mark-up language which forms the basis of Web content, which will provide new syntactical features such as enhanced video and audio elements and ultimately allow MUBI to deliver its content on a wider range of devices.

Though some users have blogged their concern that the site is transitioning away from its cinéphilic roots as a 'quality' film provider to something more mainstream, the overall focus of MUBI still seems to be dedicated to international and art house films with limited theatrical exposure. A handful of films on the site are free to watch, although the majority of content can only be viewed through a one-off purchasing scheme that sees customers paying U.S.$4.80 (£2.99) for premium and feature length films and U.S.$1.30 (£0.79) for short films. Interested patrons are also able to buy a subscription that allows unlimited viewing for U.S.$16.00 (£9.99).

The following interviews provide an entertaining and informative exploration of MUBI's rise to prominence. The first interview, conducted by Paul Fileri in 2009 for an article published in *Film Comment*, was undertaken so as to spotlight another new venture in on-line VOD distribution, one that displayed ambitions to employ social networking features and be commercially successful, while also hewing closely to auteur-centred and art house/specialty work and focusing on the international film festival scene. The second interview, conducted by Ruby Cheung, took place in May 2011 and offers the most relevant and up-to-date information about MUBI and its evolving ideas concerning the digital distribution of film to an international audience.

Beta Male: The Auteurs' Efe Cakarel Interviewed by Paul Fileri, January 2009[56]

Paul Fileri: *Roughly how many people have signed up as members in the social network?*

Efe Cakarel: We have 40,000 members on The Auteurs and 30,000 monthly active users of Movie Theater, our Facebook application.

PF:*How many films are now available for viewing by video stream? How many of these are unavailable elsewhere on DVD/video? Evidently, some are available in certain territories but not in others at this point.*

EC:We are adding new films every day. As of this moment, we have about 60 films available to stream in a variety of territories. As for what films we are showing that are unavailable on DVD, that is a difficult question to answer, as the distribution status of films in the large number of territories we exhibit in is varied. For example, we are showing Philippe Garrel's *Le Vent de le nuit* [*Night Wind*, France/Italy/U.S., 1999] in the U.S., where the film is currently unavailable on video, although it is available on DVD in France. We are proud to say we are showing a number of films in a number of territories where they were previously unavailable to watch, including Claire Denis's *Vers Mathilde* [France, 2005].

PF: As the founder, how did you bring together the group of seven that now runs the site? Were you already a friend or contact of each of these people or did you go out searching for collaborators?

EC: We believe in small teams. Small teams reduce mass – there is less formality, less fear; more flexibility, more change. We also embrace constraints – fewer resources means better use; less time means better time. With this philosophy in mind, I brought together our team one by one. Kamer, our creative director, was a friend of mine in Istanbul. He's the best designer I've ever met, so I flew him to Palo Alto. I found Gabe and Jatinder, our developers, through open source based on their contributions to the Ruby on Rails core. Gabe was in Minnesota and Jatinder was in Pune, India. I moved them both to Palo Alto. I found Daniel, our editor, through a friend at Zeitgeist Films who told me about 'this intern from NYU who was the best writer'. I met Halim, who's in charge of content, through a very close friend, and Melissa, who's in charge of user experience, is a friend of mine from Stanford that I wanted to bring in for more than a year since she's so good. We also worked with very talented individuals who contributed greatly to our effort: Chris with Flash Player, Adam and Matt for front end, and Alessandra in marketing. We hire very rarely; and we try to hire the best in the world in whatever they do. That's the way to build an organisation. Because A+ people hire A+ people, B people hire C people.

PF: Your on-line bio [studying electrical engineering and computer science at MIT, then obtaining an MBA at Stanford, working at Goldman Sachs and also becoming involved in the continuing negotiations between the EU and Turkey advising the Vice President of the European Parliament] *of course does not fit the typical picture of a 'cinephile', dedicating one's time to the appreciation and study of cinema. It's safe to say Silicon Valley/Palo Alto is not a historical Mecca of cinéphilia either. I'm wondering if you could talk a bit about your relationship with film and filmgoing over the years, both in personal and business terms? Have you always been something of a passionate filmgoer, a frequent attendee of festivals? Did you become interested only recently in the possibilities of on-line media distribution or have you been following the world of international film distribution for a longer time?*

EC: I have a confession to make: I only became a cinéphile after I founded The Auteurs. Yes, I loved *Chunking Express* [*Chung Hing* sam lam, Wong Kar-Wai, Hong Kong, 1994] and *Band of Outsiders* [*Bande à part*, Jean-Luc Godard, France, 1964], but I've never followed Cannes or Berlin, or passionately hunted down obscure films. I also knew absolutely nothing about film distribution. But I knew two things really well: 1) how to build Web applications, from concept to interface design to programming; and 2) how to do deals. Last May, I saw a very big market opportunity: nobody offered a good selection of movies, and the right user-experience, on-line. It was unbelievable; that story about me wanting to watch *In the Mood for Love* [*Fa yeung nin wa*, Wong Kar-Wai, Hong Kong/France, 2000] on-line in Tokyo is real. I would have paid anything for that, and nobody was offering it to me. I was especially excited to start this company because everybody that I talked to, especially from the industry, told me that I'd fail. They told me that not even Apple could get Criterion's films. They told me that I simply don't understand how this industry works, and that whoever had tried to build such a platform in the past had failed. But one thing I learned as an entrepreneur is that there are two reasons people tell you why something is going to fail: 1) it's been done before and 2) it's never been done before. It was a no brainer for me: big market opportunity, nobody was doing it right, everybody thinks it will fail. I founded the company at Coupa Café, a coffee shop in Palo Alto, where I worked for two months before Kamer joined me from Istanbul and we got an office, and I never looked back. After having taken shape in the latter half of 2007, the site launched in February 2008 with a media announcement at the Berlin Film Festival. Then there was the short Flip Video contest at Cannes, and the site has developed further over the course of the year, with The Notebook regularly producing content along with more streaming videos made available. Now in November, the Criterion partnership has been announced.

PF: What would you say have been the significant developmental milestones, so to speak, in the site's short history so far. Anything further to say about when you intend to take the site out of 'public beta'?

EC: You have pinpointed many of our milestones. After founding the company in May 2007, we built and deployed our Facebook application – the Movie Theater – in November 2007. Over the winter, we partnered with Celluloid Dreams not only to acquire content globally but also to create The Auteurs Europe to localise and launch The Auteurs in key European countries. We have a similar partnership with Costa Films, an early investor in The Auteurs, to launch The Auteurs Latin America in 2009 starting with Brazil. In February of 2008 we launched a private beta of The Auteurs during the Berlin Film Festival; and in Cannes 2008 we held an official short film competition called Cannes à la Flip in association with Short Film Corner, Festival de Cannes [www.theauteurs.com/competitions/1]. Over the summer, we partnered with the Criterion Collection in order to design and build their on-line cinematheque and have them programme a monthly on-line film festival at The Auteurs. At the end of the summer, we were proud to host all of the Telluride Film Festival's short films programmes on-line, as well as partner with Criterion in an on-line tribute to the Telluride Film Festival, featuring clips, trailers, and feature films from the festival's history, all viewable on-line for free at The Auteurs [www.theauteurs.com/festivals/20/tribute]. Finally, in November 2008 the Criterion cinematheque opened for the public, and likewise our closed beta has moved to an open beta, letting anybody – whether they are coming from the cinematheque or finding our site another way – access The Auteurs. The Auteurs will move out of beta and launch during Cannes Film Festival in May 2009.

PF: The site has been striking and distinctive partly for its clean, eye-catching professional design and well-planned media strategy – sponsored events at Berlin and Cannes – right from the beginning, as well as for the promising partnerships it has secured with some very prominent players with high reputations like Celluloid Dreams and Criterion: can you talk a bit about how these notable connections came about so early on for the project? Have specific individuals been key contacts/liaisons in helping The Auteurs as an initiative make this entry into the industry?

EC: When I started the company in May 2007, a week before the Cannes Film Festival, I wrote a personal letter to the director of the Festival saying that Cannes should embrace start-ups like The Auteurs in order to be at the cutting edge of film distribution. That miraculously got me accredited as a 'Film Buyer' with no money in the bank, no films ever bought, and nobody I knew in the industry. I remember being so nervous when I arrived at the Palais that I couldn't enter it for more than an hour. It's amazing that only a year later we were organising an official film competition there. Then I started meeting people. You know how Cannes is – I met a Romanian actress from that year's Camera d'Or winner who introduced me to the producer of that year's Palme d'Or winner over dinner who took me to the boat of a film financier for an after party where I met two very important distributors. The week went on like that. I met a lot of people but nobody was willing to give me their films. I quickly figured out that I had to meet the person whom I heard to be one of the most forward-looking, intelligent, and powerful in the industry: Hengameh Panahi, founder and Chairman of Celluloid Dreams. I knew Hengameh – who has access to the most significant producers and distributors in the world – could solve my content acquisition problem overnight. At the time, Hengameh did not answer my e-mails or return my calls, so I postponed my meeting her until the next film festival rolled around. After Cannes, I spent months writing to every important sales agent and distributor around the world explaining my vision and asking for their films. By Toronto, after four months, I did not have a single film. In Toronto, knowing that I simply had to meet Hengameh, I just strolled into her office, walked in the door, and demanded that I see her. They kindly walked me out of the door, but took my business card. After what seemed like the longest 18 hours, Hengameh called me and said I have 15 minutes. I said I need only 10, and went to her office to meet her. The rest is history. Hengameh immediately got what we are trying to do, and realised the vision is so fresh and strong; I was in Paris three weeks after, working and brainstorming with her. Then we met Tom Luddy, director of the Telluride Film Festival, who loved the vision and has been our informal advisor ever since. He introduced us to Dieter Kosslick, director of Berlinale, who initiated partnership discussions between us and Berlinale. In Berlin, I was introduced to Peter Becker, president of Criterion, by Eduardo Costantini, who was our investor and guardian angel. A few weeks later, I was in New York meeting Peter Becker and Jonathan Turrell, CEO of Criterion. I went there to license a few films. I walked out with a multi-year partnership where we design and build Criterion's website and power it going forward, Criterion curating a monthly festival on The Auteurs, and Criterion taking an equity stake. Since then Peter and Jonathan have been my mentors and have tremendously helped me bring The Auteurs to where it is now.

PF: *Who do you see as the site's intended audience in on-line English-language film culture versus the still developing audience it's attracted at this stage?*

EC: Those who are interested in the journalistic film coverage don't necessarily overlap with those attracted to the social networking/forums and those attracted to the on-line video content. Our goal is simply to become an on-line destination point for film lovers – anybody who loves film. The Auteurs is a place for cinéphiles as well as those just beginning to become interested in film. From our private beta to the early days of our public beta, the community we have attracted is varied but all have one thing in common: an ardent passion for film. We hope in the future to attract those who haven't yet found their passion but are willing to try. We are providing a varied experience: come to watch, come to read, come to discuss, come to discover. We have built a social network platform that spreads interest in and awareness of smaller films to a wider audience; and our platform gives our audiences a wide range of activities that can cater to different levels of interests and involvement in film, and encourage them to expand both. Those who come to talk about their favorite movies might read about something new or intriguing in our Notebook, or take a chance on one of the many films our site offers to watch for free. The ideal community would be a comprehensively active one: people who come to do everything: they watch, they discuss, they read, they write, they spread the word.

PF: What's your thinking behind the prominent framing of the site's subject as 'auteurs' and 'auteur-driven cinema', which of course places the emphasis on one particular facet of world cinema, the cinemas of the world as a whole, in all its genres and nationalities? For instance, is it the particular creativity, innovation, status/prestige of 'auteur cinema' as a niche identified with film festivals that is framed as the centre of the project?

EC: We have framed our site under The Auteurs moniker not because we are strict auteurists or wish to only view cinema from this angle, but because it represents our dedication to cinematic artistry. We want to show only distinctive, visionary films, whether their inspiration comes from the single mind of a director, or from a star, subject, country, culture, or any other deciding factor. Our niche is in using on-line distribution as a means to show these distinctive films, many of which, like those of Philippe Garrel, are tremendous works of cinematic art but which have trouble finding distribution in the current conservative climate. The library has been expanding, especially with Criterion now onboard.

PF: In what directions do you see or hope to have the offerings grow? What has the challenge been like to negotiate for Internet distribution rights with other distribution companies or the filmmakers themselves? Will you be proceeding by finding other well-established operations with which to partner, or will The Auteurs act as a distributor directly?

EC: We want our library to grow, of course, but we have always conceived The Auteurs as being a curated selection of cinema. I'm pleased to announce that just this week, one of the most respected programmers in the world, Marie-Pierre Duhamel Muller, who was in the selection committee for this year's Venice Film Festival, joined The Auteurs as a programmer to help us select the most significant films ever produced. The last thing we want is to befuddle those who are coming to the site and are open to trying these films with an overwhelming, video store like barrage of films. We are going to carefully choose great films from those that played at film festivals, those that have already been released, and those that have never been released – we are dedicated to showcasing the best of cinema, wherever we can find it, and make it available to whomever we can. The goal is not only to acquire these films, but then to be able to show them to as many audiences around the world as possible. A principle challenge has simply been to convince rights holders that Internet distribution is a viable business. This is neither theatrical distribution nor video distribution; the Internet, as a social platform, makes the availability of media work in a far different way than those arms of traditional distribution. That making films available on-line is as much a viral way of marketing films as it is a source of tremendous income is something that few rights holders have been far-seeing enough to recognise. We are overjoyed that two of the very best film companies in the world – the Criterion Collection and Celluloid Dreams – share our vision for using the Internet as a way to make films accessible to audiences in ways they never have been in the past. For the future, we conceive The Auteurs as an open platform with a broad set of partnerships globally. The vision is no less than to become a global cultural hub for cinema. Just to give you an idea about what we are up to, we are in partnership discussions with an advertising agency in UK, a publishing house in Italy, a consortium of distributors in Spain, and a film-financing company in Japan.

PF: *What shapes the editorial vision behind The Notebook? Is it largely an autonomous entity, set free to cover the film festival scene, DVD* *releases and film culture in general with an independent critical eye, from many writers' perspectives? What kind of coverage do you want to see? Do you see any publishing ventures as models or on-line outfits as ones that share a similar vision about film criticism and debate? What is the relationship between this critical project and the film library where content has to be promoted?*

EC: The Notebook is our on-line journal that has grown spontaneously through outreach to Internet-based contributors. It operates autonomously, and focuses on one of the prime goals of The Auteurs project – to explore and discover international cinema. We have selected a group of writers not through traditional sources but through on-line networks of film criticism – blogs, magazines, review sites, etc. – mirroring not just the way The Auteurs as a company was formed, but also emblemising the mission of the company to unite disparate film viewers around the world. For the most part, we give our writers independence to find their own subjects, be it reviewing, festival coverage, film theory, in-depth criticism, or image essays. The key was to find a talented and varied set of voices and give them a space to explore film in their own way. We hope to expand our criticism towards a more multi-media based approach: more images, more video, video essays, excerpts from films, etc. The subject of inquiry will always remain the same: cinema new and old, obvious and obscure – helping new readers discover these works and veteran readers push deeper into film. Because The Notebook is running in tandem with The Auteurs as a broader conception of an on-line movie social network, it has no exact equivalent on-line, but there are a great many on-line publications which have a quality of criticism that we hold up as ideal – for examples Senses of Cinema, Reverse Shot and Rouge, as well as dozens of smaller, more personal websites. Perhaps the closest example of an ideal we are pursuing is Girish Shambu's blog, which unites astute critical discussion of film with a large and active community of readers. Our desire is for the most part to keep The Notebook as a critical publication and our library separate. If we write on films in our library, it is solely from a critical standpoint and not a PR move.

MUBI Reboot: Efe Cakarel Interivewed by Ruby Cheung (May 2011)

Ruby Cheung: Why did the company change name from the original 'The Auteurs' to become the present 'MUBI'?

Efe Cakarel: The name change came at a point in time where our audience was greatly expanding beyond the original English and French language core we had at the beginning. We were showing more films in more countries and needed a name that was not burdened by being difficult to spell or say for the majority of the world. Instead of picking something invested with meaning, we decided on something without meaning that we could define through our unique platform.

RC: What is the relationship of MUBI with the other, more conventional distribution channels (such as theatrical, DVD, TV)? What is your view on the current debates on shortening the windows of distribution?

EC: Our relationship is partially symbiotic – it is often the rights holders who handle a film's theatrical or home video release that we are dealing with to secure VOD [video-on-demand] rights. VOD does not cannibalise theatrical, it is a supplemental revenue stream for a film title. For us, the debate about distribution windows is irrelevant; we'd love to show a film on MUBI the day it comes out in theatres, but we're also happy showing it when it hits traditional home video distribution lines later on. The industry is worried about competing revenue streams; they should be more concerned with maximising the ones that exist.

RC: How does MUBI differentiate itself and its services from that of other film distribution channels, in particular, new media channels?

EC: To be brief, in several ways: (1) curated content of independent, international and classic cinema. We select our titles one by one, we're about quality not quantity; we're not a video store; (2) we are a global platform – we are currently showing hundreds of films in every country in the world; and finally, (3) we unite this global audience and our curated library through a social network that helps film lovers around the world find films they love and the people who love them, investing the social aspect back into film watching.

RC: What criteria do you have in selecting films to be acquired and streamed to your audience?

EC: It's quite simple: we want to show the best films. This may mean a mainstream film or something that was never distributed in a country; it may mean a festival hit or a recent DVD release. We want to fill our library with a breadth of great cinema, emphasising both the known and unknown, the established and emerging, the distributed and undistributed.

RC: Besides the Criterion Collection, where do you find new titles to acquire? I understand that you have a presence at some of the biggest film festivals. Are these your main product sources?

EC: We acquire titles from a wide range of partners, from international sales agents to local distributors to the filmmakers or producers themselves.

RC: How do you curate film programmes? For instance, do you go by territories or purely by titles? Any other criteria?

EC: It depends on the film programme. Obviously it starts with the films, whether we are doing a director retrospective or a film festival partnership. But you are correct that territorial availability plays a part as well, as we can't show a programme of one available film in a country! Like acquisitions, one criterion is also the quality of the digital master – we won't show a film whose video quality is not up to our standards.

RC: How many subscribers does MUBI have?

EC: Confidential information.[57]

RC: Can we say that MUBI is developing a specific kind of audience and viewing experience, complete with interactive social networking platforms embedded in MUBI's website? How do you see your audience as different from audiences of conventional exhibition venues and/or home entertainment markets?

EC: Yes, I would say your first statement is accurate. To attend to your second statement, most 'audiences' as you call them are really consumers making buying decisions from a market. We want to avoid this connotation and atmosphere: our audience is a community, a group of people spread around the world but united by a love of film, a love of watching it, discussing it and sharing it.

RC: Can you tell us more about 'The Garage' and how it is meant to develop independent production projects as well as corresponding audiences?

EC: The Garage is a section of the site focusing on grassroots, community-based filmmaking. It's for both new, independent filmmakers, as well as audiences curious about the process of the indie scene.

RC: Our book features case studies of Jaman and Withoutabox, among others, and discusses a variety of new film festivals that are taking place on-line. How does MUBI interact with these and other streaming services, festival suppliers and on-line festivals?

EC: I'm afraid this question is too general to answer, but I can say that we don't deal with Jaman or Withoutabox.

RC: I understand MUBI is facilitating 'Project: New Cinéphilia' at the Edinburgh International Film Festival (EIFF) in 2011 and that this symposium aligns itself perfectly with EIFF's new focus as an 'intelligent' film festival. What I'm particularly curious about are the predicted/ encouraged outcomes of this project. For example, from my point of view, such an on-line event could revitalise of the role of the film critic at film festivals. Could you elaborate? Perhaps discussing your goal for this project and the role of MUBI in connecting EIFF to cinéphiles/critics/ writers the world over...

EC: One of the things that appealed to us when the Festival approached us with this project was the organisers' insistence that we would not be rehashing issues that have been talked to death over the past several years now. Frankly, there have been too many panels at too many festivals addressing 'the crisis in film criticism' and so on, panels that focus on the fate of old models and raise questions as to which new models will replace them. We're past that point now. Answers to those questions have long since begun to present themselves: print is going electronic, the lines between professional and amateur film critics carry on blurring – and the discourse is livelier and more robust than ever.

Project: New Cinéphilia begins, then, at the point at which so many other assessments have ended. You ask about what outcomes we might expect to see. That's precisely what excites us about getting involved with this project: We don't know. The organisers – Damon Smith, in particular – have brought together some very sharp folks who've had a hand in developing this 'New Cinephilia'. We're glad to help facilitate the exchange of ideas and look forward to taking part in the discussion.

Note

Alex Fischer edited and introduced these interviews for publication in the context of this book.

Works Cited

Fileri, Paul (2009) 'Site Specifics: The Auteurs', *Film Comment*, January-February.

Keating, Barry (2010) 'Meet the Man Behind MUBI, Efe Cakarel', *Play Station Blog*. On-line. Available HTTP: http://blog.eu.playstation.com/2010/06/11/meet-the-man-behind-MUBI-efe-cakarel/ (20 June 2011).

MUBI (2011) 'Films'. MUBI Website. On-line. Available HTTP: http://MUBI.com/films (20 June 2011).

Thompson, Anne (2010) 'The Auteurs Is Now MUBI', *Thompson on Hollywood: Digital Future*. On-line. Available HTTP: http://blogs.indiewire.com/thompsononhollywood/2010/05/13/the_auteurs_is_now_MUBI/ (22 June 2011).

Notes

[1]   The name MUBI was apparently inspired by the mispronunciation of the word 'movie' by non-English speakers (Thompson 2010).

[2]   First published as 'Site Specifics: The Auteurs', *Film Comment*, January-February 2009. Reprinted with permission.

[3]   As indicated above, in 2010 the site had '260,000 registered global members in 177 countries' (Thompson 2010).

'What Do You Do with What You See?' Patterns and Uses of Cinéphilia, Then and Now

Ben Slater

The term 'cinéphile' did not properly enter my consciousness for a long time. Without a name, it was merely a club that we belonged to, we film-lovers, an un-constituted organisation that required a certain intensity of passion and knowledge of its members. Everywhere around us were people who enjoyed films, who to larger or lesser degrees were familiar with stars, directors, new releases, classics, blockbusters, award nominations and other basic touchstones – a general knowledge of film if you will – but it took a special type of person to be a film-lover. We had moved beyond the regular bandwidth of filmic awareness. The symptoms were: a deep adoration for the work of certain directors (auteurism still abounds!), a quasi-encyclopaedic memory for titles seen and unseen, and an often overwhelming enthusiasm for the cinematic experience that 'civilians' couldn't really relate to.

'Film Buff' was the old-fashioned, less-flattering term for what I thought I was. 'Buffery' is akin to being a collector or a hobbyist; the Film Buff memorises names and dates, he (almost invariably a he) writes down all he sees on index cards and files them away. The Buff codifies and catalogues cinema, and although there's a strong strand of Buffery in the DNA of every film-lover, Buffs are perfectly content to be watchers; they rarely have an interest in entering the world of cinema, either as a participant in the process of film-making or as a critic, professional or otherwise. The true Film Buff, I suspect, could just as happily be gathering information about cars, birds or trains – film just happens, almost arbitrarily, to be the object of their neurotic desire. They know what they like – Hollywood musicals of the Thirties, say, or Gialli of the Seventies – but they are woefully inarticulate about the exact qualities of these films, quite content to revisit them endlessly and complete their knowledge. The film-lover, on the other hand, is driven to discuss, to analyse, to penetrate film, in an attempt to understand this medium that has gripped them so thoroughly.

It has been noted many times before that a peculiar characteristic of the film-lover is their desire to speak of film, to read about film, to study the form and the history, and then begin to make statements of their own. More than that, though, the film-lover needs to be deeply engaged with the form of cinema itself: contemplating its mysteries, trying to divine what this thing actually is and what it's capable of. It may be closer to religion than anything else. It certainly requires faith, and a place of worship.

The so-called 'first generation' of film-lovers came of age in the church-like hush of repertory cinemas, cinémathèques and film clubs. The self-styled 'Man of Cinema', and arguably one of the all-time great cinéphiles, Pierre Rissient told me that his interest began during screenings run by the teachers at his school; he would later graduate to the Cinémathèque Français and the programming of Henri Langlois. Simultaneously, around the major capitals of the world similarly passionate young people were gathering in smoky auditoria to experience film from the first half-century of cinema's history. What marked them out was a new seriousness in their approach to the medium. As these long unseen treasures unspooled there was no question of cinema as mere entertainment. It contained vast pleasures to be sure, but it now had to be seen as an art form.

My interest in and knowledge of film were born in a different time and through different channels. As a child, growing up in England in the Eighties, my guides were the unseen and unknown film-buyers for BBC, Channel Four and even ITV with its late night 'regional variations'. By my early teens I was hooked on films and armed with a tool to catch them all – a VHS recorder. This flourishing of interest coincided with what we could call a 'golden age' in British television's broadcasting of film. Each channel had its own 'seasons', sometimes concentrated over a few weeks, others spanning an entire year. It seems unthinkable now, but in the mid- to late-80s there was a trend for films to be 'introduced' on TV with contextual information provided by some authority. This was most famously the case with a series on BBC2 called Film Club, where I witnessed, among others, G. Cabrera Infante fondly précis Budd Boetticher's *The Rise and Fall of Legs Diamond* (U.S., 1960) and Sam Fuller's *House of Bamboo* (U.S., 1955) – my first time seeing a letter-boxed film on TV – and Bernardo Bertolucci present a revelatory double-bill of *À bout de souffle* (*Breathless*, France, Jean-Luc Godard, 1960) and *Gun Crazy* (U.S., Joseph H. Lewis, 1950).

It's all about time and place. A decade later and television had become a filmic dead zone, all thoughtful seasons and strands gone, no context available and, worse still, an allergy for films with subtitles. DVDs supplanted VHS, but what was gained in quality, rewindability, and informational 'extras' was lost in accessibility and affordability. You had to be rich (older and employed) to build a collection of discs. Each generation of cinéphiles needs to feel that film is their discovery, not that they are walking through a museum of pre-curated artefacts. Where were the new entry-points, the spaces where the precocious film-lover could stumble upon cinema?

Alexis Tioseco was a cinéphile whose interest and passion for film was inspired by and within the age of the Internet. As a teenager in Canada he'd been exposed to film on VHS via his mother's love of classic Hollywood and his brother's typically 'older brother' move of renting notorious 'cult' films such as *A Clockwork Orange* (UK/U.S., Stanley Kubrick, 1971). As Alexis stated many times, the 'turning point' would come much later and, in a way, would strike that much deeper. My epiphany upon watching *The Lady From Shanghai* (U.S., Orson Welles, 1947) at age 10 was that Orson Welles the actor was also Orson Welles the director, but the consequent understanding of what he brought to both roles seems trivial and well-rehearsed when compared to Alexis' experience of watching Lav Diaz's *Batang West Side* (Philippines/U.S., 2001) at age 20. I was travelling down an old road, whereas Alexis was heading somewhere new. Alexis had entered the cinema a 'movie fan', but when the film was complete, some five hours later, he had changed. Declaring it an 'unequivocal masterpiece', he wrote those words in a review for a (now defunct) website, Indiefilipino. It might seem like standard student-level hyperbole, but the position that Alexis had taken was a surprise even to him. Diaz's film galvanised him into a level of serious engagement with cinema (generally, but Filipino film in particular) that he'd never come close to before. That was just the beginning.

The Internet was Alexis' platform of expression and it was also his resource. He learnt more about cinema there, although he was also a prolific collector of film books and was steadily building a library of such tomes. The Web was a channel for connection with other cinéphiles (he joined and contributed to various mailing lists and closely studied many film blogs) and later on it was also a site for illicit distribution. Time and place again. Alexis was based in Manila, so art house films were few and far between on the big screen and television was semi-redundant, but he did have the pirates – and their Southeast Asian ubiquity had led to specialisation and a real market for 'non-mainstream' product. Alexis marvelled that in Manila he was able to buy DVD copies of Chris Marker's *Sans Soleil* (France, 1983) for a few pesos, and he always half-joked that he should buy them in bulk to give away as presents. By then the piracy of physical goods was rapidly becoming obsolete and digital circulation had taken its place.

The last time I saw Alexis, he had become a proud member of a notorious private network that exchanged a vast library of (again, 'non-mainstream') cinema via Bit Torrent, the ingenious method of Internet file-sharing that has proved consistently impossible to eradicate. Just as with pirate discs, for the cinéphile the ethics of such transactions are fairly straightforward: I need to see this material and the alternative options are very expensive, time-consuming or non-existent. Obviously a filmmaker wants to be rewarded for their work, but isn't it more important that this work is seen in the first place? In this way the Internet becomes the ideal 'free university' for cinéphiles. The aforementioned site, nicknamed Black Crow by the critic Quintín in an article in *Film Comment* (Quintín 2009), is a 'darknet' community (less sinister than it sounds), open only to recommended members and governed by strict rules about uploading and downloading. Intimidating for many, these add a moral imperative to participate in the circulation of films, not just to 'acquire' images, but to help others in their acquisition. Discussions on the site are often technical – file sizes and compression formats, and there is also a move to create subtitles for films never before released in English. It is a service for the dedicated, armchair cinéphile, and I'm sure there are other similar communities out there, with their own specialist areas of interest.

So now we've reached a stage where almost the entire history of cinema is on tap for those patient and persistent enough to master the networks. There are still limits (and films that slipped through the cracks, which we need as well) and there's also the major caveat that we're watching this history on a computer screen, or at best a large television. This vast library of content is folded into an ever-evolving archive of information, history and opinion on the Web, which may be partial, incomplete and frequently wrong, but is robust enough to stop any emerging film-lover from getting completely lost in the funhouse.

As a result the new cinéphile has to read more, talk to more people, refer backwards to older generations of film-lovers, who have also gone on-line and are available for discussion, debate and information via blogs and, more recently, Twitter. A spirit of generosity infuses these ad hoc cinéphile communities. On-line I've had discussions with a number of kindred spirits in their mid-20s whose knowledge and experience of cinema compared to mine at that age is truly staggering. They are so much more self-aware of their identity as cinéphiles than 'my generation' and that comes directly from a sense of interconnectedness with so many others writing, watching, showing and even making films. And that's all very well, but then there's a more important question – what do you do with all that you know and see?

Alexis' cinéphilia had a purpose and a mission and in the flattened space of the Internet, where it often felt like everyone was watching and talking about the same (new and old) films, he had something unique to offer. If everything has gone global, then dig deeper around the place where you stand – go local. Real local knowledge and an understanding of context, culture and the personalities involved, has become a more precious currency than the films themselves.

Alexis' championing of Lav Diaz had emerged not just out of the intense encounter with a powerful film, but out of a passionate advocacy generated from the lack he perceived in Filipino film culture for discussion or even serious appreciation of such films. His enthusiasm translated into a form of 'cultural work'. He spread the news about independent cinema at home and almost simultaneously, thanks to the Internet, abroad. His website Criticine became a unique resource for those wishing to learn about the new cinema of Southeast Asia. And he wasn't some one-man-band film promotion board; in fact Alexis was fiercely critical of the local industry and even his friends' films on occasion. Yet, at the same time, he needed to know about film history and criticism in a far broader context. Alexis' personality and curiosity made it relatively easy for him to make connections, be they on-line or in person (at conferences and film festivals, frequently the physical embodiment of the on-line network), and the intensity of his interest was matched by the speed of the technology.

It all happened quickly. And it's possible now, looking at his writing on-line – from early, informal blogs about films he'd just seen, to later articles for leading international publications – to trace Alexis' evolution as a watcher and a critic. In 2003 he's grooving about Scarlett Johansson's 'stoic, expressionless face' in *Lost in Translation* (U.S./Japan, Sofia Coppola, 2003) on his Livejournal blog. Then, in 2005, he's at *Senses of Cinema*.com saying that *Ruang rak noi nid mahasan* (*Last Life in the Universe*, Thailand/Japan, Pen-Ek Ratanaruang, 2003) is a much better film, while still admiring *Eternal Sunshine of the Spotless Mind* (U.S., Michel Gondry, 2004) and *Before Sunset* (U.S., Richard Linklater, 2004). By 2007, though, when selecting his Top Five for the year for the UK's *Sight & Sound* magazine, the American films are politically radical (Travis Wilkerson and John Gianvito), and he includes two young Filipino directors, Raya Martin and Sherad Anthony Sanchez, along with a quote from Jean-Marie Straub. I don't mean to present him as becoming ultra-serious – in fact he retained a keen appreciation for the pleasures of a flashy, new film – but he knew that there was absolutely no point at all in spending time writing about those things. Instead, his awareness of his role as a spokesperson for unknown cinema increased. Space was limited, so he had to be strategic.

'It's not enough to like a film, you have to like it for the right reasons' is a quote attributed to the aforementioned Pierre Rissient and printed on the back of a t-shirt distributed during the 2007 Telluride Film Festival. What he meant by that, as I understand it, is that there are those who flock to a film, extolling its brilliance, but they are not truly appreciative, they don't really 'get it'. Similarly, there may be those film-lovers who are attracted by certain elements of cinema, by the glamour, the power of images, narratives or stars, but who don't 'get' the deeper cultural value of cinema, or the endless challenge of the possibility of cinema. Alexis proved that in an era where all cinema is available, it's not enough to simply be a cinéphile – you have to love film for the right reasons. And he did.

Note: Alexis Tioseco, editor of the on-line magazine Criticine and his partner, the Slovenian film writer and programmer Nika Bohinc, were killed in their Manila home on 1 September 2009. They are greatly missed.

Works Cited

Quintín (2009) 'Black Crow Blues', *Film Comment*, 45, 4, July/August, 36-7.

RESOURCES

Appendix 1

Timeline – On-line Distribution of Feature Films

Stuart Cunningham and Jon Silver

Year	Milestone
1994	U.S.: First VOD trials (cable) in New York offer Paramount and New Line movies PPV.
1997	U.S.: **Netflix** offers an on-line movie rental service delivering DVDs to the home.
	U.S.: **Zoei Films** runs first on-line film festival.
1998	U.S.: **BitScreen** provides on-line lab for experimental filmmakers from July 1998.
1999	U.S.: **Sightsound** sells first movie on Internet as PPV – *Pi* (Darren Aronofsky, U.S., 1998).
	U.S.: **CinemaNow** launches first commercial on-line movie download service.
	Korea: **Cinero** launches a VOD site.
	US: **MovieFlix** launches movie download service.
2000	U.S.: Sightsound presents the first made-for-the-Internet movie *Quantum Project*.
	U.S.: Steven Spielberg's **Pop** launches but fails within 5 months.
	Germany: **Afilmcinado** offers local indie films on-line.
	China: **e-Donkey** P2P file sharing site launches in China facilitating on-line piracy.

2001	France: 34 producers collaborate to form **UniverseCine** VOD for independent films.
	U.S.: **Withoutabox** begins operation.
	Netherlands: Rotterdam International Film Festival launches on-line short film festival **Exploding Cinema**.
	U.S.: **Sundance Online** Film Festival launches.
	U.S.: **Intertainer** launches national VOD movie service in US.
	Korea: **Cinero** offers films in high definition.
2002	U.S.: **CinemaNow** becomes the first VOD website to offer major Hollywood studio content.
	U.S.: Five Hollywood studios launch **Movielink**, an on-line rental download service in response to the threat of piracy.
	U.S.: Disney launches **Moviebeam** – a VOD service delivering movies via a set top box.
	Sweden: **SF Anytime** – VOD film service launches and expands into Scandinavia.
	Netherlands: P2P platform **Kazaa** legally distributes Bollywood film *Supari* (Padam Kumar, India, 2002) On-line as a U.S.$2.99 rental.
2003	U.S.: **CinemaNow** movie library becomes available on- line in Japan via ADSL, fibre to the home (FTTH) broadband and set-top boxes (via NTT-Data).
	China: **BitTorrent China** (BT China) launches on-line with overseas films and TV.
	UK: **LoveFilm** goes on-line.
	Germany: **Videoload** goes on-line as Deutche Telekom's VOD division.

2004	U.S.: **CinemaNow** becomes the first major VOD site to sell movies as download-to-own.
	Italy: **Rosso Alice** offers films as VOD.
2005	China: **Tudou, Joy** and 56 sites launched.
	India: **Eros** studio launches on-line store.
	France: Five film VOD platforms launch: **24/24, CanalPlay, M6 Video, TF1** and **TPS**.
	Denmark: **Movieurope** (FIDD - Filmmakers Independent Digital Distribution) founded.
2006	U.S.: Apple **iTunes** begins offering movies and TV shows as downloads to rent or buy.
	U.S.: Amazon launches VOD service **Amazon Unbox** (merged with Withoutabox after its aqusition).
	U.S.: Apple iTunes releases the low budget indie film *Purple Violets* (Ed Burns, U.S., 2007) as the first direct-to-VOD release.
	India: NRI site **Saavn** launches in New York offering Bollywood movies on-line.
	U.S.: On-line DVD rental store **Netflix** introduces 'Watch Instantly' streaming movies.
	Australia: **BigPondMovies** launches on-line distribution service.
	Italy: **FilmIsNow** launches on-line distribution service.
	France: **Glowria** launches VOD service.
	Germany: **Maxdome** launches VOD service.
	Sweden: **Stockholm Film Festival** goes on-line.
	India: **Rajshri** film studio launches movies-on-demand.
	China: **Quacor** becomes the first legal film download site in China; it offers free movies.

2007	Spain: **Filmotech** offers 'the best of Spanish cinema' on-line as DTO and VOD.
2008	US: Nielsen Survey reveals movie streaming accounts for only 1% of on-line streaming.
	U.S.: **The Auteurs** started this year.
	U.S.: **Hulu** established as a joint venture between NBC-Universal and Fox.
	China: **Voole** becomes China's fourth licensed provider (joining **Joy**, **51tv** and **Netandtv**) and makes a deal to distribute Hollywood movies on-line in China. Chinese government shuts down all other VOD sites.
	Abu Dhabi: **Getmo**, the first Middle Eastern start-up offering movies and music downloads, fails to take-off.
	China: **Voole** makes a deal to distribute Hollywood studio content in China.
	India: Reliance establishes **BigFlix** On-line.
	Korea: **Cine21i** reaches agreement with 17 Korean Webhard (on-line data storage) sites to identify illegal films in their catalogues and seek payment from users at the point of consumption and provide a revenue sharing service between Webhards and legitimate content owners.
	U.S.: **YouTube** begins migration to long form content and adds High Definition widescreen.
2009	China: **Joy** and 80 copyright owners sue **Tudou** for copyright infringement.
	Japan: Five Major studios (Toho, Toei, Shochiku, Nikkatsu and Kadokawa) form a joint venture to launch **MaruMaru** Eiga – a PPV movie channel screening classic Japanese films over the acTVila VOD service.
	China: Government closes 162 unlicensed on-line video sites.
	Europe: 29 standalone on-line movie services close down in 2009.

2010	U.S.: **Hulu** launches a subscription service **Hulu Plus** for $10 per month and then reduces the price to U.S.$7.99 per month but projects total revenues in 2010 of U.S.$240 million (approximately 85% of which is television content).
	U.S.: **YouTube** places ads on illegally uploaded films passing revenues to rights-holders.
	AfricaFilms launches first legal movie download site on the continent.
	U.S.: **The Auteurs**, a high profile indie on-line distribution site which launched in 2008, is re-branded as **MUBI**.
	U.S.: **Netflix** establishes a $7.99 monthly subscription service for unlimited movie and TV downloads.
	U.S.: **iTunes** now offers movies via on-line distribution in U.S., Canada, Australia, New Zealand, France, Germany and Japan.
	U.S.: **Amazon Studios** launches providing independent producers and writers with an on-line script and film upload service and a first-look deal with Warner Brothers.
	China: **Youku** launches premium subscription service streaming Warners movie *Inception* (Christopher Nolan, U.S., 2010) for RMB 5 (US$0.75).
	China: **Tudou** licenses Warner Brothers movie *Twilight* (Catherine Hardwicke, U.S., 2008) to stream on its platform.
	India: **Reliance Big Entertainment** expands cross-platform VOD offerings on on-line distribution, IPTV, DTH with new acquisition DigiCable.
	India: **Eros Entertainment** plans to create a Hulu-style global streaming platform for Bollywood movies.

early 2011	U.S.: **Warner** launches *The Dark Knight* (Christopher Nolan, U.S., 2008) and *Inception* as iPad apps bypassing iTunes to offer rentals and DTO.
	Amazon acquires **LoveFilm**
	Netflix licenses its first original on-line distribution programming – a drama series starring Kevin Spacey titled *House of Cards* (David Fincher, U.S., 2011).
	YouTube becomes a content provider acquiring indie studio Next to facilitate creation of original programmes.
	Facebook begins offering on-line movie rentals with Warner Brothers' *The Dark Knight.*
	Hulu's future uncertain as expiry of its three-year term looms and its owners disagree over core business model and decide to sell it.

Appendix 2

A Selection of (Mostly Legal) VOD and On-Line Content Providers

Stuart Cunningham and Jon Silver

Except where otherwise indicated, all websites were functional in December 2010; similarly, December 2010 was the reference point in the instances where we have listed the site as 'defunct'. However, given the volatile and transitory nature of the Web, we make no guarantees that they will all still be operational by the time you read this book.

GEOGRAPHIC AREA	COUNTRY	WEBSITE
World	For global audiences	Internet Archive, Jaman, MUBI, YouTube, Zattoo.
Europe	For pan-European audiences	Brightwide, EuroCinema, Europa Film Treasures, FilmIsNow, LetMeWatchThis, MK2VoD, Movieurope (owned by FIDD), MUBI (formerly The Auteurs), Sony PSN movies on demand, Veamer, Universcine (French but expanding to Belgium, Finland, Germany, Ireland, Switzerland, Spain), XBox 360 Live Marketplace, Zune Movies on Demand.
	Austria	Filmladen.

	France	24/24 Video Orange, Arte VOD, CanalPlay, CinemaNow, Club Video (SFR), EuropaFilmTreasures, FNAC, Glowria, iTunes, M6 Video, MK2VoD, MovieFlix, Neuf VOD, TF1 Vision, TPS VOD, Universcine, VideoFutur, Virgin Mega.
	Benelux	Casema, CinemaNow, Direct Movie, Free Record Shop, Global Cinema, Keeno, MovieFlix, MoviePlay 2, Planet, Ster Videoteek, TVOPJEPC, Winkelwijs, Zeeland Net.
	Germany	Arcor, iTunes, Maxdome, One4Movie, iTunes, In2Movies, CinemaNow, MovieFlix, Videobuster, Videoload (T-Online).
	Hungary	Filmklik, Origo Teka.
	Italy	CinemaNow, Fastweb, FilmIsNow, MovieFlix, Rosso Alice.
	Spain	Carrefour, CinemaNow, Filmotech, Imagenio Videoclub (Telefonica), MovieFlix, MXP Digital, Pixbox, Yodecidio (Filmax).
	Sweden, Norway, Denmark, Finland	FIDD/Movieurope (Denmark), Film2Home, Headweb, LoveFilm, Stockholm Film Festival On-Demand, Viasatondemand, Voddler.

	UK/Ireland	4OD, AOL, Babelgum, BBC iPlayer (some films), Blinkbox, Bollywood TV, BT Vision, Channel Films, Cinebox on MovieMail Online, CinemaNow, Coolroom, FilmFlex (via Virgin), Film Is Now, FilmLounge, Go!View, iLoaded, IndieMoviesOnline, iTunes, ITV Player (some films), Jaman, Joost, LoveFilm Watch Online, MovieFlix, Moviestar (acquired by ScreenClick), Projector TV, Sammsung Movies, SkyAnytime, SkyPlayer, Talk Talk (formerly Tiscali Cinema Club and Tesco Digital, Tiscali Movies Now – IPTV, The Vid Store, Virgin Media Online, Wippit, Zune.
Asia/Pacific	For Asian audiences	Asian HorrorMovies, Asian DVD Club, Crunchyroll (US based-Asian), DramaFever (US based-Korean), FilmBuff (Cinetic), Gigantic, iLovePhim, MySoju, Pinoy24, PinoyChannel, TaiSeng (US based-Asian), TFCNow, TVCell, Video4Asian, VPhim, WatchPinoy.
	China	08 Media on demand (Hong Kong), 56, Boosj, Funshion, Gougou, Joy, Ku6, Heidou, Pplive, Ppstream, QiYi, Todou, UuSee, V.163, Vodone, Voole, Youku.
	India	Apni, Baharat, BigFlix, BollyCircle, BollyClips, Bollystic, DesiFun, Eros, Interval, OnlineMovieStation, Rajshri, Saavn, TeluguSilverScreen, WatchIndia.

197

	Japan	CinemaNow, MaruMaruEiga via AcTVila, Sony Playstation Network.
	Korea	Buxmovie, Cine21i, Cinepox, Cinetizen, Cinero, Cinewel, DonutsMovie, MaxMovie, Movieshow, OnKino, Tvee, UCine, Yasisi.
	Australia	AnytimeOnVolt (defunct), BigPondMovies, T-Box, Blockbuster-TiVo (defunct), Caspa-TiVo, EzyDownload (defunct), Fetch TV, Foxtel Download, Hybrid TV, iTunes, IndieFilmWeb (defunct), TiVo-Seven (defunct).
Middle East		972 Films (Israel), Azaval (Iran), CopticWeb, Divx4Arab, ElCinema, EgyptianCastle, Getmo, Glwiz, PersianHub, Sotwesoora.
Africa		AfricaFilms, AfricanFilmLibrary, Africa Magic, African Movie Channel, AllAfricanMovies, Ayitinou, GhanaCinema, Izogn, NollywoodMovies, VibeGhana, Video On-line Nigeria.
Latin and South America	Argentina	Cinevivo, Incaa VOD service (coming soon).
	Brazil	Saraiva, TerraTV, NetMovies, OnVideo (Telefonica & Saraiva).
	Chile	Bazuca, Cinepata, Cinematica Virtual de Chile.

	Latin movies	Lacentraldigital, Cinemania, SubCine, Sivoo and El Porta Latino. Latin American films are also offered on Amazon and Netflix.
North America	U.S.	Amazon Instant Video (formerly Amazon VOD and Unbox), AOL, MUBI (formerly The Auteurs), Bit Torrent Entertainment (defunct), Blockbuster (Movielink), B-Side (now Slated), CinemaNow, Cinequist, Clickstar (defunct), Crackle, CreateSpace (formally CustomFlix), Direc2Drive, EZ Takes, Fancast, Fandor, Fearnet, Greencine, Guba, Hulu, iArtHouse, IndieFlix, iTunes, Jaman, Joost, Moviebeam, MovieFlix, Movielink (acquired by Blockbuster), NetFlix Watch Now, Peer Impact, Sony Playstation Network Movies on Demand, Reframe, Starz, Veoh, Vongo, Vuze, Wal-Mart, Zune Xbox 360 Live Marketplace, Withoutabox, YouTube, Zune Movies on Demand.
	Canada	Bell Video Store (defunct), CineClix, iTunes, NFB (National Film Board), NSI, VirtualHighway.

Appendix 3

Comparative Internet Rankings:

40 International On-line

Movies-on-Demand Sites

Stuart Cunningham and Jon Silver

On-line service	Internet ranking October 1st, 2010	Type of site
YouTube	3 (U.S. – 4)	Video sharing site.
Amazon (Amazon VOD not ranked individually)	15 (U.S. – 5)	E-commerce store.
Youku	49 (China – 10)	Video sharing site.
Tudou	65 (China – 13)	Video sharing site.
Netflix	120 (U.S. – 22)	Free films streamed to DVD rental subscribers.
Ku6	121 (China – 21)	Video sharing site.
Hulu	220 (U.S. – 44)	Hollywood studio backed catch-up TV offering free streaming and ads.
LoveFilm	4,255 (UK – 133)	UK On-line movie store.
Carrefour	5,824 (Spain – 141)	Spanish on-line movie store.
MaxDome	9,902 (Germany – 390)	German on-line movie store.
Crackle	15.954 (U.S. – 3,979)	VOD site backed by Sony.
BigFlix	22,722 (India – 2,665)	Major studio on-line store.

Jaman	23,022 (India – 5,133)	World cinema platform (U.S. Indian backer).
Blinkbox	25,350 (UK – 857)	UK on-line movie store.
Video Buster	25,660 (Germany – 1,253)	German on-line movie store.
MUBI (The Auteurs)	26,502 (U.S. – 23,543)	Indie on-line film library.
Eros Entertainment	29,449 (India – 1,920)	Major studio on-line store.
Rajshri	32,663 (India – 3,825)	Major studio on-line store.
Voddler	34,135 (Sweden – 424)	Swedish on-line movie store.
Babelgum	36,572 (U.S. – 15,694)	World cinema platform (UK-Italian).
Bazuca	44,713 (Chile – 413)	Chilean on-line movie store.
Apple iTunes	50,008 (U.S. – 20,998)	On-line digital media store.
BigPond Movies	59,294 (Australia – 834)	Australian on-line movie store.
Voole	62,230 (China – 12,834)	On-line video store.
EZTakes	72,124	On-line indie movie site.
CinemaNow	74,515 (U.S. – 22,409)	On-line movie store.
Saavn	79,803 (India – 6,199)	Bollywood entertainment portal.
Headweb	157,441 Sweden – 1,319)	Swedish on-line movie store.
UniversCine	505,923 (France – 18,427)	European indie on-line site.
Filmotech	634,129 (Spain – 16,947)	European indie on-line site.
Filmaka	722,720 (U.S. – 440,004)	On-line digital studio and talent incubator.
Europa Film Treasures	918,259 (U.S. – 418,398)	European indie on-line site.

Movieurope	2,498,128	European indie on-line site.
iArt house	2,550,358	On-line art house film site.
Saraiva	3,698,488	Brazilian on-line movie store.
Internet Archive	3,717,597	Internet archive of historic films.
Filmaka	4,273,429	On-line digital studio and talent incubator.
UTV	10,239,526	Indian film/TV distributor.
Africa Films	13,190,260	African on-line movie store.

Note: Bracketed numbers for Internet ranking indicate the ranking within the country named. For example, 'YouTube 3 (U.S. 4) means whilst YouTube was the third most visited website across the world on that day, among U.S. IP addresses it was only the fourth most visited website visited by Americans on the day that this Internet traffic snapshot was taken.

Source: www.alexa.com; three-month rolling average of Web traffic snapshot taken 1 October 2010 3pm-4pm.

Appendix 4

Comparative Deal Terms in 2009

Stuart Cunningham and Jon Silver

On-line Aggregator (Business Model)	Terms for Independent Producers	Revenue Split	Retail Pricing U.S.$	Return to Filmmaker U.S.$	Costs U.S.$	Content Suppliers and Distribution Partners	Library
iTunes (rent or purchase download to own on demand)	3-year non-exclusive only via content aggregators	iTunes and aggregator take approximately 50% of revenue and costs for iTunes proprietary encoding	Feature length downloads for $9.99	Costs off the top then approximately 50:50 split	iTunes proprietary encoding based on running time: $4 per minute for 90-119min; $3.75 per min for over 120min HD content $11 per minute	iTunes content supplied by Hollywood studios only via known distributors and partnering content aggregators e.g. IndieFlix	'iTunes has the largest library of movies in the world.'1

Hulu (ad-supported free streaming and new Hulu+ premium content subscription service)	3-year non-exclusive only via content aggregators	Hulu takes 50% of ad revenues and up to 15% ad network fee	Free VOD streaming, ad supported	On average a $7/$3 revenue split was paid per 1,000 views Web rumours of 1.5 cents per view/ stream		Hulu content supplied by NBC, Fox & Disney and only via partnering content aggregators, e.g. IndieFlix	Catalogue count on Hulu on 27 September 2010– 1,060 movies. Hulu's film library is end-of-lifecycle back catalogue i.e. DVD and TV markets already fully exploited.
Netflix (DVD by mail subscription service with free on-line streaming to subscribers)	Feature films only	Netflix buys DVDs from producers at U.S.$10 per disc; minimum 30 units	Watch Instantly on-line streaming is free; value add service to Netflix subscribers	Popular films; Netflix buys increased quantities – 60 units or 120 units, etc.	Cost to filmmaker is shipping DVDs to Netflix	Netflix content supplied by Hollywood studios and content aggregators, e.g. IndieFlix	Over 8,000 titles available for VOD + 90,000 DVDs available for rent by postal service
Amazon Instant Video (formerly - Amazon VOD) (rent or purchase download to own on demand and personal Video Library storage locker on Amazon)	3-year non-exclusive	Amazon takes 40% of retail price	Rental $2.99; download to own $9.99	Net after 40% fee to Amazon		Amazon content supplied by NBC, Fox & Disney and also from content aggregators e.g. IndieFlix and CreateSpace. It plays to devices such as TiVo, Roku and web-enabled TVs and mobiles	75,000 titles (movies and TV)

CreateSpace (digital/virtual inventory – publishing on demand – DVDs sold on Amazon.com and producer's CreateSpace e-store and streamed as rentals on Amazon VOD)	1-year non-exclusive	Fixed charge per DVD – if sold on Amazon it takes 40% of retail price; if sold on CS e-store it takes 15%	Minimum DVD pricing $9.00 On $9.00 per	DVD sold filmmaker gets $0.45		3,523 titles on Amazon - 1,731 titles are short and long form films
				Scenario 1: selling DVD on Amazon via Create Space at $12.99 – 40% ($5.19 to Amazon) - $4.95 cost = $2.84 to filmmaker.		
				Scenario 2: retail $14.99 – 40% to Amazon - $4.95 DVD cost = $4.04 to filmmaker.		
				Scenario 3: retail $19.99 – 40% to Amazon - $4.95 DVD cost = $6.04 to filmmaker.		

Source: E-mail correspondence from Mike Williams (Filmmaker Relations & Acquisitions, IndieFlix) to Nathan Wrann (Producer-Director of Hunting Season, U.S., 2007). On-line. Available HTTP: http://nwrann.wordpress.com/2009/07/22/indieflix-vs-createspace-day-1 (14 June 2011).

Notes

1   Steve Jobs speaking at the Apple Special Event, 1 September 2010. On-line. Available HTTP: http://www.apple.com/apple-events/september-2010/ (2 September 2011).

Appendix 5
Related Websites

Alexander Marlow-Mann

Below is an alphabetical listing of the websites cited in this volume. Except where otherwise indicated, all websites were functional in September 2011; respectively, September 2011 was the reference point in the instances where we have listed the URL as 'unavailable' or 'defunct.' However, given the volatile and transitory nature of the Web, we make no guarantees that they will all still be operational by the time you read this book.

08 Media.com on Demand, URL unavailable
24/24, URL unavailable
4 on Demand, www.channel4.com/programmes/4od
51tv, www.51tv.com
56, www.56.com
60 Frames, www.youtube.com/user/60frames
972 Films, www.972films.com
acTVila, actvila.jp
AFI Fest, www.afi.com/afifest
Afilmcinado, URL unavailable
AfricaFilms, www.africafilms.tv
Africa Magic, beta.mnet.co.za/africamagic
African Film Library, www.africanfilmlibrary.com
African Movie Channel, www.africanmoviechannel.tv
African Movies, www.africanmovies.com
Ain't It Cool News, www.aintitcool.com
Alexa, www.Alexa.com
All African Movies, www.allafricanmovies.com
Amazon, amazon.com
Amazon Instant Video, www.amazon.com/Instant-Video/
    b?ie=UTF8&node=2858778011
Amazon Studios, studios.amazon.com

Ann Arbor Film Festival, www.aafilmfest.org
The Annoying Orange, www.youtube.com/watch?v=ZN5PoW7_kdA
AnytimeOnVolt, URL unavailable
Apni, apni.tv
Arcor, www.arcor.de
Arte VOD, www.artevod.com/Accueil.html
Arts Alliance Media, www.artsalliancemedia.com
Asian DVD Club, asiandvdclub.org
Asian Horror Movies, www.asian-horror-movies.com
Auteurs (The), see MUBI
Ayitinou, ayitinou.com/movies/movies-on-demand.html
Axiom Films, www.axiomfilms.co.uk
Azaval, www.azaval.com/forum/index.php
B-Side, bside.com/about
Babelgum, www.babelgum.com
Baharat, URL unavailable
Bazuca, www.bazuca.com/home
BBC iPlayer, www.bbc.co.uk/iplayer
Bell Video Store, URL unavailable
Berlin International Film Festival, www.berlinale.de
Berlin International Film Festival – European Film Market, www.efm-
    berlinale.de
Big Flix, www.bigflix.com
Big Pond Movies, bigpondmovies.com
BT China (Bit Torrent China), URL unavailable
Bit Torrent Entertainment, URL unavailable
Bitscreen, URL unavailable
BizShark, www.bizshark.com
Blinkbox, www.blinkbox.com
Blockbuster, www.blockbuster.com
Blogpulse, www.blogpulse.com
Bollycircle, www.bollycircle.com
Bollyclips, www.bollyclips.com
Bollystic, bollystic.com/Bollywood
Bollywood TV, www.bollywood.tv
Boosj, www.boosj.com
Box Office Mojo, boxofficemojo.com
Brightwide, www.brightwide.com/home
British Film Institute, www.bfi.org.uk
BT Vision, www.btvision.bt.com

Buxmovie, www.buxmovie.com

Buyacredit, www.buyacredit.com

Caachi, www.caachi.com (URL no longer active)

Cable Vision, www.cablevision.com

CanalPlay, www.canalplay.com

Cannes Film Festival, www.festival-cannes.fr

Cannes Film Festival – Marché du Film, www.marchedufilm.com

Casema, www.casema.nl

Caspa on Demand, see Caspa TiVo

Caspa TiVo, www.mytivo.com.au/whatistivo/moviestvmusic/
entertainmentondemand

Celluloid Dreams, www.celluloid-dreams.com

La central digital, www.lacentraldigital.com

Channel Films, www.channelfilms.com

Cine21i, twitter.com/#!/cine21i

Cinebox on Movie Mail, www.moviemail-online.co.uk/cinebox

CineClix, www.urbancinefile.com.au/home/view.asp?a=9521&s=Forum

El Cinema, www.elcinema.com

Cinemania TV, www.cinemania.tv

CinemaNow, www.cinemanow.com

Cinema Reloaded, www.cinemareloaded.com

Cinemateca Virtual de Chile, www.cinechileno.org

Cinépata, www.cinepata.com

Cinepox, cinepox.com

Cinequest, www.cinequest.org

Cinero, www.cinero.com

Cinetizen, www.cinetizen.com

Cinevivo, www.cinevivo.org/home/?tpl=home

Cinewel, www.cinewel.com

Cleveland International Film Festival, www.clevelandfilm.org

Clickstar, URL unavailable

Club Video (SFR), club-video.sfr.fr

Comcast, www.comcast.com

ComScore Media Metrix, www.comscore.com/Products_Services/
Product_Index/Media_Metrix_Suite/Media_Metrix_Core_Reports

CON-CAN, en.con-can.com

Content Media, www.contentmediacorp.com

Coolroom, www.coolroom.com

Coptic Web, www.azaval.com/forum/index.php

Costa Films, www.costafilms.com

Crackle, www.crackle.com

CreateSpace, www.createspace.com

Creative Commons, www.creativecommons.org.uk

Criterion Collection, www.criterion.com

Critic after Dark, criticafterdark.blogspot.com

Criticine, www.criticine.com/main.php

Crunchyroll, www.crunchyroll.com

Curzon Cinemas – Film On Demand, www.curzoncinemas.com/film_on_demand

Dances with Films, www.danceswithfilms.com

Dark Carnival Film Festival, www.darkcarnivalfilmfest.com

Dataflow, dataflowenterprises.com

Desifun, www.desifun.co.uk

Direct2Drive, www.direct2drive.com

Direct Movie, www.directmovie.nl

Disney Studio All Access, disney.go.com/disney-studio-all-access

Distribber, www.distribber.com

Distrify, www.distrify.com

Divx4Arab, www.divx4arab.com

DonutsMovie, www.donutsmovie.com

Dovetail TV, URL unavailable

Drama Fever, www.dramafever.com

e-Donkey, see eMule

Edge City Films, www.edgecityfilms.com

Egyptian Castle, www.egyptiancastle.com

eMule, www.emule-project.net/home/perl/general.cgi?l=1

Eros Entertainment, www.erosentertainment.com

Eurocinema, www.eurocinema.com

Europa Film Treasures, www.europafilmtreasures.eu

Europe's Finest, www.finest-film.com

European Independent Film Festival, www.ecufilmfestival.com

The Evening Class, theeveningclass.blogspot.com

Eventival, www.eventival.com

Eye On Films, eyeonfilms.org

EZTakes, www.eztakes.com

EzyDownload, URL unavailable

Facebook, facebook.com

Fancast, see XFinity TV

Fandor, www.fandor.com

Fastweb, URL unavailable

Fearnet, www.fearnet.com

Festival de Cine del Sahara, www.fisahara.es

Festival Scope, www.festivalscope.com

Fetch TV, www.fetchtv.com.au

Film Buff, www.filmbuffondemand.com

Film Festivals, www.filmfestivals.com

Film Lounge, www.filmlounge.com

Film2Home, www.film2home.com

Filmaka, www.filmaka.com

Filmfinder, www.filmfinder.com

Filmflex, www.filmflexmovies.co.uk

FilmIsNow, www.filmisnow.it

Filmklik, www.filmklik.eu

Filmladen, www.filmladen.at

Filmotech, www.filmotech.com/V2/ES/inicio.asp

Find Any Film, www.findanyfilm.com

Finest Film, www.finest-film.com

Flicklaunch, www.flicklaunch.com

FNAC, www.fnac.com

Fortissimo Films, www.fortissimo.nl

Fortune Star Entertainment, www.fortunestarentertainment.com

Fox Mobile Entertainment, www.foxmobileentertainment.com

Foxtel Download, www.foxtel.com.au/download/default.htm

France Televisions, www.francetelevisions.fr

Free Record Shop, www.freerecordshop.nl

Funshion, www.funshion.com/english

Future of Film Blog, www.tribecafilm.com/tribecaonline/future-of-film

The Garage, MUBI.com/garage

Gaza Sderot (film), gaza-sderot.arte.tv

Getmo, www.getmo.com

Ghana Cinema, www.ghanacinema.tv

Giganic, URL unavailable

Girish, girishshambu.blogspot.com

Global Cinema www.globalcinemadistribution.com

Glowria, www.glowria.fr

Glwiz, www.glwiz.com

Go View!, URL unavailable

Gougou, www.gougou.com

Greencine, www.greencine.com/main

Guba, www.blinkx.com/channel/Guba

Headweb, www.headweb.com/sv
Heartbreak Publishing, www.heartbreakpublishing.com
Heidu, heidou.com
Heretic, URL unavailable
Hong Kong International Film Festival, www.hkiff.org.hk/en/index.php
Hulu, www.hulu.com
Hybrid TV, www.hybridtv.com.au/home
i-Art house, www.iart house.com
I Love Phim, phim.asia
iLoaded, URL unavailable
Imagenio Videoclub (Telefonica), URL unavailable
IMDb, www.imdb.com
In2Movies, URL unavailable
Incaa VOD, URL unavailable
Independent Film Festival of Boston, www.iffboston.org
Indiefilipino, Indiefilipino.com (defunct)
IndieFilmWeb, URL unavailable
IndieFlix, www.indieflix.com
IndieGoGo, www.indiegogo.com
Indie Movies Online, www.indiemoviesonline.com
Insane Mute, www.insanemute.com
International Film Festival Rotterdam, www.filmfestivalrotterdam.com
Internet Archive, www.archive.org
Internet World Stat, www.Internetworldstats.com/stats4.htm
Intertainer, www.intertainer.com
Interval, URL unavailable
iTunes, www.apple.com/itunes
ITV Player, www.itv.com/itvplayer
Izogn, URL unavailable
Jaman, www.jaman.com
Jaman Networks, www.jaman.net
Jonathan Rosenbaum, www.jonathanrosenbaum.com
JOOST, www.joost.com
Joy, www.joy.cn
Kazaa, www.kazaa.com
Keeno, URL unavailable
Kickstarter, www.kickstarter.com
Ku6, www.ku6.com
Last FM, www.lastFM.com
LeTV, www.letv.com

Let Me Watch This, www.letmewatchthis.ch

Lionsgate, lionsgate.com

LoveFilm, www.lovefilm.com

LoveFilm Watch Online, www.lovefilm.com/browse/film/watch-online

M-Net, mnet.dstv.com

M6 Video, www.m6vod.fr

Magnolia Pictures, www.magpictures.com

Maru Maru Eiga, URL unavailable

MaxDome, www.maxdome.de

MaxMovie, www.maxmovie.com

Media That Matters Film Festival, www.mediathatmattersfest.org

MK2 VOD, www.facebook.com/group.php?gid=21456895334&v=info

Moser Baer, www.moserbaerhomevideo.com

Movie Mobz, www.moviemobz.org

Movie Star, now Screen Click

The Movie Theatre, www.facebook.com/apps/application.
    php?id=5409810948

MovieBeam, www.moviebeam.com

Movieflix, www.movieflix.com

MovieLink, www.movielinkguide.com

Moviepilot, www.MoviePilot.de

MoviePlay 2, URL unavailable

Movieshow, URL unavailable

Movieurope, www.movieurope.com

MUBI, www.MUBI.com

MUBI – The Notebook, mubi.com/notebook

MUBI – Project Cinéphilia, projectcinéphilia.MUBI.com

MXP Digital, URL unavailable

My Film Station, www.myfilmstation.com

My Soju, www.mysoju.com

My Space, www.myspace.com

Napster, www.napster.co.uk

NDTV Lumiere, www.ndtvlumiere.com

Net Movies, www.netmovies.com.br

Netflix, www.netflix.com

Neuf VOD, URL unavailable

NFB: National Film Board, Canada, www.nfb.ca

Nollywood Movies, www.nollywoodmovies.tv

NSI: National Screen Institute, www.nsi-canada.ca

One4movie, URL unavailable

OnKino, onkino.com
Online Film, www.onlinefilm.org
Online Movie Station, onlinemoviestation.com
OnVideo, www.speedy.com.ar/onvideo
Orange 24/24 Video Orange, www.apple.com/downloads/dashboard/
    movie_tv/orange2424video.html
Origo Téka, teka.origo.hu
Palm Springs International Film Festival, www.psfilmfest.org
Pandora, www.pandora.com
Paramount Digital Entertainment, www.paramount.com/studio/
    divisions#paramount-digital-entertainment
Pathé International, www.patheinternational.com
Peer Impact, URL unavailable
People for Cinema, www.peopleforcinema.com
Persian Hub, www.persianhub.org
Ping, www.apple.com/itunes/ping
Pinoy 24, www.pinoy24.com
The Pirate Bay, thepiratebay.org
Pixbox, www.pixbox.es
Pop, www.pop.com (defunct)
El Portal Latino, www.elportallatino.com
Pottermore, www.pottermore.com
Power to the Pixel, powertothepixel.com
PP Live, www.synacast.com
PP Stream, www.ppstream.com
Projector.tv, www.projector.tv/index.aspx
Pure Grass Films, www.puregrassfilms.com
QiYi, www.qiyi.com
Quacor, URL unavailable
Quickflix, www.quickflix.com.au
Rage (film), www.babelgum.com/rage
RAIN, www.rain.com.br/Cached
Rajshri, www.rajshri.com
Red Films, www.redfilms.com.my/company.htm
Reframe, reframefilmfestival.blogspot.com/2011/01/reframe-bazaar.
    html
Reframe Collection, www.reframecollection.org
Reliance Big Entertainment, www.rbe.com.in
Reverse Shot, reverseshot.com
Rightsline, www.rightsline.com

Rome Film Festival, www.romacinemafest.it
Rosso Alice, URL unavailable
Rotten Tomatoes, www.rottentomatoes.com
Rotterdam International Film Festival, www.filmfestivalrotterdam.
    com/en
Rouge, www.rouge.com.au
Rue Morgue, www.Rue-morgue.com
Saavn, www.saavn.com
Samsung Movies, movies.uk.samsungmobile.com
San Francisco International Film Festival, www.sfiff.org/festival
Saraiva, www.livrariasaraiva.com.br
Screen Click, www.screenclick.com
Screenwriter, www.screenwriter.com
Secret Cinema, www.secretcinema.org
Sellaband, www.sellaband.com
Senses of Cinema, www.sensesofcinema.com
SF Anytime, sfanytime.com
SightSound, www.sightsound.com
Sivoo, www.sivoo.com
Skeletons The Movie – Facebook page, www.facebook.com/pages/
    Skeletons-The-Movie/260736678117
Skeletons The Movie – Twitter feed, twitter.com/#!/SkeletonsMovie
Sky Anytime, www.sky.com/shop/tv/anytime
Sky Player, go.sky.com/vod/page/default/home.do
Slated, www.slated.com
SnagFilms, www.snagfilms.com
Soda Pictures, www.sodapictures.com
Sony Playstation Network, us.playstation.com/psn
Sony PSN Movies on Demand, us.playstation.com/psn/playstation-
    store/moviestv/index.htm
Sotwesoora, www.sotwesoora.tv
Spanner Films, www.spannerfilms.net
Spotify, www.spotify.com
Starz, www.starz.com
Ster Videotheek, www.stervideotheek.nl
Stockholm Film Festival, www.stockholmfilmfestival.se/en
SubCine, www.subcine.com
Sundance Film Festival, www.sundance.org/festival
Sundance Online Film Festival, www.sundanceonlinefilmfestival.org
Taiseng, www.taiseng.com

Tallinn Black Nights Film Festival, 2011.poff.ee
T-Box, www.telstra.com.au/tv/tbox
Technorati, technorati.com
Telluride Film Festival, www.telluridefilmfestival.org
TeluguSilverScreen, URL unavailable
Terra TV, terratv.terra.com.br
TF1, www.tf1.fr
TF1 Vision, www.tf1vision.com
TFC Now, tfcnow.abs-cbn.com
TH_NK, www.think.eu
TiVo, www.tivo.com
TiVo-Seven, URL unavailable
Toronto International Film Festival, tiff.net
Torrent Freak, www.torrentfreak.com
Touscoprod, www.touscoprod.com
TPS, www.tps.uk.com
Tribeca Film Festival, www.tribecafilm.com/festival
Trust Film, URL unavailable
Tudou, www.tudou.com
TV Cells, www.tvcells.org
TV OP JE PC, www.tvopjepc.nl
TVee, URL unavailable
Twitch, twitchfilm.com
Twitter, twitter.com
Ucine, www.ucine.edu.ar
UltraViolet, www.uvvu.com
Undergroundfilm, URL unavailable
Universcine, www.universcine.com
UTV, www.utvgroup.com
UUSee, www.uusee.com
V.163, v.163.com
Veamer, www.veamer.nl
Venice Film Festival, www.labiennale.org/en/cinema
Ventana Sur, www.ventanasur.com.ar
Veoh, www.veoh.com
Verizon, www.verizonbusiness.com
Viasat Ondemand, viaplay.se
Vibe Ghana, vibeghana.com
Video 4 Asian, www.video4asian.com
Video Buster, www.videobuster.de

Video Online Nigeria, video.onlinenigeria.com/default.aspx
Videofutur, www.videofutur.fr
Videoload, www.videoload.de
The Vid Store, thevidstore.co.uk
Virgin Media Online, onlinemovies.virginmedia.com
Virgin Mega, virginmega.com
Virtual Highway, URL unavailable
Voddler, www.voddler.com/en
VODO, vodo.net
Vodone, www.vodone.com
Vongo, www.vongo.com
Voole, www.voole.com
VPhim, vphim.com
Vuze, www.vuze.com
Wal Mart, www.walmart.com/cp/movies-tv/4096
Watch India, www.watchindia.tv
Watch Pinoy TV, www.watchpinoytv.info
Wild Bunch, www.wildbunch.biz
Winkelwijs, URL unavailable
Wippit, www.wippit.com
Withoutabox, www.withoutabox.com
Xbox 360 Live Marketplace, marketplace.xbox.com/en-GB
XFinitiy TV, xfinitytv.comcast.net
Yasisi, yasisi.co.kr
Yodecidio, URL unavailable
Youku, www.youku.com
YouTube, www.youtube.com
YouTube – Screening Room, www.youtube.com/user/ytscreeningroom
Zattoo, zattoo.com/view
Zeeland, www.zeelandnet.nl
Zoei Films, URL unavailable
Zune, www.zune.net/en-GB
Zune Movies on Demand, URL unavailable
Zune Xbox 360 Live Marketplace, www.zune.net/en-us/products/
zuneonxbox/default.htm

About Dynamics of World Cinema

Carried out under the aegis of The Leverhulme Trust, Dynamics of World Cinema was a major research project undertaken by the Centre for Film Studies at the University of St Andrews in Scotland, UK (2008-2011). It was headed by the Centre's Director, Prof. Dina Iordanova and Prof. Stuart Cunningham, Director of the ARC Centre of Excellence for Creative Industries and Innovation at the Queensland University of Technology in Australia. The project employed several post-doctoral researchers, including Dr. Ruby Cheung, Dr. Ragan Rhyne and Dr. Alex Fischer.

Dynamics of World Cinema examined the patterns and cycles of distinctly active circuits of contemporary transnational film distribution and exhibition and the dynamic patterns of complex interaction between them. Attention was focused on four areas of the global circulation of film: the global film festival circuit, the various Internet-enabled forms of dissemination, the penetration of international blockbusters into global mainstream distribution and film circulation via diasporic channels. The project's distinctiveness is in its endeavour to correlate these diverse strands and foreground their dynamic interactions.

As part of Dynamics of World Cinema we established the series of *Film Festival Yearbooks*, published by St Andrews Film Studies under the auspices of the Leverhulme Trust. Publications so far include: *The Festival Circuit* (2009), *Film Festivals and Imagined Communities* (2010), *Film Festivals and East Asia* (2011) and *Film Festivals and Activism* (2012). The work published out of the project has been widely reviewed and presented at international venues.

The project benefited from the expertise of our International Advisory Board members: in the UK – Yoram Allon, Peter Buckingham, Rajinder Dudrah, Rachel Dwyer, Simon Field, Catherine Grant, Karsten-Peter Grummitt, Michael Gubbins, Terry Illot, Paul MacDonald, Nick Roddick and Annabelle Sreberny; in the U.S. – Michael Curtin, Geoffrey Gilmore, Faye Ginsburg, Toby Miller, Richard Porton, B. Ruby Rich, Jonathan Rosenbaum and John Trumpbour; in other parts of the world – Irene Bignardi, Henning Camre, Emmanuel Ethis, Koichi Iwabuchi, Kang Han-sup, Adrian Martin and John Sinclair. Thank you!

For more information about Dynamics of World Cinema, visit: http://www.st-andrews.ac.uk/worldcinema/

St Andrews Film Studies
International Advisory Board

CPSIA information can be obtained at www.ICGtesting.com
Printed in the USA
BVOW021137270812

298911BV00016B/221/P

9 780956 373076